Jesse George Cross

Dictionary of Eclectic Shorthand

Jesse George Cross

Dictionary of Eclectic Shorthand

ISBN/EAN: 9783744645966

Printed in Europe, USA, Canada, Australia, Japan

Cover: Foto ©Andreas Hilbeck / pixelio.de

More available books at **www.hansebooks.com**

DICTIONARY

OF

ECLECTIC SHORTHAND,

GIVING THE

PHONETIC AND SHORTHAND EQUIVALENTS

OF THE PRIMITIVE WORDS AND THE VARIOUS CLASSES OF
DERIVATIVE WORDS OF THE ENGLISH
LANGUAGE.

ALSO, SEVERAL

VOCABULARIES OF TECHNICAL TERMS.

BY J. G. CROSS, M.A.,
AUTHOR OF ECLECTIC SHORTHAND.

FIFTH THOUSAND

CHICAGO:
S. C. GRIGGS AND COMPANY,
1894.

CONTENTS.

iii

PREFACE.

The text-book of Eclectic Shorthand was designed to be a complete instructor. The lists of words and illustrations it contains were supposed to be sufficient to enable the thoughtful student to acquire a practical knowledge of the art. For some time, however, there has been a growing conviction in the mind of the author that a dictionary, similar to those used in other systems, would be very helpful. This conviction, strengthened by the frequent inquiry from Eclectic writers for the authoritative writing of some word, and by friendly suggestions of some of the most intelligent teachers and writers of the system, has led to the preparation of this volume.

It is believed by the author that it will be of great advantage in three ways:

1. It will aid teachers, students and writers of Eclectic Shorthand to a prompt settlement of questions that are constantly arising.

2. It will greatly lessen the length of time required to master the art, both of the private learner and of the student in school.

3. It will give a stability to the system, and a uniformity in the application of its principles that can be secured in no other way.

It is intended for writers of all grades of proficiency. Not only the beginner, but also the most practiced writer is liable to feel uncertain and perplexed as to the best expression of a new or unfamiliar word; hence the importance of having at hand a dictionary of phonetic and shorthand words.

To write through this work will be equivalent to writing the entire language; hence it should be written through repeatedly by all who wish to become expert in the use of Eclectic Shorthand.

A few words unavoidably omitted from the list of primitive words are given in a supplement.

That the work will prove invaluable to both learners and practical writers is the belief of

THE AUTHOR

INTRODUCTORY.

PRIMITIVE words are those which can be reduced to no fewer letters and still remain significant English words; as, boy, good, firm.

Derivative words are those which are formed by prefixing, or adding other letters or syllables to primitives; as, boyish, goodness, goodly, firmness, infirm.

There are some words of Latin origin; as, abdicate, convene, adhere, etc., which, although derivatives in the language to which they belong, are generally treated as primitives in English, because they not only have no English root word, but the root which they have is generally, in English, employed as a prefix or suffix.

Compound words are such as are formed from two or more primitive words; as, car-load, type-writer.

It will be seen from these facts that the primitives are the *root words* from which other words are derived, and that to become a proficient shorthand writer requires perfect familiarity with all the primitive words, and with the prefixes and suffixes which are used with the primitives in producing the derivative words.

In the writing of primitive words the initial part of each is fully expressed, with enough of its termination to clearly indicate the intended word.

In writing derivatives, occasionally a short prefix may be safely omitted, while terminations are either written or clearly indicated, and vice versa, when the initial part of a derivative is fully written, short, uncharacteristic terminations may be omitted.

The student who has thoroughly learned the principles of Eclectic Shorthand, as embodied in the text-book of instructions and the chapter on abbreviations in this work, is prepared to write this dictionary systematically and repeatedly through. Placing this and the practice book side by side, a word should be written, first, carefully and thoughtfully, and then rapidly, but as nearly perfect as possible, as many times as may be on a line, or more, of the practice book.

Each word is accompanied by a skeleton word which indi-cates exactly what is written in the shorthand outline following it. The shorthand words are written without ruled lines to indicate their position, but the italic character used in each skeleton word is the positional letter of the word; thus, in the first primitive word, *aback*, the outline a*b*c, having the italic *b*, indicates that *a* is to be written on the *b*, or first position, to ex-press the *b* and then *c* added. This means of expressing the position of the first part of a word renders unnecessary the use of ruled lines in this work, yet indicating clearly to the learner the positions of the first letter as well as the character to be ex-pressed by position. Of course the learner will use ruled paper in practice, because he cannot dispense with the ruled lines safely until very proficient in the use of the system, when his familiarity with the outlines of words will enable him to write with perfect confidence on unruled paper.

In the skeleton word a prefix or suffix is indicated by sepa-rating the letter which represents it from the rest of the word by a short dash, as in the words, abbreviate, abdicate and accommodate, which see.

ABBREVIATION.

ABBREVIATION in Eclectic Shorthand is accomplished by the following means:

I. An alphabet of simple characters representing the English alphabet of twenty-six letters, each letter being expressed by a single line.

II. The representation of each diphthong, digraph, trigraph and coalescent compound of the language by a simple, distinct character.

III. A positional alphabet representing each letter of the entire alphabet by a definite position with reference to the line of writing, in which position each character representing a letter, digraph or trigraph may be written to express the letter following it, represented by the position.

IV. The representation of uncoalescent consonant compounds of frequent occurrence by a single character.

V. The lengthening of the long alphabetic characters and the *p* and *g* to express a following *m* or *n*, and enlarging the surface characters, viz., *p*, *g*, *h*, *r*. *l*, *sh*, *ch*, *wh*, *sp*, *st*, *ns*, *pch* and *retraced r*, to express a following *t* or *d*.

VI. The shortening the short alphabetic characters to express a following *t* or *d;* also diminishing them to mere ticks to express a following *m*, *n* or *y*, and diminishing the surface characters to express a following *l*, *ly*, *ling*, *fl*, *fly*, *fling*.

VII. The representation of frequent lengthy and compound prefixes and suffixes by a single character.

VIII. The representation of a few frequent words, each by a single character called a word sign.

IX. The representation of frequent simple phrases and phrase words, each by a simple character of one line.

By these principles, singly and combined, are produced an almost endless number of two, three, four and five letter syllables, each expressed by a single simple character, affording ample means of brevity for verbatim writing, probably unequaled in the history of practical shorthand.

A	**Abject**
an	abj
Aback	**Abjure**
abc	abjr
Abacus	**Ablative**
abcs	abl-t
Abaft	**Able**
abft	abl
Abandon	**Ablution**
abnn	ab-l
Abase	**Abnegation**
abas	abn-g
Abash	**Abnormal**
absh	ab-nr
Abate	**Aboard**
abat	abrd
Abatis	**Abode**
abts	abd
Abba	**Abolish**
aba	ablsh
Abbess	**Abolition**
abs	ab-l
Abbey	**Abominable**
aby	abm-n
Abbot	**Aboriginal**
abot	abrgnl
Abbreviate	**Aborigines**
abr-v	abrjns
Abdicate	**Abortion**
abd-c	abrshn
Abdomen	**Abortive**
abdmn	abr-t
Abduct	**Abound**
ab-d	abnd
Abed	**About**
abd	abt
Aberrant	**Above**
abrnt	abv
Abet	**Abrade**
abt	abrad
Abeyance	**Abreast**
abns	abrst
Abhor	**Abridge**
` abhr	abrj
Abide	**Abroach**
abid	abrch
Ability	**Abroad**
ablt	abrd

Accustom acstm		**Acrobat** acrbt
Ace as		**Acronycal** acrncl
Acephalous actls		**Acropolis** acropls
Acerbety asrb-t		**Across** acros
Acescent assnt		**Acrostic** acrstc
Acetify astfi		**Act** act
Acetimetry astm-tr		**Action** ac-shn
Acetous asets		**Active** ac-t
Ache ac		**Actuary** actry
Achieve achv		**Aculeate** aculat
Achromatic ac-rm		**Acumen** acumn
Acid asd		**Acuminate** acum-n
Acknowledge acnl		**Acute** acut
Acme acm		**Adage** adj
Acorn acrn		**Adagio** adjo
Acoustic acstc		**Adamant** admnt
Acquaint quant		**Adapt** dapt
Acquiesce quis		**Add** ad
Acquire quir		**Addendum** adndm
Acquit quit		**Adder** adr
Acre acr		**Addict** ad-i
Acrid acrd		**Addle** adl
Acrimony actmny		**Address** adrs
Acritude acrtd		**Adduce** adus

Adept dpt	**Ado** ado
Adequate ad-q	**Adore** adr
Adhere adhr	**Adorn** adrn
Adieu adu	**Adrift** adrft
Adipose adpos	**Adroit** adrot
Adit adt	**Adscititious** ads-t
Adjacent jsnt	**Adulation** adu-l
Adjective ad-j	**Adult** adt
Adjoin jin	**Adumbrate** admbrt
Adjourn jurn	**Aduncity** adnst
Adjudge juj	**Adust** adst
Adjunct junct	**Advance** vans
Adjure jur	**Advantage** vntj
Adjust just	**Advent** advnt
Adjutant jutnt	**Adverb** advrb
Adjuvant juvnt	**Adversary** advrsry
Administer a-tr	**Adverse** advrs
Admirable mrbl	**Advert** advrt
Admire mr	**Advertise** advrts
Admission mshn	**Advice** advs
Admit mt	**Advocate** advct
Admix mix	**Advowee** adve
Admonish m nsh	**Advowson** advsn
Adnascent nsnt	**Adynamic** adnm-i

Adz	Afflatus
Aeolian	Afflict
Aerial	Affluent
Aerie ery. ary)	Afflux
Aerify	Afford
Aerography	Affray
Aerolite	Affright
Aerology	Affront
Aeromancy	Affuse
Aerometry	Afield
Aeronaut	Afloat
Aerostatic	Afoot
Aerostation	Afore
Aesthetic	Afraid
Afar	Afresh
Afeard	Aft
Affable	After
Affair	Again gen)
Affect	Against geast
Affiant	Agape
Affiliate	Agate
Affinity	Age
Affirm	Agent
Afflx	Agglomerate

Aggrandize	agrnds	
Aggravate	agr-v	
Aggregate	agr g	
Aggression	agrshn	
Aggrieve	agrv	
Aggroup	agrp	
Aghast	agst	
Agile	ajl	
Agitate	aj-t	
Aglet	aglt	
Agnail	agnal	
Agnate	ag n	
Agnomen	agnmn	
Ago	ago	
Agog	agg	
Agony	agny	
Agrarian	agrryn	
Agree	agr	
Agriculture	agrcltr	
Aground	ground	
Ague (agu)	agu	
Ah	ah	
Aba	aha	
Aiddecamp(kong)	adcmg	

Aim — am
Air — ar
Airy — ary
Aisle (il) — il
Ajar — jar
Akimbo — cmbo
Akin — akn
Alabaster — albstr
Alack — alc
Alacrity — alcr-t
Alamode — alamd
Alarm — alrm
Alas — alas
Alb — alb
Albeit — albt
Albescent — albsnt
Albino — albno
Album — albm
Albumen — albmn
Alburnum — albrnm
Alcahest — alchst
Alchemy — alcmy
Alcohol — alchl
Alcoran — alcrn

Alcove
a/cv

Alder
a/dr

Alderman
a/drmn

Ale
al

Alembic
a/mbc

Alert
a/rt

Algebra
a/gbr

Alias
a/is

Alibi
a/ib

Alien (yen)
a/yn

Alight
a/t

Alignment
a/inmnt

Alike
a/k

Aliment
a/mnt

Alimony
a/mny

Aliquant
a/qnt

Aliquot
a/qt

Alive
a/v

Alkali
a/kli

Alkaloid
a/kloid

All
al

Alay
a/a

Allege
a/j

Allegory
a/gry

Allegro
a/gro

Alleluia (ya)
a/ya

Alleviate
a/c-v

Alley
a/y

Alliance
a/ns

Alligation
al g

Alligator
a/gtr

Alliteration
a/t r

Allocation
al c

Allocution
al c

Allodial
a/odl

Allodium
a/odm

Allot
a/ot

Allow
low

Alloy
loy

Allspice
a/sps

Allude
a/-l

Allure
a/ur

Allusion
a/-l

Alluvial
a/vl

Alluvium
a/vm

Ally
a/i

Almanac
a/mnc

Almighty (mit)
a/m-t

Almond a/md		**Alveolate** a/vo l	
Almoner a/mnr		**Alvine** a/vn	
Almost a/mst		**Always** a/ws,	
Aloe (alo) a/o		**Am** am	
Aloft a/lt		**Amain** aman	
Alone a/n		**Amalgam** amlgm	
Along a/ng		**Amanuensis** mannss	
Aloof a/l		**Amaranth** amrnth	
Aloud a/d		**Amass** amas	
Alpaca a/pca		**Amateur (tur)** amtr	
Alpha (fa) a/fa		**Amative** am-t	
Alphabet a/fbt		**Amatory** amtr	
Alpine a/pn		**Amaze** amaz	
Already a/rdy		**Amazon** amzn	
Also a/s		**Ambassador** ambsdr	
Altar a/tr		**Amber** ambr	
Alter a/tr		**Ambergris** ambrgrs	
Althea a/thea		**Ambient** ambnt	
Although (tho) a/th		**Ambiguous (us)** am-gs	
Altimetry a/tm-try		**Ambition** am-b	
Altitude a/t t		**Amble** ambl	
Alto a/to		**Ambrosial** am-br	
Altogether a/tgtr		**Ambrotype** ambrtp	
Alumnus a/mns		**Ambulance** ambulns	

Ambulatory
ambltry

Ambush
ambsh

Ameliorate
aml-r

Amen
amn

Amend
amnd

Amende(amongd)
amngd

Amenity
amn-t

Ameree
amrs

American
amrcn

Amethyst
amthst

Amiable
amabl

Amicable
amcbl

Amidst
amdst

Amiss
amis

Amity
am-t

Ammonia
amna

Ammunition
am-n

Amnesty
amnst

Amongst
amngst

Amorous
amors

Amorphous
amrfs

Amount
amnt

Amour
amoor

Amphibian
am-bn

Ample
ampl

Amplify
amplf

Amply
ampl

Amputate
amp-t

Amulet
amult

Amuse
amus

Amygdaline
amgdln

Amylaceous
amy-l

An
an

Anabaptist
anbptst

Anachronism
ancr-n

Anaconda
ancnd

Anagram
anagrm

Analogy
anlj

Analysis
anlss

Analyze
anlis

Anapest
anapst

Anarchy
ancry

Anathema
anthma

Anatomy
antmy

Anbury
anbry

Ancestor
ansstr

Anchor
ancr

Anchovy
ancv

Ancient (shent) an-shnt	**Ankle** ancl
And and	**Annals** anls
Andante andn-t	**Annats** anats
Andiron andrn	**Anneal** anel
Androgynous andrjns	**Annex** anx
Anecdote ancdt	**Annihilate** ani-hl
Anemone anmne	**Anniversary** anvrsry
Aneurism anrsm	**Annotate** ano-t
Anew anu	**Announce** nouns
Angel anjl	**Annotto** anoto
Anger angr	**Annoy** anoy
Angle angl	**Annual** anul
Angler anglr	**Annular** anlr
Anglican anglcn	**Amulet** amlt
Angry angry	**Annunciate** nun-sh
Anguish angwsh	**Anodyne** anodn
Angular angular	**Anoint** noint
Anile anil	**Anomalous** nomals
Animadvert anmd-v	**Anon** non
Animal anml	**Anonymous** nonms
Animalcule anmlcl	**Another** anr
Animate anmt	**Anserine** ansrin
Animosity anmst	**Answer (ser)** ansr
Anise anis	**Ant** ant

Antagonism antg-n	**Antiphonal** antfnl
Antalgic antaljc	**Antipodal** antpdl
Antarctic antrctc	**Antipode** antpd
Ante an-t	**Antiquary** ant-q
Antarthritic antrthrtc	**Antiquated** ant-q
Antecedent antsdnt	**Antique** antk
Antedate ant-d	**Antithesis** antthss
Antediluvian antd-l	**Antithetic** antthtc
Antelope antlop	**Antitype** anttp
Antenna antna	**Antler** antlr
Anterior antrr	**Anvil** anvl
Anthem anthm	**Anxiety** anxt
Anther anthr	**Anxious (ankshus)** an-shs
Anthology anth-o	**Any** en
Anthracite anthrst	**Aorta** aort
Anthropology anthrplj	**Apace** afas
Anthropomorphism anthrp-mr	**Apart** afrt
Anti an-t	**Apathy** afthy
Antic antc	**Ape** ap
Antichrist antcrst	**Aperient** afrnt
Anticipate antspt	**Aperture** afrtur
Antidote antdt	**Apex** afx
Antimony antmny	**Aphelion** aflyn
Antipathy antpth	**Aphorism** afrsm

Apiary a/ary		**Appeal** a/l	
Apiece a/s		**Appear** a/r	
Apish a/sh		**Appease** a/s	
Apocalypse a/clps		**Appellate** a/lat	
Apocope a/cp		**Appellant** a/lnt	
Apocrypha a/crf		**Appellee** a/le	
Apogee a/j		**Appellor** a/lr	
Apologetic a/l-j		**Append** a/nd	
Apologue (log) a/-l		**Appertain** a/rtn	
Apology a/lj		**Appetence** a/tns	
Apothegm (them) a/thm		**Appetite** a/tt	
Apoplexy a/plx		**Applaud** a/ld	
Apostasy a/stsy		**Applause** a/ls	
Apostle (apossl) a/sl		**Apple** a/l	
Apostrophe a/strf		**Apply** apli, pli	
Apostrophize a/strfs		**Apportion** a/r-shn	
Apothecary a/thcry		**Apposite** a/st	
Apotheosis a/thoss		**Appraise** a/ras	
Appall a/al		**Appreciate (shi)** a/r-sh	
Appanage a/nj		**Apprehend** a/rnd	
Apparatus a/rats		**Apprentice** a/rnts	
Apparel a/rl		**Apprise** a/ris	
Apparent a/rnt		**Approach** a/rch, proch	
Apparition a/-r		**Approbation** a/r b	

Appropriate a/rprt		**Arbor** a/br	
Approve a/rv		**Arc** arc	
Approximate a/rxmt		**Arcade** arcad	
Appulse a/pls		**Arcanum** arcnm	
Appurtenance a/rtnns		**Arch** arch	
Apricot a/rct		**Archaeology** arc-o	
April a/rl		**Archaic** arc-i	
Apron a/rn		**Archangel** arcngl	
Apropos a/rpo		**Archbishop** archbshp	
Apt a/t		**Arched (archt)** archt	
Apterous a/trus		**Archer** archr	
Aptitude a/t-t		**Archery** archry	
Aptly a/tly		**Archetype** archtp	
Aptness a/tns		**Archfiend** archfnd	
Aquafortis acfrts		**Archipelago** arcpl	
Aquatic a-q		**Architect** arc-t	
Aqueduct acw-d		**Architrave** arctrv	
Aquiline acwln		**Archives** arcvs	
Arab a/b		**Archness** archns	
Arabesque (besk) a/bsk		**Archway** archw	
Arable a/bl		**Arctic** arc-t	
Arbiter a/btr		**Ardent** a/dnt	
Arbitrary a/btry		**Ardor** a/dr	
Arbitrate arb-tr		**Arduous** a/dus	

Area	area	**Armor**	armr
Arena	arna	**Armpit**	armpt
Argal	argl	**Arms**	arms
Argent	argnt	**Army**	army
Argillaceous	arg-l	**Aroma**	arma
Argosy	argosy	**Aromatic**	arm a
Argue	arg	**Arose**	aros
Arian	aryn	**Around**	arnd
Arid	ard	**Arouse**	arous
Aright	arit	**Arquebuse**	arqbs
Arise	aris	**Arrack**	arrc
Aristocrat	arstcrt	**Arraign (ran)**	aran
Arithmetic	arth	**Arrange**	arng
Ark	ark	**Arrant**	arnt
Arm	arm	**Arras**	arrs
Armada	armada	**Array**	arra
Armament	armmnt	**Arrears**	artrs
Armature	armatr	**Arrest**	arst
Armful	armfl	**Arrive**	arv
Armillary	arm-l	**Arrogate**	ar-g
Armenian (yan)	armnyn	**Arrow**	aro
Armipotent	armptnt	**Arsenal**	arsnl
Armistice	armsts	**Arsenic**	arsnc
Armlet	armlt	**Arson**	arsn

Art art		**Ashamed** shamd	
Arterial artrl		**Ashes** ashs	
Artery artry		**Ashore** shor	
Artful artfl		**Ashy** ashy	
Arthritic arthrtc		**Aside** asid	
Artichoke artchk		**Asinine** asnn	
Article artcl		**Ask** ask	
Articulate artclt		**Askance** askns	
Artifice atrfs		**Askant** asknt	
Artificer artfsr		**Askew (sku)** askew	
Artificial art f		**Asleep** aslp	
Artillery artlry		**Asp** asp	
Artisan artsn		**Asparagus** asprgs	
Artist artst		**Aspect** aspct	
Artless artls		**Aspen** aspn	
As as		**Asperity** asprt	
Asafetida asftd		**Asperse** asprs	
Asbestos asbsts		**Aspersion** aspr-shn	
Ascend asnd		**Asphalt** asflt	
Ascent asnt		**Asphyxia** asfxa	
Ascertain asrtn		**Aspirant** asprnt	
Ascetic as-c		**Aspirate** asprt	
Ascribe ascrb		**Aspire** aspr	
Ash ash		**Asquint** asqnt	

Assail		**Astern**	
asl		astrn	
Assassin		**Asteroid**	
asasn		astroid	
Assault		**Asthma (az)**	
asalt		asma	
Assay		**Astonish**	
asa		astnsh	
Assemble		**Astound**	
asmbl		astound	
Assent		**Astral**	
asnt		astral	
Assert		**Astray**	
asrt		astra	
Assess		**Astride**	
asss		astrid	
Assets		**Astringent**	
assts		astrnjnt	
Asseverate		**Astrology**	
asvrat		astrlj	
Assiduity		**Astronomy**	
asdu-t		astronmy	
Assiduous		**Astute**	
asidus		astut	
Assign		**Asunder**	
asn		asndr	
Assimilate		**Asylum**	
asmlt		aslm	
Assist		**At**	
asst		at	
Assize		**Ate**	
assis		at	
Associate		**Atheism**	
as-s		athism	
Assonant		**Atheist**	
asonnt		athist	
Assort		**Atheneum**	
asrt		athnm	
Assuage		**Athirst**	
as-sw		athrst	
Assume		**Athlete**	
asum		athlt	
Assure		**Athwart**	
asur		athrt	
Aster		**Atlantean**	
astr		atlntn	
Asterisk		**Atlantic**	
astrsk		atlntc	

Atlas
a/ls

Atmosphere
a/mstr

Atom
a/m

Atone
a/n

Atrocious
a/rshs

Atrocity
a/rst

Atrophy
a/rf

Attach
a/ch

Attache (atasha)
a/sha

Attack
a/c

Attain
a/an

Attaint
a/ant

Attemper
a/mpr

Attempt
a/mt

Attend
a/nd, tend

Attention
atnshn, tenshn

Attentive
a/n-t

Attenuate
a/n-w

Attest
a/st

Attic
a/-i

Atticism
a/ssm

Attire
a/r

Attitude
a/-t

Attorney (tur)
a/rny

Attribute
a/rbt

Attrition
a/-tr

Attune
a/tn

Auburn
au/rn

Auction
auc-shn

Audacious
au-d

Audible
aud/bl

Audience
aud/ns

Audit
aud/t

Auger
augr

Aught (awt)
au/

August
angst

Aulic
au/-i

Aunt
au/t

Aureola
aurola

Auricle
aurcl

Auriferous
aurfrs

Aurist
aurst

Aurora
aurora

Auscultation
auscl-t

Auspices
auspss

Austere
austr

Austral
austrl

Authentic
au/hn-t

Author
   au*th*r

Autobiographer
   au*t*b-g

Autocracy
   au*t*cr s

Autocrat
   au*t*crt

Autodafe
   au*t*df

Autograph
   au*t*-g

Automatic
   au*t*mt i

Autumn (tum)
   au*t*m

Auxiliary
   auxlry

Avail
   a*v*l

Avalanche
   a*v*lnch

Avarice
   a*v*rs

Avast
   a*v*st

Avaunt
   a*v*nt

Ave-Mary
   a*v*mry

Avenaceous
   a*v* n

Avenge
   a*v*ng

Avenue
   a*v*new

Aver
   a*v*r

Average
   a*v*rg

Averment
   a*v*rmnt

Aversion
   a*v*rshn

Avert
   a*v*rt

Aviary
   a*v*ary

Avidity
   a*v*d-t

Avocation
   a*v*-c

Avoid
   a*v*d

Avoirdupois
   a*v*rdps

Avouch
   a*v*ouch

Avow
   a*v*ow

Avulsion
   a*v*l-shn

Await
   a*w*t

Awake
   a*w*k

Award
   a*w*rd

Aware
   a*w*r

Away
   a*w*a

Awe
   a*w*

Awful
   a*w*fl

Awhile
   a*w*l

Awkward
   aw*k*rd

Awl
   aw*l*

Awn
   a*w*n

Awning
   a*w*n-ing

Awoke
   a*w*k

Awry
   a*r*i

Ax
   a*k*s

Axial
   a*k*shl

Axiform
   a*k*sfrm

Axillary akslry		**Baffle** bafl
Axiom aksm		**Bag** bag
Axis akss		**Bagatelle** bagtl
Axle aksl		**Baggage** bagj
Aye i		**Bagnio (banyo)** banyo
Azure azr		**Bagpipe** bagpp

B.

Baa ba		**Bail** bal
Babble babl		**Bailiff** balf
Babe bab		**Balliwick** balwc
Baboon babn		**Bailor** balr
Baby baby		**Bairn** barn
Baccalaureate bac-l		**Bait** bat
Bacchanal bacnl		**Baize** baz
Bachelor bachlr		**Bake** bac
Back bac		**Baker** bakr
Backbite bacbt		**Balance** balns
Backbone bacbn		**Balcony** balcny
Backward bacrd		**Bald** bald
Bacon bacn		**Balderdash** baldrsh
Bad bad		**Baldric** baldrc
Bade bad		**Bale** bal
Badge baj		**Balk (bawk)** bak
Badger bajr		**Ball** bal
		Ballad balad

Ballast
balst

Ballet
balet

Balloon
baln

Ballot
balt

Balm (bam)
bam

Balsam
balsm

Baluster
balstr

Balustrade
balstrd

Bamboo
bamboo

Bamboozle
bambzl

Ban
ban

Banana
banana

Band
band

Bandage
bandj

Bandana
bandna

Bandit
bandt

Bandy
bandy

Bane
ban

Bang
bang

Banian
banyn

Banish
bansh

Banister
banstr

Bank
bank

Bank-bill
bankbl

Bank-note
banknt

Bankrupt
bankrpt

Bank-stock
bankstc

Banner
banr

Banquet
banqt

Bans
bans

Bantam
bantm

Banter
bantr

Bantling
bantl-ing

Banyan
banyn

Baptism
baptsm

Baptist
baptst

Baptize
baptz

Bar
bar

Barb
barb

Barbarian
barbrn

Barbaric
barbrc

Barbarism
barbsm

Barbarous
barbrs

Barbecue
barbcu

Barber
barbr

Barberry
barbry

Bard
bard

Bare
bar

Bargain
bargn

Barge
barj

Barilla
barla

Bark
bark

Barley
barly

Barm
barm

Barn
barn

Barnacle
barncl

Barometer
barmtr

Baron
barn

Baronial
barnl

Barouche (roosh)
barush

Barrack
barc

Barrator
baratr

Barratry
bara-tr

Barrel
barl

Barren
barn

Barricade
bar-c

Barrier
baryr

Barrister
barstr

Barrow
baro

Barter
bartr

Barytone
bartn

Basalt
baslt

Base
bas

Bashful
bashfl

Basic
bas-i

Basilisk
baslsk

Basin (sn)
basn

Basis (ses)
bass

Bask
bask

Basket
baskt

Bass
bas

Bass
bas

Bassoon
basn

Bastard
bastrd

Baste
bast

Bastile
bastl

Bastinade
bastnd

Bastion (ynn)
bastyn

Bat
bat

Batch
bach

Bate
bat

Batteau (batto)
bato

Bath
bath

Baton (tong)
batng

Battalion
batlyn

Batten
batn

Batter		**Beast**
battr		best
Batting		**Beat**
bat-ing		bet
Battle		**Beaten**
batl		betn
Bawble		**Beatific**
bawbl		betfc
Bawd		**Beatitude**
baud		beat-t
Bawl		**Beau (bo)**
bawl		bo
Bay		**Beauteous**
ba		beutus
Bayberry		**Beautiful**
babry		beutil
Bayonet		**Beauty**
bant		beuty
Bayou		**Beaver**
baoo		bevr
Bay-rum		**Becalm**
barm		becm
Bazar		**Became**
bazr		becm
Be		**Because**
be		becs
Beach		**Bechance**
bech		bechns
Beacon		**Beck**
becn		bec
Bead		**Beckon**
bed		becn
Beadle		**Bed**
bedl		bed
Beagle		**Bedabble**
begl		bedabl
Beak		**Bedash**
bek		bedsh
Beam		**Bedaub**
bem		bedb
Bean		**Bedazzle**
ben		bedzl
Bear		**Bedeck**
bar		bedk
Beard		**Bedew**
berd		bedew
Bearer		**Bedim**
barr		bedm

Bedizen bedzn		**Begrime** begrm	
Bedlam bedlm		**Begrudge** begrj	
Bedraggle bedragl		**Beguile** begil	
Bedrench bedrnch		**Begun** begn	
Bee be		**Behalf** behf	
Beech bech		**Behave** behv	
Beef bef		**Behead** behd	
Been (bin) bin		**Beheld** behld	
Beer ber		**Behemoth** behmth	
Beet bet		**Behest** behst	
Beetle betl		**Behind** behnd	
Beeves bevs		**Behold** behld	
Befit beft		**Behoof** behf	
Befool befl		**Behoove** behv	
Before fro		**Being** be-ing	
Befoul befl		**Belabor** belbr	
Befriend befrnd		**Belate** belat	
Beg beg		**Belay** bela	
Beget begt		**Belch** belch	
Beggar begr		**Beldam** beldm	
Begin begn		**Beleaguer** belegr	
Begird begrd		**Belfry** belfry	
Begone begn		**Belie** beli	
Begot begt		**Belief** blef	

Believe
blev

Bell
bel

Belles-lettres
beltr

Belligerent
beljrnt

Bellman
belmn

Bellow
belo

Belly
bely

Belong
belng

Beloved
belvd

Below
blo

Bemire
bemr

Bemoan
bemn

Bench
bench

Bend
bend

Beneath
benth

Benedict
bend-i

Benediction
ben-d

Benefactor
benfktr

Benefice
benefs

Beneficial
ben-f

Benefit
benft

Benevolent
benvlnt

Benight (nit)
be-nt

Benign (nin)
be-nn

Benignant
be-ng

Benison
bensn

Bent
bent

Benumb (num)
benm

Benzoin
benzoin

Bepraise
bepras

Bequeath
beqth

Berate
berat

Bereave
brv

Bereft
berft

Bergamot
bergmt

Berth
berth

Beryl
beril

Beseech
besh

Beseem
besm

Beset
beset

Beshrew
beshru

Beside
besid

Besiege
besj

Besmear
besmr

Besom
besm

Besot
besot

Besought
besaut

Bespatter
besptr

Bespeak
bespc

Besprinkle
besprnkl

Best
best

Bestial (yal)
bestl

Bestir
bestr

Bestow
besto

Bestrew (stru)
bestru

Bestride
bestrid

Bet
bet

Betake
betk

Betel
betl

Bethink
bethnk

Betide
betid

Betime
betm

Betook
betk

Betray
betra

Betroth
betrth

Better
betr

Betty
be-ty

Between
twen

Betwixt
twixt

Bevel
bevl

Beverage
bevrj

Bevy
bevy

Bewail
bewl

Beware
bewr

Bewilder
bewldr

Bewitch
bewch

Bey (ba)
ba

Beyond
beyn

Bezel
bezl

Bias
bras

Bib
bib

Bibber
bibr

Bible
bibl

Bicker
bicr

Bid
bid

Bide
bid

Biennial
binl

Bier
ber

Bifarious
bi-fr

Bifid
bifd

Biform
bifrm

Bifurcate
bifrct

Big
big

Bigamy
bigmy

Biggin
bign

Bigot
bigt

Bilberry bilbry	**Bipartite** biprtit
Bilbo bilbo	**Biped** bipd
Bile bil	**Biquadrate** bi-q
Bilge bilj	**Birch** birch
Biliary bilary	**Bird** bird
Bilingual bilngl	**Birth** birth
Bilious (yus) bilys	**Biscuit** bisct
Bilk bilk	**Bisect** bis-e
Bill bil	**Bishop** bi-hp
Billet bilet	**Bismuth** bismth
Billet-doux (doo) bildoo	**Bison** bisn
Billiards bilyrs	**Bissextile** bisxtl
Billingsgate bil-insgt	**Bister** bistr
Billion bilyn	**Bit** bit
Billow bilo	**Bite** bit
Bin bin	**Bitter** bitr
Binary bi-n	**Bittern** bitrn
Binate binat	**Bitumen** bitumn
Bind bind	**Bivalve** bivlv
Binnacle bincl	**Bivouac (wak)** bivc
Binocular bin-o	**Blab** blab
Binomial binml	**Black** blac
Biographer bio-g	**Bladder** bladr
Biology bi-o	**Blade** blad

Blain blan	**Blink** blink
Blame blam	**Bliss** blis
Blanch blanch	**Blister** blistr
Blanc-mange (blomonj) blomnj	**Blithe** blith
Bland bland	**Bloat** blot
Blank blank	**Block** bloc
Blarney blarny	**Blood** blood
Blaspheme blas-f	**Bloom** bloom
Blast blast	**Blossom** blosm
Blatant blatnt	**Blot** blot
Blaze blaz	**Blotch** bloch
Blazon blazn	**Blouse** blous
Bleach blech	**Blow** blo
Bleak blek	**Blowze** blowz
Blear bler	**Blubber** blubr
Bleat blet	**Bludgeon** blujn
Bleed bled	**Blue** blu
Blemish blemsh	**Bluff** bluf
Blench blench	**Blunder** blundr
Blend blend	**Blunt** blunt
Bless bles	**Blur** blur
Blew blew	**Blurt** blurt
Blight (blit) blit	**Blush** blush
Blind blind	**Bluster** blustr

Boa
boa

Boar
ber

Board
bord

Boast
bost

Boat
bot

Bob
bob

Bobbin
bobn

Bocking
boc-ing

Bode
bod

Bodice
bodis

Bodily
bodly

Bodkin
bodkn

Body
body

Bog
bog

Boggle
bogl

Bohea
bohe

Boil
boil

Boisterous
boistrs

Bold
bold

Bole
bol

Bolt
bolt

Bolus
bols

Bomb (bum)
bum

Bombard
bumbrd

Bombazine
bumbzn

Bombast
bumbst

Bombazette
bumbzt

Bombketch
bumkch

Bond
bond

Bone
bon

Bonfire
bonfr

Bonnet
bont

Bonny
bonny

Bony
bony

Bonus
bons

Booby
booby

Book
book

Bookcase
bookks

Book-keeping
bookp-ing

Boom
boom

Boon
boon

Boor
boor

Boosy
boo-s

Boot
boot

Booth
booth

Booty
boo-t

Borax
borx

Border
bordr

Bore
bor

Boreas
bores

Born
born

Borne
born

Borough (o)
buro

Borrow
boro

Boss
bos ·

Bosom (boozum)
boosm

Botanic
botnc

Botany
botny

Botch
boch

Both
both

Bother
bothr

Bots
bots

Bottle
botl

Bottom
botm

Boudoir (boodwor)
boodwr

Bough (bou)
bou

Bought (bawt)
baut

Bounce
bouns

Bound
bound

Bounty
boun-t

Bouquet (booka)
booka

Bourgeois (burjois)
burjs

Bourn
brn

Bourse
bers

Bout
bout

Bovine
bovn

Bow (bou)
bow

Bow
bo

Bowel
bowel

Bower
bower

Bowie-knife (boe)
b nf

Bowl
bol

Bowlder
b ldr

Bowsprit
bosprt

Box
box

Boy
by

Brace
bras

Brachygraphy
brac-gr

Bracket
bracet

Brackish
bracsh

Bract
bract

Brad
brad

Brag
brag

Brahmin
bramn

Braid
brad

Brain
bran

Brake
brak

Bramble
brambl

Bran
bran

Branch
branch

Brand
brand

Brandy
bran-d

Brasier (zhur)
brazr

Brass
bras

Brat
brat

Bravado
bra-v

Brave
brav

Bravo
bravo

Brawl
brawl

Brawn
brawn

Brawny
brawny

Bray
bra

Braze
braz

Breach
brech

Bread
bred

Breadth
bredth

Break
brak

Bream
brem

Breast
brest

Breath
breth

Breathe
breth

Bred
bred

Breech
brech

Breed
bred

Breeze
brez

Brethren
brethrn

Brevet
brevt

Breviary
brevry

Brevier
brevr

Brevity
brev-t

Brew (bru)
bru

Brewer
brur

Brewis
bruis

Bribe
brib

Brick
bric

Bride
brid

Bridge
brij

Bridle
bridl

Brief
bref

Brier
brir

Brig
brig

Bright (brit)
brit

Brilliant
brilynt

Brim
brim

Brindle brindl	**Brood** brood	
Brine brin	**Brook** brook	
Bring bring	**Broom** broom	
Brink brink	**Broth** broth	
Brisk brisk	**Brother** bruthr	
Brisket briskt	**Brought (brawt)** brawt	
Bristle (brisl) brisl	**Brow** brow	
Britannia britny	**Brown** brown	
British britsh	**Browse** browz	
Briton britn	**Browse** brows	
Brittle britl	**Bruin** brun	
Broach broch	**Bruise** bruz	
Broad brod	**Bruit** brut	
Brocade brocd	**Brunette** brunet	
Broccoli brocli	**Brunt** brunt	
Brogan brogn	**Brush** brush	
Brogue brog	**Brutal** brutl	
Broil broil	**Brute** brut	
Broke brok	**Bubble** bubl	
Broker brokr	**Buccaneer** bucnr	
Bronchial broncl	**Buck** buc	
Bronchitis broncts	**Bucket** buct	
Bronze bronz	**Buckle (l)** bucl	
Brooch brooch	**Bucolic** buclc	

Bud
bud

Budge
buj

Budget
bujt

Buff
buf

Buffalo
buflo

Buffet
buft

Buffoon
bufn

Bug
bug

Buggy
bugy

Bugle
bugl

Buhl (bul)
bul

Buhrstone
burstn

Build
bild

Built
bilt

Bulb
bulb

Bulge
bulj

Bulk
bulk

Bull
bul

Bullet
bulct

Bulletin
bultn

Bullion
bulyn

Bulwark
bulwrk

Bumblebee
bumblb

Bump
bump

Bumper
bumpr

Bumpkin
bumpkn

Bun
bun

Bunch
bunch

Bundle
bundl

Bung
bung

Bungle
bungl

Bunion
bunyn

Bunk
bunk

Bunting
bunt-ing

Buoy (bwooy)
booy

Bur .
bur

Burden
burdn

Burdock
burdc

Bureau (ro)
buro

Burgess
burjs

Burgher
burgr

Burglar
burglr

Burgomaster
burgmstr

Burgundy
burgndy

Burial (berial)
beryl

Burin
burn

Burlesque (lesk)
burlsk

Burly
burly

Burn burn	**Buttock** butc
Burnt burnt	**Button** butn
Burrow buro	**Buttress** butrs
Bursar bursr	**Buxom** buxm
Burst burst	**Buy (bi)** bi
Burthen burthn	**Buyer** bir
Bury (bery) bery	**Buzz** buz
Bush bush	**Buzzard** buzrd
Bushel bushl	**By** bi
Busily bisly	**Byzantine** bizntn
Business bisns	**C.**
Busk busk	**Cab** cab
Buskin buskn	**Cabal** cabl
Buss bus	**Cabala** cabla
Bust bust	**Cabbage** cabj
Bustard bustrd	**Cabin** cabn
Bustle (l) busl	**Cabinet** cabnt
Busy bisy	**Cable** cabl
But but	**Caboose** caboos
Butcher buchr	**Cacao** cacao
Butler butlr	**Cackle** cacl
Butment butmnt	**Cactus** cacts
Butt but	**Cadaver** cadvr
Butter butr	**Caddy** cady

Cadence
cadns

Cadet
cadt

Caesura
sesura

Cag
cag

Cage
caj

Cairn
carn

Caitiff
catf

Cajole
cajl

Cake
cak

Calabash
calbsh

Calamitous
calmts

Calash
calsh

Calcareous
calcrs

Calcination
cals-n

Calcine
calsn

Calculate
calclt

Calculus
calcls

Caldron
caldrn

Calefactive
calfc-t

Calendar
calndr

Calender
calndr

Calends
calnds

Calenture
calntr

Calf (kaf)
caf

Caliber
calbr

Calico
calco

Calipers
calprs

Caliph
calf

Calisthenics
cals-thn

Calk
cawk

Call
cal

Calligraphy
cal g

Calling
cal ing

Callosity
calost

Callous
calus

Callow
calo

Calm (kam)
calm

Calomel
calml

Calorie
calrc

Calorific
calrfc

Calumet
calmt

Calumny
calmny

Calve (kav)
cav

Calvinist
calvnst

Calyx
calx

Cam
cam

Cambric
cambrc

Came
cam

Camel	**Cannibal**
caml	canbl
Camelopard	**Cannon**
camlprd	cann
Cameo	**Cannot**
cameo	cant
Camlet	**Can't**
camlt	cant
Camp	**Canoe (noo)**
camp	canoo
Campaign	**Canon**
campn	cann
Campaniform	**Canopy**
campnfrm	canpy
Camphene	**Cant**
camfn	cant
Camphor	**Cantalope**
camfr	cantlp
Can	**Cantata**
can	cantta
Canal	**Canteen**
canl	cantn
Canary	**Canter**
canry	cantr
Cancel	**Cantiele**
cansl	cantcl
Cancer	**Canto**
cansr	canto
Candelabrum	**Canton**
candlbrm	cantn
Candid	**Canvas**
candd	canvs
Candidate	**Canvass**
canddt	canvs
Candle	**Canzonet**
candl	canznt
Candor	**Caoutchoue (koo-**
candr	coochk (ehook
Candy	**Capable**
candy	capbl
Cane	**Capacious**
can	ca p
Canine	**Capacity**
cann	capst
Canister	**Capapie**
canstr	capap
Canker	**Caparison**
cankr	caprsn

Cape	**Carat**
cap	carat
Caper	**Caravan**
capr	carvn
Capillament	**Caraway**
caplmt	carw
Capillary	**Carbine**
caplry	carbn
Capital	**Carbon**
captl	carbn
Capitation	**Carboy**
cap-t	carboy
Capitol	**Carbuncle**
captl	carbncl
Capitulate	**Caress**
capt-l	carcs
Capon (pu)	**Card**
capn	card
Cap-paper	**Cardiac**
capapr	card-a
Caprice	**Cardinal**
capres	cardnl
Capsize	**Care**
capss	care
Capstan	**Careen**
capstn	carn
Capsule	**Career**
capsl	carr
Captain	**Careful**
captn	carfl
Caption	**Careless**
capshn	carls
Captivate	**Caress**
capt-v	cars
Captive	**Caret**
cap-t	caret
Captor	**Cargo**
captr	cargo
Capture	**Caricature**
captur	carctr
Capuchin (sheen)	**Caries**
capshn	cares
Car	**Cariole**
car	caril
Carabine	**Carious**
carabn	caris
Caracole	**Carl**
caracl	carl

Carmine carmn	**Cartridge** cartrj
Carnage carnj	**Carve** carv
Carnal carnl	**Cascade** cascd
Carnation car-n	**Case** cas
Carnelian carnln	**Caseous** casys
Carnival carnvl	**Cash** cash
Carnivorous car-nv	**Cashmere** cashmr
Carol carol	**Casing** cas-ing
Carotid carotd	**Cask** cask
Carouse carous	**Casket** caskt
Carp carp	**Casque** cask
Carpenter carpntr	**Cassation** cas-s
Carpet carpt	**Cassia (kasha)** casha
Carriage (rig) carj	**Cassimere** casmr
Carrier caryr	**Cassock** cas-o
Carrion caryn	**Cassowary** caswry
Carrot carot	**Cast** cast
Carry cary	**Castanet** castnt
Cart cart	**Castaway** castw
Cartel cartl	**Caste** cast
Carter cartr	**Castellated** castl-l
Cartilage cartlj	**Caster** castr
Cartoon cartn	**Castigate** cast-g
Cartouch (tooch) cartch	**Casting** cast-ing

Castle (l)
casl

Castor
castr

Casual (eazh)
casyl

Casuist
casust

Cat
cat

Catacomb (kom)
catcm

Catacoustics
catcst-i

Catalepsy
catlps

Catalogue (log)
catlg

Catamount
catmnt

Cataplasm
catplsm

Cataract
catrct

Catarrh (tar)
catr

Catastrophe
catstrf

Catcall
catcl

Catch
cach

Catching
cach-ing

Catchup
cachup

Catechetic
catct-i

Catechise
catcis

Catechu
catcu

Catechumen
catcmn

Categorical
catgrcl

Catenary
catnry

Cater
catr

Caterwaul
catrwl

Catfish
catfsh

Cathartic
cathrtc

Catheter
cathtr

Catholic
cathlc

Catholicon
cathlcn

Catkin
catcn

Catnip
catnp

Cat-o'-nine-tails
catnntls

Cattle
catl

Caucus
caucs

Caudal
caudl

Caught (kawt)
caut

Caul
caul

Cauliflower
caulflr

Causality
causlt

Causative
caus-t

Cause
caus

Causeway
causw

Caustic
caustc

Cauter
cautr

Cauterize
cautris

Caution
caushn

Cautious caushs		**Cell** sel	
Cavalcade cavlcd		**Cellar** selr	
Cavalier cavlr		**Cellular** selylr	
Cavalry cavlry		**Celt** selt	
Cave cav		**Celtic** seltc	
Cavern cavrn		**Cement** semnt	
Caviar cavyr		**Cemetery** sem-tr	
Cavil cavl		**Cenobite** senbt	
Cavity cav-t		**Cenotaph** sentf	
Caw caw		**Censer** sensr	
Cayenne (en) can		**Censor** sensr	
Cazique (zeek) cazk		**Censure** senshr	
Cease ses		**Census** senss	
Cedar sedr		**Cent** sent	
Cede sed		**Centaur** sentaur	
Cedilla sedla		**Centennial** sentnl	
Ceil sel		**Center** sentr	
Ceiling sel-ing		**Centigrade** sentgrd	
Celebrate selbrt		**Centiped** sentpd	
Celebrity selbr-t		**Cento** sento	
Celerity selrt		**Central** sentrl	
Celery selry		**Centric** sentrc	
Celestial selstl		**Centricity** sentrst	
Celibacy selbs		**Centrifugal** sentrfgl	

Centripetal sentrptl		**Chain** chan	
Centuple sentpl		**Chair** char	
Centurion sentrn		**Chaise** shaz	
Century sentry		**Chalcedony** calsdny	
Cephalic seflc		**Chaldron** caldrn	
Cerate serat		**Chalice** chals	
Cere ser		**Chalk** chak	
Cerebral serbrl		**Challenge** chalnj	
Ceremonial sermnl		**Chalybeate** calbat	
Certain sertn		**Chamber** chambr	
Certificate sertfct		**Chameleon** camln	
Certify sertf		**Chamfer** chamfr	
Certitude sert-t		**Chamois** shamy	
Cerulean serlyn		**Chamomile** camml	
Ceruse serus		**Champ** champ	
Cervical servcl		**Champagne** shampn	
Cessation sesashn		**Champion** champn	
Cession seshn		**Chance** chans	
Cesura sesra		**Chancel** chansl	
Cetacean se-t		**Chancellor** chanslr	
Chafe chaf		**Chancery** chansry	
Chaff chaf		**Chandelier** shandlr	
Chagreen shagren		**Chandler** chandlr	
Chagrin shagrn		**Change** chanj	

Chanticleer chantclr		**Chastise** chasts	
Chantry chantry		**Chastity** chastt	
Chaos caos		**Chat** chat	
Chap chap		**Chateau (shato)** shato	
Chapel chapl		**Chattel (tl)** chatl	
Chaperon (shap) shaprn		**Chatter** chatr	
Chaplain chapln		**Chatty** chaty	
Chaplet chaplet		**Cheap** chep	
Chapman chapmn		**Cheat** chet	
Chaps (chops) chops		**Check** chck	
Chapter chaptr		**Cheek** chek	
Char char		**Cheer** cher	
Character carctr		**Cheese** ches	
Charade (sha) sharad		**Chemical** crmcl	
Charcoal charcl		**Chemise** shemes	
Charge charj		**Chemist** crmst	
Charily charily		**Cherry** chery	
Chariot charot		**Chersonese** chrsnes	
Charity char-t		**Cherub** cherb	
Charm charm		**Chess** ches	
Charnel-house charnlous		**Chest** chest	
Chart chart		**Chestnut** chesnt	
Chary chary		**Chevalier (shev)** shevlr	
Chase chas		**Chew (choo)** choo	

Chicane (shi) shican		**Chockfull** chckfl	
Chicken chicn		**Chocolate** choclt	
Chide chid		**Choice** chois	
Chief chef		**Choir (kwir)** quir	
Chilblain chilbln		**Choke** chok	
Child child		**Choler** colr	
Chill chil		**Cholera** colra	
Chime chim		**Choose** choos	
Chimera cimra		**Chop** chop	
Chimney chimny		**Choral** corl	
China china		**Chord** cord	
Chine chin		**Chore** chor	
Chink chink		**Chorister** corstr	
Chintz chintz		**Chorography** coro-g	
Chip chip		**Chorus** cors	
Chirography ciro-g		**Chose** chos	
Chiromancy cirmn-s		**Chough (chuf)** chuf	
Chiropodist cirpdst		**Chowder** chowdr	
Chirp chirp		**Chrism** crism	
Chisel chisl		**Christ** x	
Chit chit		**Christian** xn	
Chivalry shivlry		**Christianity** xnt	
Chives chivs		**Christmas** xms	
Chlorine clorn		**Chromatic** crom-a	

Chrome
crom

Chronic
cron-i

Chronicle
croncl

Chronology
cron-o

Chronometer
cronmtr

Chrysalis
crisls

Chrysolite
crislt

Chub
chub

Chuck
chuc

Chuff
chuf

Chum
chum

Chunk
chunk

Church
church

Churl
churl

Churn
churn

Chyle
cil

Chyme
cim

Cicatrice
sictrs

Cider
sidr

Cigar
sigr

Ciliary
silry

Cincture
sinctr

Cinder
sindr

Cinnamon
sinmn

Cinque (sink)
sink

Cion
sion

Cipher
sifr

Circle
sircl

Circuit (kit)
sirct

Circulate
sirc-l

Circumambient
sm-ambnt

Circumcise
sm-sis

Circumference
sm-frns

Circumflex
sm-flx

Circumfuse
sm-fs

Circumjacent
sm-jsnt

Circumlocution
sml-cshn

Circumlocutory
sml-ctr

Circumnavigate
sm-vgt

Circumpolar
sm-plr

Circumscribe
sm-scrb

Circumspect
sm-spt

Circumstance
sm-tns

Circumvallation
sm-vlshn

Circumvent
sm-vnt

Circus
sircs

Cisalpine
sisalpn

Cisatlantic
sisatlntc

Cistern
sistrn

Cit
sit

Citadel
sitdl

Citation
si-t

Cite
sit

Citizen
sitzn

Citric
sitrc

Citron
sitrn

City
si-t

Civet
sivet

Civic
siv-i

Civil
sivl

Clack
clac

Clad
clad

Claim
clam

Clairvoyant
clarvnt

Clam
clam

Clamber
clambr

Clammy
clamy

Clamor
clamr

Clamp
clamp

Clandestine
clandstn

Clang
clang

Clangor
clangr

Clank
clank

Clap
clap

Clapboard
clapbrd

Clapper
clapr

Claptrap
claptrp

Claret
clart

Clarify
clarf

Clarinet
clarnt

Clarion
clarn

Clash
clash

Clasp
clasp

Class
clas

Classic
clas-i

Classify
clasf .

Clatter
clatr

Clause
claus

Claw
claw

Clay
cla

Clean
clen

Cleanse
clens

Clear
cler

Cleat
clet

Cleave
clev

Clef
clef

Cleft
cleft

Clement
clemnt

Clergy
clerjy

Clerk
clerk

Clever
clevr

Clevis
clevis

Clew
clu

Click
clic

Client
clint

Cliff
clif

Climacteric
climctr-i

Climate
climt

Climax
climx

Climb
clim

Clime
clim

Clinch
clinch

Cling
cling

Clinic
clin-i

Clink
clink

Clinker
clinkr

Clip
clip

Cloak
clok

Clock
cloc

Clod
clod

Cloff
clof

Clog
clog

Cloister
cloistr

Close
cloz

Close
clos

Closet
closet

Closing
clos-ing

Closure
closyr

Clot
clot

Cloth
cloth

Clothe
cloth

Cloud
cloud

Clout
clout

Clove
clov

Clover
clovr

Clown
clown

Cloy
cloy

Club
club

Cluck
cluc

Clue
clu

Clump
clump

Clumsy
clum-s

Clung
clung

Cluster
clustr

Clutch cluch	**Cod** cod
Clutter clutr	**Code** cod
Clyster clistr	**Codger** cojr
Coach coch	**Codicil** codisl
Coadjutor co-j	**Codify** codf
Coagent co-agnt	**Coddle** codl
Coagulate coaglt	**Coefficient** coe-f
Coal col	**Coequal** coekl
Coalesce coles	**Coerce** coers
Coalition coa-l	**Coessential** co-sn
Coarse cors	**Coeternal** co-tr
Coast cost	**Coeval** coevl
Coat cot	**Coexist** coxst
Coax cox	**Coextend** coxtnd
Cob cob	**Coffee** cofe
Cobalt coblt	**Coffer** cofr
Cobble cobl	**Coffin** cofn
Cobweb cobwb	**Cog** cog
Cochineal cochnl	**Cogent** cojnt
Cochleary coclry	**Cogitate** coj-t
Cock coc	**Cognate** c g-n
Cockle cocl	**Cognac (konyak)** conyc
Cocoa (koko) coco	**Cognition** cog-n
Cocoon cocn	**Cohabit** cohbt

Coheir (ar) coar	
Cohere cohr	
Cohort cohrt	
Coif coif	
Coil coil	
Coin coin	
Coincide consd	
Coke cok	
Colander (kul) culndr	
Cold cold	
Colie colc	
Collapse colps	
Collar colar	
Collate co-l	
Collateral co-l	
Collation co-l	
Colleague clg	
Collect col-e	
Collect' colct	
College colj, col	
Collide colid	
Collier (yer) colyr	
Collision col-l	
Collocate col-c	

Collop colp	
Colloquy col-q	
Collude colud	
Colon coln	
Colonel (kurnel) curnl	
Colonial colnl	
Colony colny	
Color culr	
Colossal c-losl	
Collossus coloss	
Colt colt	
Coulter coltr	
Columbine colmbn	
Column (kolum) colm	
Colure colur	
Coma coma	
Comatose comts	
Comb com	
Combat comba-t	
Combine combi-n	
Combustion combu-stn	
Come (kum) cum	
Comedy come-dy	
Comely cumly	

Comet
come-t

Comfit
comfi-t

Comfort (kum)
cumfor-t

Comfrey
cumfre-y

Comic
comi-c

Coming
cumi-ng

Comity
comi-ty

Comma
coma

Command
comma-nd

Commemorate
comme-mrat

Commence
comme-ns

Commend
comme-nd

Commensurate
comme-nsrt

Comment
comme-nt

Commerce
commer-s

Commingle
commi-ngl

Comminute
commi-nut

Commiserate
commi-srt

Commissary
commi-sry

Commission
commi-shn

Commissure (yur)
commi-sr

Commit
commi-t

Committee
commi-te

Commix
commi-x

Commode
commo-d

Commodore
commo-dr

Common
commo-n

Commons
commo-ns

Commotion
commo-sn

Commune
commu-n

Communicate
commu-nct

Communion
commu-nn

Community
commu-nt

Commutation
commu-tsn

Commute
commu-t

Compact
compa-ct

Companion
compa-nn

Compare
compa-r

Compass
compa-s

Compassion
compa-sn

Compatible
compat-bl

Compatriot
compat-rt

Compeer
compe-r

Compel
compe-l

Compend
compe-nd

Compete
compe-t

Competent
compet-nt

Compile
compi-l

Complacent
compla-snt

Complain
compla-n

Complaisant
compla-snt

Complement
comple-mnt

Complete
comple-t

Complex
comple-x

Comply
pli

Component
compo-nnt

Comport
compo-rt

Compose
compo-s

Compost
compo-st

Composure
compo-shr

Compotation
compo-tsn

Compound
compou-nd

Compound′
compou-nd

Comprehend
compre-nd

Compress
compre-s

Compress′
compre-s

Comprise
compri-s

Compromise
compro-ms

Comptroller (kon)
contro-lr

Compulsory
compul-sry

Compunction
compu-ncshn

Compute
compu-t

Comrade
comrad

Con
cen

Concatenate
concat-nat

Concave
conca-v

Conceal
conse-l

Conceit
conse-t

Concentrate
consen-trt

Concentric
consen-trc

Concern
conser-n

Concession
conses-sn

Conch (konk)
conc

Conciliate
consil-at

Concise
consi-s

Conclude
conclu-d

Concoct
conco-ct

Concord
concor-d

Concourse
concors

Concrete
concre-t

Concubine
concu-bn

Concur
concr

Concussion
concu-sn

Condemn
conde-m

Condense
conden-s

Condign
condi-n

Condition
condi-sn

Condole
condo-l

Condor
condo-r

Conduce
condu-s

Conduct
condu-ct

Conduct′
condu-ct

Conduit (dit)
condi-t

Cone
con

Confabulate
confa-blt

Confect
confe-ct

Confederate
confed-rt

Confer
confe-r

Confess
fes

Confessor
fesr

Confidant
confi-dnt

Confide
fid

Confident
confi-dnt

Configuration
config-rsn

Confine
confi-n

Confirm
confir-m

Confiscate
confi-sct

Conflagration
confla-grsn

Conflict
flict

Confluent
conflu-nt

Conform
confor-m

Confound
confou-nd

Confront
confru-nt

Confuse
confu-s

Confute
confu-t

Conge
conj

Congeal
conjl

Congener
conje-nr

Congenial
conje-nl

Congenital
conje-ntl

Congeries
conjer-es

Congestion
conje-sn

Conglobate
conglo-bt

Conglomerate
conglo-mrat

Congratulate
congrat-lt

Congregate
congre-gt

Congregation
congre-gshn

Congress
congre-s

Congruent
congru-nt

Conic
coni-c

Conics
coni-x

Coniferous
coni-frs

Conjecture
conje-ctr

Conjoin
conjoj-n

Conjugal
conju-gl

Conjugate
conju-gt

Conjunct
conju-nct

Conjure
conju-r

Connate
conna-t

Connect
conne-ct

Connive
conni-v

Connoisseur (nissur)
conni-sr

Conoid
conoi-d

Connubial
connu-bl

Conquer (conker)
conke-r

Consanguinity
consan-gwnty

Conscience
conshns

Conscientious
consi-nshs

Conscionable
conshi-nbl

Conscious
conshs

Conscript
conscri-pt

Consecrate
conse-crt

Consecutive
consec-tv

Consent
conse-nt

Consentaneous
consen-tns

Consequent
conse-qnt

Conserve
conser-v

Consider
consi-dr

Consign
consi-n

Consist
consi-st

Consociation
conso-sshn

Consolable
consol-bl

Consolation
conso-lashn

Console
conso-l

Consolidate
consol-dt

Consols
consol-s

Consonance
conso-nns

Consort
consor-t

Consort
consor-t

Conspicuous
conspi-cs

Conspire
conspi-r

Constable
consta-bl

Constant
consta-nt

Constellation
conste-lashn

Consternation
conster-nshn

Constipate
consti-pt

Constitute
consti-tut

Constitution
stushn

Constrain
constra-n

Constrict
constri-ct

Constringent
constri-njnt

Construct
constru-ct

Construe
stru

Constupration
constu-prshn

Consubstantial
consub-stnshl

Consubstantiation
consub-stnshn

Consuetudinal
conse-tdnl

Consul
consu-l

Consult
consu-lt

Consume
consu-m

Consummate
consu-mt

Consummate´
consum-t

Consumption
sumshn

Contact
conta-ct

Contagion
conta-jn

Contain
conta-´n

Contaminate
contam-nt

Contemn (tem)
conte-m

Contemplate
contem-plt

Contemporary
contem-pry

Contempt
contem-t

Contend
conten-d

Content
conten-t

Contention
conten-sn

Conterminous
conter-mns

Contest
conte-st

Contest
conte-st

Context
conte-xt

Contiguity
conti-gty

Continence
conti-nns

Continent
conti-nnt

Contingent
conti-njnt

Continue
conti-n

Continuity
conti-nt

Contort
contor-t

Contour
contu-r

Contraband
contra-bn

Contract
contra-ct

Contract´
contra-ct

Contradistinction
contra-stnkshn

Contralto
contral-to

Contrary
trary

Contrast
contra-st

Contrast´
contra-st

Contravallation
contra-vlshn

Contravene
contra-vn

Contribute
contri-bt

Contrite
contri-t

Contrive
contri-v

Control
contro-l

Controversy
contro-vrs

Contumacy
contu-ms

Contumely
contu-mly

Contusion
contu-sn

Conundrum
connun-drm

Convalescence
conva-lsns

Convene
ven

Convenient
vennt

Convent
vent

Convention
venshn

Conventual
ventl

Converge
verj

Converse
vers

Conversion
vershn

Convert
vert

Convert'
vert

Convex
vex

Convey
va

Convict
vict

Convict'
vict

Convince
vins

Convivial
convi-vl

Convocation
convo-cshn

Convoke
convo-c

Convolve
convol-v

Convoy
voy

Convulse
convul-s

Cony
cony

Coo
coo

Cook
cook

Cooky
cooky

Cool
cool

Cooler
coolr

Coolly
cooly

Coomb (koom)
coomb

Coop
coop

Cooper
coopr

Co-operate
co o

Co-ordinate
cord-n

Coot
coot

Copaiba
copba

Copal
copl

Coparcenary
coprs-n

Copartner
coprtnr

Cope
cop

Copier
copyr

Coping
cop-ing

Copious
copus

Copper copr	**Corollary** corlary
Copse cops	**Coronal** cornl
Copulative copl-t	**Coronation** cor-n
Copy copy	**Coroner** cornr
Coquet (ket) cokt	**Coronet** cornt
Coquette (ket) cokt	**Corporate** corprt
Coral corl	**Corporeal** corprl
Cord cord	**Corporeity** corprit
Cordial cordl	**Corpse** corps
Cordon cordn	**Corpulent** corplnt
Corduroy cordroy	**Corpuscle (pussl)** corpsl
Core cor	**Correct** cor-c
Coriaceous corashs	**Correlative** corel-t
Coriander corandr	**Correspond** cor-sp
Cork cork	**Corridor** cordr
Cormorant cormrnt	**Corroborate** corb-r
Corn corn	**Corrode** corod
Cornea cornea	**Corrosive** coro-s
Cornel cornl	**Corrugate** cor-g
Corner cornr	**Corrupt** cor-u
Cornet cornt	**Corsair** corsr
Cornice cornis	**Corse** cors
Cornucopia corncpa	**Corselet** corslt
Corolla corla	**Corset** corst

Cortege (kortazh) cortzh	**Could (kood)** cu
Cortical cortcl	**Coulter** cultr
Coruscate corusct	**Council** counsl
Corvette corvt	**Counsel** counsl
Cosey cosy	**Count** count
Cosmetic cos-mt	**Counter** countr
Cosmography cosm-gr	**Counterfeit** countrît
Cosmology cosm-o	**Countess** countes
Cosmopolite cosmplit	**Countless** countls
Cosset coset	**Country (kuntry)** countr
Cost cost	**County** coun-t
Costal costl	**Couple** cupl
Costive costv	**Coupon (koopong)** coopng
Costly costly	**Courage (kurej)** curj
Costume costm	**Courier (koorier)** coorer
Cotemporary cotmpry	**Course** cours
Coterie cotre	**Courser** coursr
Cotillion (yun) cotlyn	**Court** court
Cottage cotj	**Courteous** curts
Cotter cotr	**Courtesan** curtsn
Cotton cotn	**Courtesy** curt-s
Cotyledon cotldn	**Courtier (yer** curtr
Couch couch	**Courtly** courtly
Cough (kawf) cauf	**Courtship** courtshp

Cousin	**Cranberry**
cusn	crnbry
Cove	**Crane**
cov	cran
Covenant	**Cranium**
cuvnnt	cranym
Cover	**Crank**
cuvr	crank
Covert	**Cranny**
cuvrt	crany
Coverture	**Crape**
cuvrtur	crap
Covet	**Crash**
cuvt	crash
Covey	**Crate**
cuvy	crat
Cow	**Craunch**
cow	craunch
Coward	**Cravat**
cowrd	cravt
Cower	**Crave**
cowr	crav
Cowl	**Craven**
cowl	cravn
Coxcomb	**Craw**
cocscm	craw
Coy	**Crawfish**
coy	crawfsh
Cozy	**Crawl**
co-s	crawl
Crab	**Crayon**
crab	craon
Crack	**Craze**
crac	craz
Cradle	**Crazy**
cradl	craz
Craft	**Creak**
craft	crek
Crag	**Cream**
crag	crem
Cram	**Crease**
cram	cres
Crambo	**Create**
crambo	creat
Cramp	**Creator**
cramp	creatr
Crampoons	**Creature**
crampns	cretr

Credence crɛdns	**Cried** crid
Credentials crɛdnshls	**Crime** crɪm
Credible crɛdbl	**Criminal** crɪmnl
Creditor crɛdtr	**Crimp** crɪmp
Credulous crɛdls	**Crimson** crɪmsn
Creed crɛd	**Cringe** crɪnj
Creek crɛk	**Crinkle** crɪnkl
Creel crɛl	**Cripple** crɪpl
Creole crɛol	**Crisis** crɪss
Creosote crɛost	**Crisp** crɪsp
Crepitate crɛp-t	**Criterion** crɪtrn
Crept crɛpt	**Critic** crɪtc
Crepuscular crɛpsclr	**Criticise** crɪtss
Crescent crɛsnt	**Critique** crɪtc
Cress crɛs	**Croak** crok
Crest crɛst	**Crock** crɔc
Cretaceous crɛ-t	**Crocodile** crɔcdl
Crevice crɛvis	**Crocus** crɔcs
Crew (kru) crɛw	**Croft** crɔft
Crewel crɛwl	**Crone** crøn
Crib crɪb	**Crony** crøny
Cribbage crɪbj	**Crook** crøck
Crick crɪc	**Crop** crøp
Cricket crɪct	**Crosier (kroshᵣ** croshr

Cross cros		**Crutch** cruch	
Crotch croch		**Cry** cri	
Crouch crouch		**Crypt** cript	
Croup (kroop) croop		**Crystal** cristl	
Crow crow		**Crib** crib	
Crowbar crobr		**Cube** cub	
Crowd crowd		**Cubeb** cubb	
Crow-foot croft		**Cubic** cubc	
Crown crown		**Cuckold** cucld	
Crucial crushl		**Cuckoo** cucoo	
Cruciate crushat		**Cucumber** cucmbr	
Crucible crusbl		**Cud** cud	
Crucify crusf		**Cuddle** cudl	
Crude crud		**Cudgel** cugl	
Cruel crul		**Cue** cu	
Cruet cruet		**Cuff** cuf	
Cruise crus		**Cuirass (kwe)** queras	
Crumb crum		**Culinary** culnry	
Crupper crupr		**Cull** cull	
Crusade crusd		**Cullender** culndr	
Cruse crus		**Culler** culr	
Crush crush		**Culminate** culm-n	
Crust crust		**Culpable** culpbl	
Crustacean crus t		**Culprit** culprt	

Culvert
culvrt

Cumber
cumbr

Cumin
cumin

Cumulate
cum-l

Cuneiform
cunefrm

Cunning
cun-ing

Cup
cup

Cupel
cupel

Cupellation
cup-l

Cupidity
cupd-t

Cupola
cupla

Cupping
cup-ing

Cur
cur

Curable
curabl

Curacoa
curaso

Curate
curat

Curative
cur-t

Curator
curatr

Curb
curb

Curd
curd

Curdle
curdl

Cure
cur

Curfew
curfu

Curiosity
curost

Curious
curys

Curlew
curlu

Curmudgeon
curmjn

Currant
curnt

Currency
curn-s

Current
curnt

Curricle
curcl

Currish
cursh

Curry
cury

Curse
curs

Cursive
cur-s

Cursory
cursry

Curtail
curtl

Curtain
curtn

Curve
curv

Curvet
curvet

Cushion
cushn

Cusp
cusp

Custard
custrd

Custodian
custdn

Custom
custm

Cut
cut

Cutaneous
cu-tn

Cuticle
cutcl

Cutlass
cutls

Cutler
cutlr

Cutlet
cutlt

Cutpurse
cutprs

Cutter
cutr

Cutthroat
cutthrt

Cutting
cut-ing

Cycle
sycl

Cyclopic
syclpc

Cyclopedia
syclpda

Cygnet
sygnt

Cylinder
sylndr

Cymbal
symbl

Cynic
syn-i

Cynosure
synshr

Cypress
syprs

Cyst
syst

Czar (zar)
zar

D.

Dab
dab

Dace
das

Dactyl
dactl

Dad
dad

Daff
daf

Daffodil
dafdl

Dagger
dagr

Daguerreotype
dagrtp

Dahlia
dalya

Daily
daly

Dainty
dan-t

Dairy
dary

Daisy
da-s

Dale
dal

Dally
daly

Dam
dam

Damage
damj

Damask
damsk

Damasse
damas

Dame
dam

Damn
dam

Damp
damp

Damsel
damsl

Damson
damsn

Dance
dans

Dandle
dandl

Dandruff
dandrf

Dandy
dandy

Danger
danjr

Dangle dangl	**Dazzle** dazl
Dank dank	**Deacon** decn
Dapper dapr	**Dead** ded
Dapple dapl	**Deaf** def
Dare dar	**Deal** del
Dark dark	**Dean** den
Darling darl-ing	**Dear** der
Darn darn	**Dearth** derth
Darnel darnl	**Death** deth
Dart dart	**Debar** debr
Dash dash	**Debase** debs
Dastard dastrd	**Debate** debt
Data data	**Debauch** debch
Date dat	**Debenture** debntr
Dative da-t	**Debility** deblt
Daub daub	**Debit** debt
Daughter dautr	**Debonair** debnar
Daunt daunt	**Debouch (boosh)** debsh
Dauphin dauin	**Debris (bree)** debre
Davit davt	**Debt** det
Dawdle dawdl	**Debut (dabu)** dabu
Dawn dawn	**Decade** decad
Day da	**Decagon** decgn
Daze daz	**Decalogue (log)** dec-l

Decamp	**Decorate**
decmp	dec-r
Decant	**Decorous**
decnt	decrus
Decapitate	**Decorticate**
decp-t	decrt-c
Decay	**Decorum**
deca	decrm
Decease	**Decoy**
deses	decoy
Deceit	**Decrease**
deset	decres
Deceive	**Decree**
desv	decr
December	**Decrement**
desmbr	decrmnt
Decent	**Decrepit**
desnt	decrpt
Deception	**Decretal**
despshn	decrtl
Decide	**Decry**
desd	decri
Deciduous	**Decumbent**
desdus	decmbnt
Decimal	**Decuple**
desml	decupl
Decipher	**Decurion**
desfr	decurn
Decision	**Decussate**
dec-s	decusat
Deck	**Dedicate**
dec	ded-c
Declare	**Deduce**
declr	dec-d
Declaim	**Deduct**
declm	ded-u
Declension	**Deed**
declnshn	ded
Decline	**Deem**
decln	dem
Decoct	**Deep**
dec-o	dep
Decoloration	**Deer**
decul-r	der
Decompose	**Deface**
decmps	defs
Decompound	**Defalcation**
decmpnd	defl-c

Defame defam	
Default deflt	
Defeasance defsns	
Defeat deft	
Defecate def-c	
Defect defct	
Defence defns	
Defend defnd	
Defendant def	
Defense defns	
Defer defr	
Defiant defnt	
Deficit defst	
Defile defl	
Define defn	
Deflagrate defl-gr	
Deflect deflct	
Deflour deflr	
Defoliation defo-l	
Deform defrm	
Defraud defraud	
Defy defi	
Degenerate dejnrat	
Deglutition degl-t	

Degrade degrd	
Degree degr	
Deify deif	
Deign (dan) dan	
Deism deism	
Deist deist	
Deity de-t	
Deject de-j	
Delay dela	
Delectable del-e	
Delegate del-g	
Delf delf	
Deliberate delbrt	
Delicacy delc-s	
Delicious de-l	
Delight delit	
Delineate delnat	
Deliquesce delqs	
Delirious delrs	
Deliver delvr	
Dell del	
Delude delud	
Deluge delj	
Delusion de-l	

Demand
demnd

Demain
demn

Demarcation
demr-c

Demean
demn

Demented
demntd

Demerit
demrit

Demigod
demgd

Demijohn
demjn

Demise
demis

Democrat
demcrt

Demolish
demlsh

Demon
demn

Demonstrate
demnstrt

Demoralize
demrlis

Demulcent
de-ml

Demur
demr

Demure
demr

Demurrage
demrj

Demurrer
demrr

Demy
demy

Den
den

Dendrology
dendrlj

Denial
denil

Denizen
denzn

Denominate
de-nm

Denote
dent

Denounce
dcnns

Dense
dens

Dent
dent

Dentil
dentl

Dentist
dentst

Dentition
den-t

Denude
denud

Denunciate
denn-sh

Deny
deni

Deodand
dednd

Deontology
dent-o

Depart
deprt

Depend
depnd

Depict
depct

Depilatory
depl-tr

Depletion
de-pl

Deplore
deplr

Deploy
deploy

Deplume
deplm

Deponent
depnnt

Depopulate
depp-l

Deport
deprt

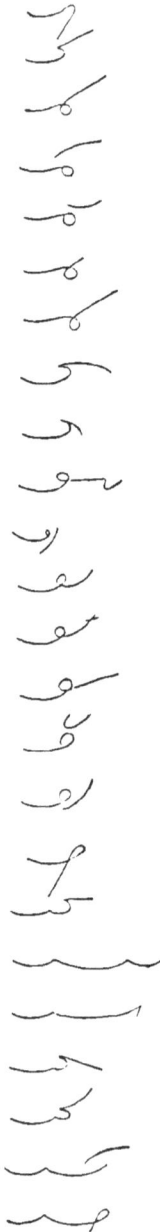

Depose depos		**Desert** desrt
Depot depo		**Deserve** desrv
Deprave deprv		**Deshabille** deshbl
Deprecate depr-c		**Desiccate** des-c
Depredate depr-d		**Desiderate** desdrt
Depress deprs		**Design** desn
Deprive deprv		**Desire** desr
Depth depth		**Desist** desst
Depute deput		**Desk** desk
Derange derng		**Desolate** des-l
Derelict derl-i		**Despair** despr
Deride derid		**Despatch** despch
Derisive deri-s		**Desperate** desprat
Derive derv		**Despise** desps
Derogate der-g		**Despoil** despl
Derrick der-i		**Despond** despnd
Dervis dervs		**Despot** despt
Descant descnt		**Despumation** desp-m
Descend desnd		**Desquamation** desq-m
Descent desnt		**Dessert** desrt
Describe descrb		**Destine** destn
Descry descry		**Destitute** dest-t
Desecrate des-cr		**Destroy** destr
Desert desrt		**Destruction** destr-u

Desuetude
desw-t

Desultory
desltry

Detach
detch

Detail
detl

Detain
detn

Detect
det-e

Deter
detr

Deteriorate
detr-r

Determine
detrmn

Detersive
detr-s

Detest
detst

Dethrone
dethrn

Detinue
detnu

Detonate
det-n

Detort
detrt

Detract
detr-a

Detriment
detrmnt

Detruncate
detrn-c

Detrusion
de-tr

Deuce
dus

Devastate
devs-t

Develop
velp

Deviate
de-v

Device
devs

Devil
devl

Devise
devs

Devisee
devse

Devisor
devsr

Devoid
devoid

Devoir (devwor)
devwr

Devolve
devlv

Devote
de-v

Devour
dev

Devout
devout

Dew (du)
dew

Dexter
dextr

Diabetes
dibts

Diabolical
diblcl

Diacritical
dicrtcl

Diadem
didm

Diaereses
dirss

Diagonal
dignl

Diagram
digrm

Dial
dil

Dialect
dil-e

Dialing
dil-ing

Dialogue
di-l

Diameter
diamtr

Diamond
dimnd

Diapason
dipsn

Diaper
diapr

Diaphanous
difns

Diaphragm
difrm

Diarrhea
direa

Diary
diry

Diatonic
ditn-i

Diatribe
ditrb

Dibble
dibl

Dice
dis

Dicky
dicy

Diction
dicshn

Dictum
dictm

Did
did

Die
di

Dieresis
dirss

Diet
diet

Differ
difr

Difficult
diliclt

Diffidence
difdns

Diffuse
difus

Dig
dig

Digest
dijst

Digit
dijt

Dignify
dignf

Dignitary
dign-tr

Dignity
dign-t

Digraph
di-gr

Digress
digrs

Dike
dik

Dilapidate
dilp-d

Dilate
di-l

Dilatory
dil-try

Dilemma
dilma

Diligent
diljnt

Dilute
di-l

Diluvial
dilvl

Dim
dim

Dime
dim

Dimension
dimnshn

Diminish
dimnsh

Dimissory
dimsry

Dimity
dim-t

Dimness
dimns

Dimple
dimpl

Din
din

Dingy
dinj

Dinner dinr	**Disarm** disarm
Dint dint	**Disarrange** disarnj
Diocese diss	**Disarray** disara
Diorama dirma	**Disaster** disastr
Dip dip	**Disavow** disavow
Diphtheria difthra	**Disband** disband
Diphthong difthng	**Disbelief** disblef
Diploma diplma	**Disburden** disbxrdn
Dipper dipr	**Disburse** disbxrs
Dire dir	**Disc** disc
Direct dir-e	**Discard** discard
Dirge dirj	**Discern** disern
Dirk dirk	**Discharge** discharj
Dirt dirt	**Disciple** dissipl
Disable disabl	**Disclaim** disclm
Disabuse disabus	**Disclose** discls
Disaffect disafct	**Discolor** discolr
Disadvantage disad	**Discomfit** d-ft
Disagree disagr	**Discomfort** d-frt
Disallow disal	**Discommode** d-md
Disannul disanl	**Discompose** d-pos
Disappear disafr	**Disconcert** d-srt
Disappoint disafnt	**Disconnect** d-nct
Disapprove disafrv	**Disconsolate** d-slt

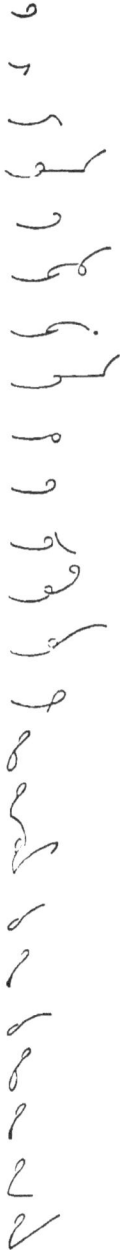

Discontent		**Dishabille**		
d-tnt		disbl		
Discontinue		**Dishearten**		
d-tnu		dishrtn		
Discord		**Dishevel**		
discord		dishvl		
Discount		**Dishonest (onest)**		
discount		disonst		
Discourage		**Dishonor (onor)**		
discurj		disonr		
Discourse		**Disingenuous**		
discors		disin-j		
Discourteous		**Disintegrate**		
discurts		disint-gr		
Discover		**Disinthrall**		
discuvr		disinthrl		
Discredit		**Disjoin**		
discredt		disjoin		
Discreet		**Disjunct**		
discret		disjunct		
Discrepant		**Disk**		
discrepnt		disc		
Discrete		**Dislodge**		
discret		disloj		
Discretion		**Dismal**		
dis-creshn		dismal		
Discriminate		**Dismay**		
discrim-n		disma		
Discursion		**Dismiss**		
discurshn		dismis		
Discursive		**Disparage**		
discur-s		disparj		
Discuss		**Dispatch**		
discus		dispach		
Disdain		**Dispel**		
disdan		dispel		
Disease		**Dispense**		
dises		dispens		
Disembark		**Disperse**		
disembrk		dispers		
Disgrace		**Display**		
disgras		displa		
Disguise		**Disport**		
disgis		disport		
Disgust		**Dispose**		
disgust		dispos		
Dish		**Dispute**		
dish		disput		

Dissect
dissect

Dissemble
dissembl

Dissent
dissent

Dissident
dissidnt

Dissipate
dissipat

Dissolute
dissolt

Dissonant
dissonnt

Dissuade
disswad

Distaff
distf

Distain
distn

Distend
distnd

Distill
distl

Distinct
distnct

Distort
distrt

Distract
distrct

Distrain
distrn

Distress
distrs

Distribute
distrbt

District
distrct

Distrust
distrust

Disturb
distrb

Disuse
disus

Ditto
dito

Ditty
dity

Diurnal
dirnl

Divan
divn

Divaricate
divr-c

Dive
div

Diver
divr

Diverge
divrj

Diverse
divrs

Divert
divrt

Divest
divst

Divide
divd

Divine
divn

Division
di-v

Divorce
divrs

Divulge
divlg

Dizzy
diz

Do
do

Docile
dosl

Dock
doc

Doctor
doctr, dr

Doctrine
doctrn

Document
docmnt

Dodecagon
dodcgn

Dodge
doj

Doe
do

Doer
door

Does (duz)
duz

Doff
dof

Dog
dog

Dogma
dogm

Doily
doily

Doing
do-ing

Doit
doit

Dole
dol

Doll
dol

Dollar
dolr

Dolor
dolor

Dolphin
dolfn

Dolt
dolt

Domain
domn

Dome
dom

Domestic
domstc

Domicil
domsl

Dominant
domnnt

Domineer
domnr

Dominical
domncl

Dominion
domnyn

Domino
domno

Don
don

Donate
do n

Donative
do-n

Done (dun)
dun

Donkey
dunky

Donor
donr

Doom
doom

Door
door

Doric
dor-i

Dormant
dormnt

Dormer
dormr

Dormouse
dorms

Dorsal
dorsl

Dose
dos

Dot
dot

Dotage
dotj

Dotard
dotrd

Dotation
do-t

Double
dubl

Doubloon
dubln

Doubt
dout

Douceur (doosur)
doosr

Dough
do

Doughty (dow)
dow-t

Douse
dous

Dove	duv		**Dramatist**	dramtst
Dowager	dowejr		**Drank**	drank
Dowdy	dowdy		**Drape**	drap
Dowel	dowel		**Drastic**	drast-i
Dower	dower		**Draught (draft)**	draft
Down	down		**Draw**	draw
Dowry	dowry		**Dray**	dra
Doxology	dox-o		**Dread**	dred
Doze	doz		**Dream**	drem
Dozen	duzn		**Drear**	drer
Dozy	do-s		**Dredge**	drej
Drab	drab		**Dregs**	dregs
Drachm	dram		**Drench**	drench
Draff	draf		**Dress**	dres
Draft	draft		**Dribble**	dribl
Drag	drag		**Drift**	drift
Dragoman	dragmn		**Drill**	dril
Dragon	dragn		**Drink**	drink
Dragoon	dragn		**Drip**	drip
Drain	dran		**Drive**	driv
Drake	drak		**Drivel**	drivl
Dram	dram		**Drizzle**	drizl
Drama	drama		**Droll**	drol
Dramatic	dram a		**Dromedary**	dromdry

Drone dron		**Ducal** ducl	
Droop droop		**Ducat** duct	
Drop drop		**Duchy** duchy	
Dropsy drop-s		**Duck** duc	
Dross dros		**Duct** duct	
Drouth (drowt) drowt		**Ductile** ductl	
Drove drov		**Dudgeon** dugn	
Drown drown		**Duds** dudz	
Drowse drowz		**Due** du	
Drub drub		**Duel** dul	
Drudge druj		**Duenna** duena	
Drug drug		**Duet** duet	
Drugget druget		**Dug** dug	
Druid druid		**Duke** duk	
Drum drum		**Dulcet** dulst	
Drunk drunk		**Dulcimer** dulsmr	
Drupe drup		**Dull** dul	
Dry dry		**Duly** duly	
Dryad dryad		**Dumb** dum	
Dryly dryly		**Dumpish** dumpsh	
Dryness dryns		**Dun** dun	
Dual dual		**Dunce** duns	
Dub dub		**Dungeon** dunjn	
Dubious dubs		**Duo** duo	

Duodecimal
dudsml

Duodecimo
dudsmo

Dupe
dup

Duplicate
dupl-c

Duplicity
dupls-t

Durable
durbl

Durance
durns

Duration
du-r

Duress
dures

During
dur-ing

Durst
durst

Dusk
dusk

Dust
dust

Duteous
duts

Dutiful
dutfl

Duty
du-t

Dwarf
dwarf

Dwell
dwel

Dwindle
dwindl

Dye
dy

Dynamics
dynm-i

Dynasty
dyns-t

Dysentery
dysn-tr

Dyspepsy
dyspp-s

E.

Each
ech

Eager
egr

Eagle
egl

Ear
er

Earl
erl

Early
erly

Earn
ern

Earth
urth

Ease
es

Easel
esl

East
est

Eat
et

Eaves
evs

Ebb
eb

Ebon
ebn

Ebriety
ebr-t

Ebullition
eb-l

Eccentric
xentre

Ecclesiastic
eclst

Echo
eco

Eclectic
ec-lc

Eclipse
eclips

Eclogue
ec-l

Economy ecnmy	**Effuse** efus
Ecstacy ecsts	**Eft** eft
Ecumenical ecmncl	**Egg** eg
Eddy edy	**Eglantine** eglntn
Edge ej	**Egotism** egtism
Edible edbl	**Egregious** egrjs
Edict ed-i	**Egret** egret
Edify edf	**Egypt** ejpt
Edile edl	**Eider-down (ider)** idrdn
Edit edt	**Eight (at)** at
Educate ed-c	**Either** ethr, ithr
Educe edus	**Ejaculate** ejc-l
Efface efas	**Eject** ej-e
Effect ef-c	**Eke** ek
Effeminate efm-n	**Elaborate** elbrt
Effervesce efrvs	**Elapse** elps
Effete efet	**Elastic** elstc
Efficacy efcsy	**Elate** elat
Effigy efj	**Elbow** elbo
Effloresce eflrs	**Elder** eldr
Effluence eflns	**Elect** el-c
Effort efrt	**Electric** el-c
Effrontery efrntry	**Electrotype** elctr-t
Effulgent efljnt	**Electuary** el-etry

Eleemosynary
e/msnry

Elegance
e/gns

Elegiac
e/eg-a

Elegy
e/jy

Element
e/mnt

Elephant
e/fnt

Elevate
e/-v

Eleven
e/vn

Elf
e/f

Elicit
e/ist

Eligible
e/jbl

Eliminate
e/m-n

Elision
e/shn

Elixir
e/xr

Elk
e/k

Ell
e/

Ellipse
e/ps

Elm
e/m

Elocution
e/-c

Elongate
e/n-g

Elope
e/p

Eloquence
e/-q

Else
e/s

Elucidate
e/us-d

Elude
e/ud

Elvish
e/vsh

Elysian
e/shn

Emaciate
ema-sh

Emanate
em-n

Emancipate
emnspt

Embalm
embm

Embank
embnk

Embargo
embrgo

Embark
embrk

Embarrass
embrs

Embassador
embsdr

Embed
embd

Embellish
emblsh

Embers
embrs

Embezzle
embzl

Emblazon
emblzn

Emblem
emblm

Embody
embdy

Embolden
embldn

Embonpoint
ongbnpwng

Emboss
embs

Embouchure
ongbshr

Embowel
embl

Embower
embor

Embrace
embrs

Embrasure
embrsr

Embrocate
embr-c

Embroider
embrdr

Embroil
embrl

Embryo
embro

Emendation
emn-d

Emerald
emrld

Emerge
emrj

Emersion
emrshn

Emery
emry

Emetic
em-e

Emigrant
emgrnt

Eminence
emnns

Emissary
emsry

Emit
emt

Emmet
emet

Emolliate
emlat

Emolument
emlmnt

Emotion
e-m

Empale
empl

Emperil
emprl

Emperor
emprr

Emphasis
emfss

Empire
empr

Empiric
emprc

Employ
empl

Emporium
emprm

Empower
empr

Empress
emprs

Emprise
empris

Empty
em-t

Empyreal
empral

Emulate
em-l

Emulous
emls

Emulsion
emlshn

Enable
enabl

Enact
en-a

Enamel
enml

Enamor
enmr

Encamp
encmp

Encaustic
encstc

Enchain
enchn

Enchant
enchnt

Enchase
enchas

Encircle
ensrcl

Enclitic
encltc

Enclose enclos		**Enervate** enr-v
Encomium encmym		**Enfeeble** enfbl
Encompass encmps		**Enfeoff** enff
Encore (ongkor) ongcr		**Enfilade** enfld
Encounter encntr		**Enforce** enfrs
Encourage encrj		**Enfranchise** enfrnchs
Encroach encrch		**Engage** engj
Encumber encmbr		**Engender** engndr
Encyclical ensclcl		**Engine** enjn
Encyclopedia ensclpd		**Engird** engrd
Encysted ensstd		**English (ing)** inglsh
End end		**Engrain** engrn
Endanger endngr		**Engrave** engrv
Endear endr		**Engross** engrs
Endeavor endvr		**Engulf** englf
Endemic endm-i		**Enhance** enhns
Ending end-ing		**Enigma** engm
Endless endls		**Enjoin** enjn
Endorse endrs		**Enjoy** joy
Endow endow		**Enkindle** enkndl
Endue endu		**Enlarge** enlrj
Endure endur		**Enlighten** enltn
Enemy enmy		**Enlist** enlst
Energy enrj		**Enliven** enlvn

Enmity
enm-t

Ennoble
enobl

Ennui (ongnwee)
ongw

Enormity
enrm-t

Enough (nuf)
enf

Enquire
quir

Enrage
enrj

Enrapture
enrptr

Enravish
enrvsh

Enrich
enrch

Enroll
enrl

Ensample
ensmpl

Ensconce
enscns

Enshrine
enshrn

Ensiform
ensfrm

Ensign
ensn

Enslave
enslv

Ensue
ensu

Ensure (shur)
enshr

Entablature
entbltr

Entail
entl

Entangle
entngl

Enter
entr

Enterprise
entrprs

Entertain
entrtn

Enthrone
enthrn

Enthusiasm
en-ths

Entice
ents

Entire
entr

Entitle
enttl

Entity
ent-t

Entomb (toom)
entm

Entomology
entm-o

Entrails
entrls

Entrance
entrns

Entrance'
entrns

Entrap
entrp

Entreat
entrt

Entry
entry

Entwine
entwn

Entwist
entwst

Enumerate
numrat

Enunciate
nun-sh

Envelop
envlp

Envenom
envnm

Enviable
envbl

Envious
envs

Environ
envrn

Envoy
envoy

Envy
envy

Epact
ep-a

Epaulet
eplt

Ephemeral
epmrl

Ephod
epod

Epic
ep-i

Epicure
epcr

Epidemic
epdm-i

Epidermis
epdrms

Epiglottis
epglts

Epigram
ep-gr

Epilepsy
eplp-s

Epileptic
epl-c

Epilogue (log)
ep-l

Epiphany
epfny

Episcopacy
epscps

Episode
epsd

Epistle (epistl)
epsl

Epitaph
eptf

Epithet
eptht

Epitome
eptmy

Epoch
ep-o

Epode
epod

Equal
ekl

Equation
e-q

Equator
quatr

Equery
ekwry

Equestrian
ekstrn

Equilateral
ek-ltrl

Equidistant
ek-dstnt

Equilibrium
ek-lbrm

Equine
ekn

Equinox
ek-nx

Equip
ekp

Equipoise
ek-ps

Equity
ek-t

Equivalent
eh-lnt

Equivocal
ek-cl

Equivoke
ek-vk

Era
era

Eradiation
eradshn

Eradicate
erd-c

Erase
eras

Ere (ar)
ar

Erect
er-c

Erelong
erlng

Ergot
ergt

Ermine
crmn

Erosion
e-r

Err
er

Errand
crnd

Errant
crnt

Erratum
cr-r

Erring
cr-ing

Erroneous
crons

Erst
crst

Erubescent
erbsnt

Eructation
crc-t

Erudite
cru-d

Eruption
cr-u

Eruptive
cr-u

Erysipelas
crspls

Escalade
escld

Escape
cscp

Escharotic
escr-o

Escheat
cscht

Eschew
eschu

Escort
cscrt

Escritoir (twor)
cscrtwr

Esculent
csclnt

Escutcheon
cscchn

Esoteric
csotr-i

Espalier
csplcr

Especial
cspshl, spcshl

Espionage
cspni

Esplanade
csplnd

Espouse
cspous

Espy
cspi

Esquire
squir

Essay
csa

Essence
csns

Establish
estblsh

Estate
cstat

Esteem
cstm

Estimate
cstmt

Estop
cstp

Estrange
cstrnj

Estray
estra

Estuary
estry

Etch
cch

Eternal
cfrnl

Eternity
cfrn-t

Ether
cthr

Ethic
cth-i

Ethiop
cthop

Ethnic
 ethnc

Ethnography
 ethn-gr

Ethnology
 ethn-o

Etiolate
 etolt

Etiquette (ket)
 etct

Etymology
 etm-o

Etymon
 etymn

Eulogy
 eulj

Eunuch
 eunc

Euphony
 eufny

European
 eurpn

Euthanasy
 euthnsy

Evacuate
 evc-w

Evade
 evad

Evanescent
 evnsnt

Evangelist
 evnjlst

Evaporate
 evprat

Evasion
 e-v

Eve
 ev

Even
 evn

Event
 evnt

Ever
 evr

Every
 evry

Evict
 ev-i

Evident
 evdnt

Evil
 evl

Evince
 evns

Evoke
 ev-o

Evolution
 ev-l

Ewe (yu)
 yu

Ewer
 ewr

Exacerbate
 xasrbt

Exact
 xact

Exaggerate
 xajrt

Exalt
 xalt

Examine
 xamn

Example
 xampl

Exasperate
 xasprat

Excavate
 xca-v

Exceed
 xcd

Excel
 xcl

Except
 xcpt

Excerpt
 xcrpt

Excess
 xcs

Exchange
 xchang

Exchequer
 xchekr

Excise
 xis

Excite
 xit

Exclaim xclam	**Exhibit** x*i*bt
Exclude xcl*u*d	**Exhilarate** x*i*l-r
Excogitate xc*o*j-t	**Exhort** x*o*rt
Excommunicate xc*o*mn-ct	**Exhume** x*u*m
Excoriate xc*o*rat	**Exigence** x*i*jns
Excrement xcr*e*mnt	**Exile** x*i*l
Excrescence xcr*e*sns	**Exist** x*i*st
Excrete xcr*e*t	**Exit** x*i*t
Excruciate xcr*u*-sh	**Exodus** x*o*ds
Exculpate xc*u*lpt	**Exonerate** x*o*nrat
Excursion xc*u*rshn	**Exorbitant** x*o*rbtnt
Excuse xc*u*s	**Exorcise** x*o*rss
Execrate x*e*crat	**Exordium** x*o*rdm
Execute x*e*ct	**Exotic** x*o*tc
Exegesis x*e*jss	**Expanse** x*p*ans
Exemplar x*e*mplr	**Expatiate** xp*a*-sh
Exempt x*e*mt	**Expatriate** xp*a*-tr
Exequator x*e*qtr	**Expect** xp*e*t
Exequies x*e*qs	**Expectorate** xp*e*t-r
Exercise x*e*rss	**Expedience** xp*e*dns
Exert x*e*rt	**Expedite** xp*e*dt
Exfoliate xf*o*-l	**Expel** xp*e*l
Exhale x*a*l	**Expend** xp*e*nd
Exhaust x*a*ust	**Expense** xp*e*ns

Experience
xperns

Experiment
xpermnt

Expert
xpert

Expiate
xpiat

Expire
xpir

Explain
xplan

Expletive
xple-t

Explicate
xpli-c

Explicit
xplist

Explode
xplod

Explore
xplor

Explosive
xplo-s

Exponent
xponnt

Export
xport

Export'
xport

Expose
xpos

Expose (expoza)
xposa

Exposition
xpo-s

Expositor
xpostr

Expostulate
xpost-l

Exposure
xposhr

Expound
xpound

Express
xpres

Expugn (pun)
xpun

Expulsion
xpulshn

Expunge
xpunj

Expurgate
xpur-g

Exquisite
xkist

Exsiccant
xicnt

Extant
xtant

Extempore
xtempr

Extend
xtend

Extent
xtent

Extenuate
xten-w

Exterior
xter

Exterminate
xtermnt

External
xternl

Extinct
xtinct

Extinguish
xtinsh

Extirpate
xtirpt

Extol
xtol

Extort
xtort

Extract
xtract

Extract
xtract

Extradition
xtra-d

Extrajudicial
xtra-j

Extraneous
xtrans

Extravagant
xtrav

Extravasate
xtrav-s

Extreme
xtrem

Extricate
xtri-c

Extrinsic
xtrinsc

Extrude
xtrud

Exuberant
xubrnt

Exude
xud

Exult
xult

Eye (i)
i

Eyrie (ary)
ary

F.

Fable
fabl

Fabric
fabrc

Facade
facad

Face
fas

Facile
fasl

Facetious
fa-s

Facing
fas-ing

Fac-simile
facsml

Faction
facshn

Factitious
fac-t

Factor
factr

Factotum
facttm

Faculty
facl-t

Fade
fad

Fag
fag

Fagot
fagot

Fail
fal

Fain
fan

Faint
fant

Fair
far

Fairy
fary

Faith
fath

Falcate
falct

Falcon
falcn

Fall
fal

Fallacious
fa-l

Fallen
faln

Fallible
fa/bl

Fallow
falo

False
fals

Falsetto
falsto

Falter
faltr

Fame
fam

Familiar
famlr

Family
famly

Famine
famn

Famish
famsh

Famous
fams

Fan
fan

Fanatic
fan-a

Fancy
fan-s

Fandango
fandngo

Fane
· fan

Fang
fang

Fantasy
fant-s

Far
far

Faree
fars

Fare
far

Farewell
farwl

Farina
farna

Farm
farm

Faro
faro

Farrago
fargo

Farrier
farr

Farrow
faro

Farthing
farthing

Fascinate
fasnt

Fashion
fashn

Fast
fast

Fat
fat

Fatal
fatl

Fate
fat

Father
fathr

Fathom
fathm

Fatigue
fatg

Fatuity
fatu-t

Faucet
fauset

Fault
fault

Faun
faun

Fauna
fauna

Favor
favr

Fawn
fawn

Fay
fa

Fealty
fel-t

Fear
fer

Feasible
fesbl

Feast
fest

Feat
fet

Feather
fethr

Feature
fetr

Febrifuge
febrfj

Febrile
febrl

February
feb

Fecundate
fecn-d

Fed
fed

Federal
fedrl

Fee
fe

Feeble
febl

Feed
fed

Feel
fel

Feet
fet

Feign (fan)
fan

Feint
fant

Felicitate
fels-t

Feline
feln

Fell
fel

Fellow
felo

Felly
fely

Felodese
felodse

Felonious
felons

Felt
felt

Female
feml

Fen
fen

Fence
fens

Fend
fend

Fennel
fenl

Fenny
feny

Feoff (fef)
fef

Ferment
fermnt

Fern
fern

Ferocious
feroshs

Ferreous
ferus

Ferret
feret

Ferruginous
ferujns

Ferrule (ril)
feril

Ferry
fery

Fertile
fertl

Ferule
ferul

Fervent
fervnt

Fervor
fervr

Festive
festv

Fetch
fech

Fete (fat)
fat

Fetid
fetd

Fetlock
fetlk

Fetter
fetr

Fetus
fetus

Feud
fud

Fever
fevr

Few
few

Fiat
fiat

Fib
feb

Fiber
febr

Fibril			**Filch**	
f*i*brl			f*i*lch	
Fickle			**File**	
f*i*kl			f*i*l	
Fiction			**Filial**	
f*i*cshn			f*i*lyl	
Fiddle			**Filigree**	
f*i*dl			f*i*lgr	
Fidelity			**Filings**	
f*i*dl-t			f*i*lings	
Fidget			**Fill**	
f*i*jt			f*i*l	
Fiducial			**Fillet**	
f*i*-d			f*i*let	
Fie			**Fillibuster**	
f*i*			f*i*lbstr	
Fief			**Fillip**	
f*e*f ¹			f*i*lp	
Field			**Filly**	
f*e*ld			f*i*ly	
Fiend			**Film**	
f*e*nd			f*i*lm	
Fierce			**Filter**	
f*e*rs			f*i*l-tr	
Fiery			**Filth**	
f*i*ry			f*i*lth	
Fife			**Filtrate**	
f*i*f			f*i*ltr	
Fifteen			**Fin**	
f*i*ftn			f*i*n	
Fifth			**Final**	
f*i*th			t*i*nl	
Fifty			**Finance**	
f*i*f-t			f*i*ns	
Fig			**Finch**	
f*i*g			f*i*nch	
Fight			**Find**	
f*i*t			f*i*nd	
Figment			**Fine**	
f*i*gmnt			f*i*n	
Figure			**Finesse**	
f*i*gr			f*i*nes	
Filament			**Finger**	
f*i*lmnt			f*i*ngr	
Filature			**Finical**	
f*i*latr			f*i*ncl	
Filbert			**Finis**	
f*i*lbrt			f*i*nis	

Finish finsh	**Flagon** flagn
Finite finit	**Flagrant** flagrnt
Finny finy	**Flail** flal
Fir fur	**Flake** flak
Fire fir	**Flam** flam
Firkin firkn	**Flambeau** flambo
Firm firm	**Flame** flam
Firmament firmmnt	**Flamingo** flamngo
First first	**Flange** flanj
Fiscal fiscl	**Flank** flank
Fish fish	**Flannel** flanl
Fissile fisl	**Flap** flap
Fissure fisr	**Flare** flar
Fist fist	**Flash** flash
Fistula fistla	**Flask** flask
Fit fit	**Flat** flat
Five fiv	**Flatulent** flatlnt
Fix fix	**Flaunt** flaunt
Fizz fiz	**Flavor** flavr
Flabby flaby	**Flaw** flaw
Flaccid flasid	**Flax** flax
Flag flag	**Flay** fla
Flageolet flajolt	**Flea** fle
Flagitious fla-g	**Fleam** flem

Fleck flec		**Flood** flood
Fled fled		**Floor** flor
Fledge flej		**Flora** flora
Flee fle		**Floret** floret
Fleece fles		**Florin** florn
Fleer fler		**Flotage** flotj
Fleet flet		**Flotilla** flotla
Flesh flesh		**Flotsam** flotsm
Flew flu		**Flounce** flouns
Flex flex		**Flounder** floundr
Flicker flicr		**Flour** flower
Flier flir		**Flout** flout
Flight (flit) flit		**Flow** flo
Flimsy flim-s		**Flower** flower
Flinch flinch		**Fluctuate** fluct-w
Fling fling		**Flue** flu
Flint flint		**Fluent** fluent
Flip flip		**Fluid** fluid
Flirt flirt		**Fluke** fluk
Flitch flich		**Flume** flum
Float flot		**Flung** flung
Flock floc		**Flurry** flury
Floe flo		**Flush** flush
Flog flog		**Fluster** flustr

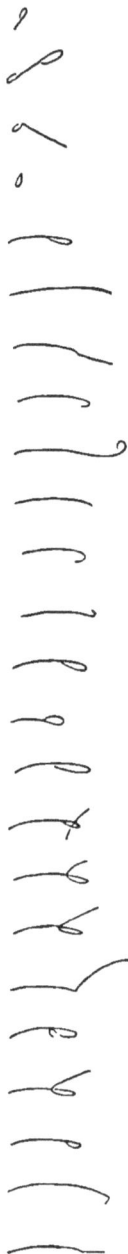

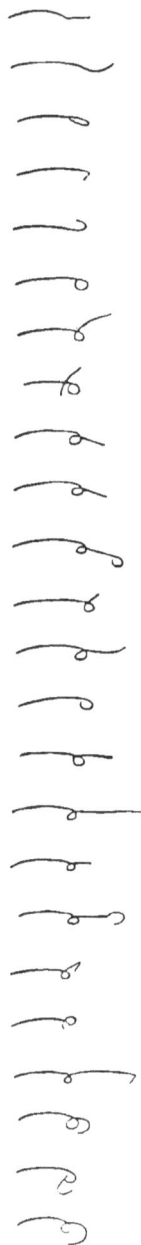

Flute
flut

Fluvial
fluvl

Flux
flux

Fly
fly

Foal
fol

Foam
fom

Fob
fob

Focal
focl

Fodder
fodr

Foe
fo

Fog
fog

Foible
foibl

Foil
foil

Foist
foist

Fold
fold

Foliage
fol-a

Foliate
folat

Folio
folo

Folk (fok)
fok

Follicle
folcl

Follow
folo

Folly
foly

Foment
fomnt

Fond
fond

Font
font

Food
food

Fool
fool

Foot
foot

Fop
fop

For
for

Foray
fora

Forage
for-a

Forbade
forbd

Forbid
forbd

Forbear
forbr

Force
fors

Ford
ford

Fore
for

Foreign (in)
forn

Foreman
formn

Forenoon
fornn

Forensic
fornsc

Forest
forst

Forever
forr

Forfeit
forft

Forgave
forg

Forge
forj

Forget
f rgt

Forgive
forg

Fork
fork

Forlorn
forlrn

Form
form

Forsake
forsk

Forsooth
forsth

Fort
fort

Forte
fort

Forth
forth

Fortify
fortfy

Fortitude
fort-t

Fortress
fortrs

Fortuitous
for-t

Forty
forty

Forum
form

Forward
ford

Fosse
fos

Fossil
fosl

Foster
fostr

Fother
fothr

Fought (fawt)
faut

Foul
foul

Found
found

Fount
fount

Four
for

Fourth
forth

Fowl
fowl

Fox
fox

Fracas
fracs

Fraction
fracshn

Fractious
fracshs

Fragile
frajl

Fragment
fragmnt

Fragrant
fragrnt

Frail
fral

Frame
fram

Franc
franc

Franchise
franchs

Frangible
franjbl

Frank
frank

Frantic
frantc

Fraternal
fratrnl

Fratricide
fratrsd

Fraud
fraud

Fraught (frawt)
frawt

Fray
fra

Freak
frck

Freckle
frecl

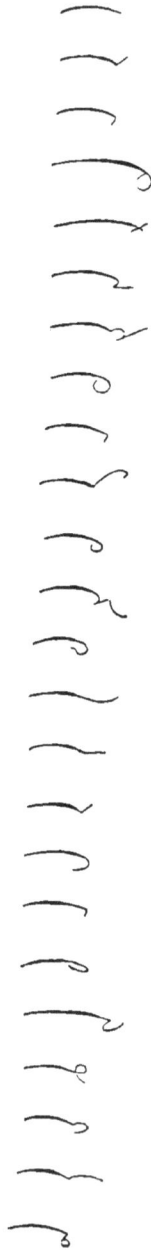

Free
fre

Freeze
frez

Freight
frat

French
french

Frenzy
fren-s

Frequent
frent

Fresco
fresco

Fresh
fresh

Fret
fret

Friable
friabl

Friar
frir

Fricassee
fricse

Friction
fricshn

Friday
frid

Friend
frend

Frieze
frez

Frigate
frigt

Fright (frit)
frit

Frill
fril

Fringe
frinj

Frippery
fripry

Frisk
frisk

Frith
frith

Fritter
fretr

Frivolous
frivls

Friz
friz

Fro
fro

Frock
froc

Frog
frog

Frolic
frolc

From
from

Frond
frond

Front
front

Frost
frost

Froth
froth

Frounce
frouns

Frouzy
frou-s

Froward
frord

Frown
frown

Froze
froz

Fructify
fructf

Frugal
frugl

Fruit
frut

Fruition
frushn

Frumenty
frumn-t

Frush
frush

Frustrate
frustr

Frustum
frustm

Fry
fry

Fuddle
fudl

Fuel
fuel

Fugacious
fu-g

Fugitive
fuj t

Fugleman
fuglmn

Fugue (fug)
fug

Fulcrum
fulcrm

Fulfill
fulfl

Full
ful

Fuller
fulr

Fulminate
fulm-n

Fulsome
fulsm

Fumble
fumbl

Fume
fum

Function
funcshn

Fund
fund

Fundament
fundmnt

Funeral
funrl

Fungous
fungs

Fungus
fungs

Funicular
funclr

Funnel
funl

Funny
funy

Fur
fur

Furbelow
furblo

Furbish
furbsh

Furcate
furct

Furious
furs

Furl
furl

Furlong
furlng

Furlough
furlo

Furnace
furns

Furnish
furnsh

Furniture
furntr

Furrier
furr

Furrow
furo

Furry
fury

Further
furthr

Furtive
fur-t

Furze
furz

Fury
fury

Fuse
fus

Fusee
fuse

Fusible
fusbl

Fusil
fusl

Fusileer
fuslr

Fusion
fushn

Fuss
 fus

Fustian
 fustyn

Futile
 futl

Futtock
 fut-o

Future
 futr

Fuzz
 fuz

Fy
 fy

G.

Gab
 gab

Gabardine
 gabrdn

Gabion
 gabyn

Gable
 gabl

Gad
 gad

Gaff
 gaf

Gag
 gag

Gage
 gaj

Gaily
 galy

Gain
 gain

Gairish
 garsh

Gait
 gat

Gaiter
 gatr

Gala
 gala

Galaxy
 galxy

Gale
 gal

Gall
 gal

Gallant
 galnt

Gallant´
 galnt

Galleon
 galen

Gallery
 galry

Galley
 galy

Gallic
 gal-i

Gallinaceous
 gal-n

Gallipot
 galipt

Gall-nut
 galnt

Gallon
 galn

Gallop
 galp

Gallows (lus)
 gals

Galoche (losh)
 galsh

Galvanic
 galvn-i

Gamble
 gambl

Gamboge
 gambj

Gambol
 gambl

Gambrel
 gambrl

Game
 gam

Gammon
 gamn

Gamut
 gamt

Gander
 gandr

Gang
 gang

Ganglion		**Gas**	
gangln		gas	
Gangrene		**Gasconade**	
gangrn		gascnd	
Gangue (gaug)		**Gash**	
gang		gash	
Gantlet		**Gasometer**	
gantlt		gasmtr	
Gaol (jal)		**Gasp**	
jal		gasp	
Gap		**Gastric**	
gap		gastrc	
Gape		**Gastronomer**	
gap		gastrnmr	
Garb		**Gate**	
garb		gat	
Garble		**Gather**	
garbl		gatr	
Garden		**Gaudiness**	
gardn		gaudns	
Garget		**Gange (gaj)**	
gargt		gaj	
Gargle		**Gaunt**	
gargl		gaunt	
Garland		**Gauntlet**	
garlnd		gauntlt	
Garlic		**Gauze**	
garl-i		gauz	
Garment		**Gave**	
garmnt		ga	
Garner		**Gavel**	
garnr		gavl	
Garnet		**Gawk**	
garnt		gawk	
Garnish		**Gay**	
garnsh		ga	
Garniture		**Gaze**	
garntr		gaz	
Garret		**Gazelle**	
garet		gazl	
Garrison		**Gazette**	
garsn		gazt	
Garrote		**Gear**	
garot		ger	
Garrulous		**Geese**	
garuls		ges	
Garter		**Gelatine**	
gartr		jeltn	

Geld
geld

Gelid
jeld

Gem
jem

Gender
jendr

Genealogy
jen-a

Genera
jenra

General
jenrl

Generate
jenrat

Generic
jenrc

Generous
jenrs

Genesis
jenss

Genial
jenl

Genie
jene

Genitive
jen-t

Genius
jenus

Genius'
jenys

Gens-d'arms (zhong
zhongdrm **darm)**

Genteel
jentl

Gentile
jentl

Gentle
jentl

Gently
jently

Gentry
jen-try

Genuflection
jen-fl

Genuine
jenn

Genus
jenus

Geocentric
jeosntrc

Geodesy
jeodesy

Geographer
jeo-gr

Geology
jeo-o

Geometry
jem-tr

Georgic
jorj-i

Geranium
jernym

Germ
jerm

German
jermn

Germane
jerman

Germinate
jerm-n

Gerund
jerund

Gestation
jes-t

Gesticulate
jestc-l

Gesture
jestur

Get
get

Gewgaw
guga

Ghastly (gast)
gastly

Ghost (gost)
gost

Giant
jint

Giaour (jour)
jour

Gibber
jibr

Gibbet
jibt

Gibe		**Girt**
jīb		gïrt
Giblets		**Gist**
jïblts		jïst
Giddy		**Give**
gïdy		gï
Gifted		**Gizzard**
gïftd		gïzrd
Gig		**Glacial**
gïg		glashl
Gigantic		**Glacis**
jïgnt-i		glass
Giggle		**Glad**
gïgl		glad
Gild		**Glade**
geld		glad
Gill		**Gladiator**
jïl		gladtr
Gillyflower		**Glair**
jïlflr		glar
Gilt		**Glance**
gïlt		glans
Gimbals		**Gland**
gïmbls		gland
Gimcrack		**Glare**
jïmcrc		glar
Gimlet		**Glass**
gïmlt		glas
Gimp		**Glaze**
gïmp		glaz
Gin		**Gleam**
jïn		glem
Ginger		**Glean**
jïnjr		glen
Gingham		**Glebe**
gïngm		gleb
Ginseng		**Glee**
jensng		gle
Gipsy		**Glen**
jïpsy		glen
Giraffe		**Glib**
jïrf		glib
Gird		**Glide**
gïrd		glid
Girdle		**Glimmer**
gïrdl		glïmr
Girl		**Glimpse**
gïrl		glïmps

Glisten (glisn)	**Gnome (nom)**
glisn	nom
Glitter	**Gnomon**
glitr	nomn
Gloat	**Gnu**
glot	nu
Globose	**Go**
globos	go
Globule	**Goad**
globl	god
Gloom	**Goal**
gloom	gol
Glory	**Goat**
glory	got
Gloss	**Gobble**
glos	gobl
Glottis	**Goblin**
glots	gobln
Glover	**God**
glovr	god
Glow	**Goggles**
glo	gogls
Gloze	**Going**
gloz	go-ing
Glue	**Goiter**
glu	goitr
Glum	**Gold**
glum	gold
Glume	**Gondola**
glum	gondla
Glut	**Gone**
glut	gon
Gluten	**Gong**
glutn	gong
Glutton	**Good**
glutn	good
Glycerine	**Goods**
glysrn	goods
Gnarl (narl)	**Goose**
narl	goos
Gnash (nash)	**Gore**
nash	gor
Gnat (nat)	**Gorge**
nat	gorj
Gnaw (naw)	**Gorgeous**
naw	gorjs
Gneiss (nis)	**Gorgon**
nis	gorgn

Gorilla	gorla	**Graduate**	grad-w
Gormand	gormnd	**Graft**	graft
Gorse	gors	**Grain**	gran
Gory	gory	**Gramineous**	gramnes
Gosling	goslng	**Grammar**	gramr
Gospel	gospl	**Grampus**	gramps
Gossamer	gosmr	**Granary**	granry
Gossip	gosp	**Grand**	grand
Got	got	**Grandam**	grandm
Goth	goth	**Grandchild**	granchld
Gothic	gothc	**Grandeur**	grandeur
Gouge (gowj)	gouj	**Grandfather**	granthr
Gourd	gord	**Grandmother**	granmthr
Gourmand (goor)	goormnd	**Grand-jury**	granjry
Gout	gout	**Grandsire**	gransr
Govern	guvrn	**Grandson**	gransn
Gown	gown	**Grange**	granj
Grab	grab	**Granite**	granit
Grace	gras	**Granivorous**	granvrs
Gracious	grashs	**Grant**	grant
Gradation	gra-d	**Granulate**	granult
Grade	grad	**Granule**	granul
Gradient	gradnt	**Grape**	grap
Gradual	gradul	**Graphic**	grafc

Grapnel
grapnl

Grasp
grasp

Grass
gras

Grate
grat

Grater
gratr

Gratify
gratf

Gratis
gratis

Gratitude
gratud

Gratulation
gratu-l

Grave
grav

Gravel
gravl

Gravitation
grav-t

Gravy
gravy

Gray
gra

Graze
graz

Grease
gres

Grease'
grez

Great
grat

Grecian
greshn

Greedy
gredy

Green
gren

Greet
gret

Gregarious
gre-g

Grenade
grenad

Grew (gru)
gru

Griddle
gridl

Gridiron
gridrn

Grieve
grev

Griffin
grifn

Grim
grim

Grimace
grimas

Grime
grim

Grin
grin

Grind
grind

Gripe
grip

Grisly
grisly

Grist
grist

Gristle
grisl

Grit
grit

Grizzly
grizly

Groan
gron

Grocer
grosr

Grog
grog

Groin
groin

Groom
groom

Groove
groov

Grope
grop

Gross
gros

Grotto groto	**Guest** gest
Grotesque (tesk) grotsk	**Guide** gid
Ground ground	**Guild** gild
Group grup	**Guile** gil
Grouse grous	**Guillotine** giltn
Grove grov	**Guilt** gilt
Grovel grovl	**Guinea** giny
Grow gro	**Guitar** gitr
Growl growl	**Gulf** gulf
Grown gron	**Gull** gul
Growth groth	**Gullet** gult
Grub grub	**Gullible** gulbl
Grudge gruj	**Gulp** gulp
Gruel grul	**Gum** gum
Gruff gruf	**Gump** gump
Grum grum	**Gun** gun
Grumble grumbl	**Gunwale** gunwl
Grunt grunt	**Gurge** gurj
Guano gwano	**Gurgle** gurgl
Guard gard	**Gush** gush
Gubernatorial gubrn	**Gusset** guset
Gudgeon gujn	**Gust** gust
Guerrilla gurla	**Guttapercha** gutprcha
Guess ges	**Gutter** gutr

Guttle
gutl

Guttural
gutrl

Guy
gy

Guzzle
guzl

Gymnastics
jimnstx

Gypsum
jipsm

Gypsy
jipsy

Gyral
jirl

Gyration
ji-r

Gyve
jiv

II.

Ha
ha

Habeas
habs

Haberdasher
habrdshr

Habiliment
hablmnt

Habit
habt

Hack
hac

Hackney
hacny

Had
had

Haddock
hadc

Haft
haft

Hag
hag

Haggard
hagrd

Haggle
hagl

Hagiography
hago-g

Hair
har

Hake
hak

Halberd
halbrd

Halcyon
halsyn

Hale
hal

Half
haf

Hall
hal

Halloo
haloo

Hallow
halo

Hallucination
halus-n

Halo
halo

Halt
halt

Halve
hav

Halyard
halyrd

Ham
ham

Hames
hams

Hamlet
hamlt

Hammer
hamr

Hammock
ham-o

Hamper
hampr

Hamstring
hamstrng

Hand
hand

Handkerchief
hanchf

Handsome handsm		**Harpy** harpy	
Handy han-d		**Harrier** haryr	
Hang hang		**Harrow** haro	
Hank hank		**Harsh** harsh	
Hap hap		**Hart** hart	
Happen hapn		**Harvest** harvs	
Happy hap		**Hash** hash	
Harangue (rang) harng		**Haslet** haslet	
Harass hars		**Hasp** hasp	
Harbinger harbnjr		**Hassock** has-o	
Harbor harbr		**Hast** hast	
Hard hard		**Haste** hast	
Harden hardn		**Hat** hat	
Hardware hardwr		**Hatch** hach	
Hare har		**Hatchet** hachet	
Harem harm		**Hate** hat	
Hark hark		**Hatter** hatr	
Harlequin harlqn		**Haughty** hauty	
Harlot harlt		**Haul** haul	
Harm harm		**Haunch** hanch	
Harmony harmny		**Haunt** hant	
Harness harns		**Hautboy (ho)** hoby	
Harp harp		**Have** hav	
Harpoon harpn		**Haven (vn)** havn	

Havoc hav-o		**Hecatomb** hectm	
Hawk hawk		**Hectic** hectc	
Hawser hawsr		**Hedge** hej	
Hawthorne hawthrn		**Heed** hed	
Hay ha		**Heel** hel	
Hazard hazrd		**Hegira** hejra	
He he		**Heifer** hefr	
Head hed		**Height** hit	
Heal hel		**Heinous (ha)** hanus	
Health helth		**Heir (ar)** ar	
Heap hep		**Held** held	
Hear her		**Heliotrope** heltrop	
Hearse hers		**Hell** hel	
Hearth harth		**Helm** helm	
Hearty harty		**Helmet** helmt	
Heat het		**Helot** helot	
Heath heth		**Help** help	
Heathen hethn		**Helve** helv	
Heather hethr		**Hem** hem	
Heave hev		**Hemisphere** hemspr	
Heaven hevn		**Hemlock** hemlc	
Heaves hevs		**Hemorrhage** hemr-a	
Heavy hevy		**Hemp** hemp	
Hebrew hebrew		**Hen** hen	

Hence hens		**Heron** hern	
Hepatic hepatc		**Herring** her-ing	
Heptagon heptgn		**Hers** hers	
Heptarchy heptrcy		**Hesitate** hes -t	
Her her		**Heterodox** hetrdx	
Herald herld		**Heterogeneous** hetr-j	
Herbaceous her-b		**Hew** hew	
Herbage erbj		**Hexagon** hexgn	
Herbivorous herbvrs		**Hexahedron** hexhdrn	
Herculean hercln		**Hexameter** hexmtr	
Herd herd		**Hexangular** hexnglr	
Here her		**Hey** ha	
Hereditament herdtment		**Hiatus** hiats	
Hereditary herd-tr		**Hibernate** hibrnt	
Herein herin		**Hiccough (hikup)** hikp	
Hereupon herpn		**Hickory** hikry	
Heresiarch hers-a		**Hid** hid	
Heresy hersy		**Hide** hid	
Hereto herto		**Hic** hi	
Heritage heritj		**Hierarch** hir-a	
Hermeneutics herm-n		**Hieroglyph** hirglf	
Hermit hermt		**Higgle** higl	
Hernia herna		**High (hi)** hi	
Hero hero		**Hilarity** hilrty	

Hill
hil

Hilt
hilt

Him
him

Hind
hind

Hinder
hindr

Hindoo
hindoo

Hinge
hinj

Hint
hint

Hip
hip

Hippodrome
hipdrm

Hippogriff
hip-gr

Hippopotamus
hipptms

Hip-roof
hiprf

Hire
hir

Hirsute
hirsut

His
his

Hiss
his

History
histry

Hit
hit

Hitch
hich

Hither
hither

Hive
hiv

Ho
ho

Hoar
hor

Hoard
hord

Hoarse
hors

Hoax
hoks

Hobble
hobl

Hobby
hoby

Hobgoblin
hobgbln

Hock
hoc

Hodgepodge
hojpj

Hoe
ho

Hog
hog

Hoiden
hoidn

Hoist
hoist

Hold
hold

Hole
hol

Holiday
holyd

Holloa
holoa

Holland
holnd

Hollow
holo

Holly
holy

Holm
hohn

Holocaust
holcst

Holster
holstr

Holy
holy

Homage
omj

Home
hom

Homely
homly

Homeopathy
homopthy

Homicide
homisd

Homily
homily

Hominy
homny

Hommock
hom-o

Homogeneal
homjnl

Hone
hon

Honest (on)
onst

Honey
huny

Honor
onr

Hood
hood

Hoof
huf

Hoop
hup

Hoot
hoot

Hop
hop

Hope
hop

Hopper
hopr

Horde
hord

Horizon
horzn

Horn
horn

Horography
horo-gr

Horology
horlj

Horrible
horbl

Horse
hors

Hortative
hortv

Horticulture
hortcltr

Hosanna
hosana

Hose
hos

Hosiery
hosry

Hospitable
hosptbl

Host
host

Hostile
hostl

Hostler
hoslr

Hot
hot

Hotel
hotl

Hotly
hotly

Hough (hok)
hok

Hound
hound

Hour (our)
our

House
hous

Hovel
hovl

Hover
huvr

How
how

Howitzer
howitzr

Howl
howl

Hoy
hoy

Hub
hub

Hubbub
hubb

Huckster
hucstr

Huddle
hudl

Hue
hew

Huff
huf

Hug
hug

Huge
huj

Hulk
hulk

Hull
hul

Hum
hum

Human
humn

Humble
humbl

Humbug
humbg

Humdrum
humdrm

Humid
humid

Humility
huml-t

Humming
hum-ing

Humor
humr

Hump
hump

Hunch
hunch

Hundred
hundrd

Hung
hung

Hunger
hungr

Hunks
hunks

Hunt
hunt

Hurdle
hurdl

Hurl
hurl

Hurra
hura

Hurricane
hurcn

Hurry
hury

Hurt
hurt

Husband
husbn

Hush
hush

Husk
husk

Hussar
husr

Hussy
husy

Hustings
hust-ings

Hustle
husl

Hut
hut

Huzza
huza

Hyacinth
hisnth

Hybrid
hibrd

Hydra
hidra

Hydrant
hidrnt

Hydraulic
hidrl-c

Hydrogen
hidrjn

Hydrography
hidr-gr

Hydromel hidrml		**I.**	
Hydrometry hidrmtr		**I**	
Hydropathy hidropthy		**Icicle** iscl	
Hydrophobia hidro-f		**Iconoclast** icnclst	
Hydrostatic hydro-st		**Iconography** icno-gr	
Hyena hiena		**Icy** isy	
Hygiene hijn		**Idea** ida	
Hymen himn		**Identical** idntcl	
Hymn (him) him		**Identify** idntf	
Hyperbola hiprbla		**Ides** ids	
Hyperborean hiprbrn		**Idiocy** id-s	
Hypercritic hiprcrtc		**Idiom** idm	
Hyphen hifn		**Idiosyncrasy** idsncr-s	
Hypochondria hypo-cn		**Idiot** idot	
Hypocrite hipcrt		**Idle** idl	
Hypostatic hypo-stt		**If** if	
Hypotenuse hipot-n		**Igneous** ignes	
Hypothecate hipth-c		**Ignis Fatuus** igns-f	
Hypothesis hipthss		**Ignite** ignt	
Hyson hisn		**Ignoble** ignbl	
Hysop hisp		**Ignominy** ignmny	
Hysterics histr-i		**Ignoramus** ign-r	
		Ignorant ignrnt	
		Ignore ignr	

Ill	
il	
Illation	
il-l	
Ill-bred	
i/brd	
Illegal	
ilgl	
Illegible	
i/jbl	
Illegitimate	
i/jtmt	
Ill-favored	
i/fvrd	
Illiberal	
i/brl	
Illicit	
i/lst	
Illiterate	
i/itrat	
Ill-natured	
i/ntrd	
Illness	
i/ns	
Illogical	
i/ljcl	
Ill-starred	
i/strd	
Illude	
i/ud	
Illume	
i/um	
Illusion	
il-l	
Illustrate	
i/us-tr	
Ill-will	
i/wl	
Image	
imj	
Imagine	
imjn	
Imbank	
imbnk	
Imbecile	
imbsl	
Imbed	
imbd	

Imbibe	
imbb	
Imbitter	
imbtr	
Imbosom	
imbsm	
Imbricate	
imbr-c	
Imbrue	
imbru	
Imbrute	
imbrut	
Imbue	
imbu	
Imitate	
im-t	
Immaculate	
imclt	
Immanent	
imnnt	
Immaterial	
imatrl	
Immature	
imatur	
Immeasurable	
imesrbl	
Immediate	
imedt	
Immense	
imns	
Immerge	
imrj	
Immerse	
imrs	
Immethodical	
imthdcl	
Immigrate	
imgrt	
Imminent	
imnnt	
Immission	
im-m	
Immobility	
imoblt	
Immoderate	
imodrat	
Immodest	
imodest

Immolate im-l	**Imperial** imprl
Immoral imrl	**Imperil** imprl
Immortal imrtl	**Imperious** imprys
Immovable imvbl	**Imperishable** imprshbl
Immunity imn-t	**Impermeable** imprmbl
Immure imur	**Impersonable** imprsnbl
Immutable imutbl	**Impertinence** imprtnns
Imp imp	**Impervious** imprvs
Impact impct	**Impetuous** imptus
Impair impr	**Impetus** impts
Impale impal	**Impiety** impi-t
Impalpable implpbl	**Impinge** impnj
Impanel impnl	**Implacable** implcbl
Impart imprt	**Implant** implnt
Impartial imprshl	**Implead** impld
Impassible impasbl	**Implicate** implct
Impatient impshnt	**Implicit** implst
Impeach pech	**Implore** implr
Impeccable impcbl	**Imply** impli
Impede impd	**Impolite** implit
Impel impl	**Import** imprt
Impend impnd	**Important** imprtnt
Impenitent impntnt	**Importune** imprtn
Imperative impr-t	**Impose** impos

Imposing *im*pos-ing	**Inception** *in*spshn
Imposition *im*p-s	**Inch** *in*ch
Impost *im*post	**Inchoate** *in*coat
Impostor *im*postr	**Incident** *in*sdnt
Impotence *im*ptns	**Incipient** *in*spnt
Imprecate *im*pr-c	**Incisive** *in*ssv
Impregnate *im*prg-n	**Incite** *in*sit
Impress *im*prs	**Incline** *in*cln
Imprint *im*prnt	**Inclose** *in*clos
Imprint′ *im*prnt	**Include** *in*cld
Impromptu *im*prmtu	**Incog** *in*cg
Improve *im*prv	**Income** *in*cm
Improvise *im*prvs	**Increase** *in*cres
Impudence *im*pdns	**Incubate** *in*cbt
Impugn *im*pn	**Indeed** *in*dd
Impulse *im*pls	**Indent** *in*dnt
Impunity *im*pn-t	**Indicate** *in*d-c
Impute *im*put	**Indigent** *in*djnt
Inane *in*an	**Indigo** *in*dgo
Inarch *in*rch	**Indorse** *in*drs
Inaugurate *in*augrt	**Induce** *in*dus
Incarnate *in*crnt	**Indulge** *in*dlj
Incense *in*sns	**Indurate** *in*d-r
Incentive *in*sn-t	**Industry** *in*ds-tr

Inebriate
   *in*ebrt

Ineffable
   *in*fbl

Inert
   *in*rt

Inevitable
   *in*vtbl

Infamy
   *in*fmy

Infant
   *in*fnt

Infect
   *in*fct

Inferior
   *in*frr

Infernal
   *in*frnl

Infest
   *in*fst

Infidel
   *in*fdl

Inflame
   *in*flm

Inflate
   *in*flt

Inflect
   *in*fl-e

Influence
   *in*flns

Influx
   *in*flx

Inform
   *in*frm

Infringe
   *in*frnj

Infuse
   *in*fs

Ingenious
   in-j

Ingot
   *in*gt

Ingrate
   *in*grt

Ingredient
   *in*grdnt

Ingress
   *in*grs

Ingulf
   *in*glf

Inhabit
   *in*hbt

Inhale
   *in*hl

Inhere
   *in*hr

Inherit
   *in*hrit

Inhibit
   *in*hbt

Inhume
   *in*hm

Inimical
   in mcl

Iniquity
   *in*iqt

Initial
   *in*shl

Initiate
   in-sh

Inject
   in-j

Injure
   *in*jr

Ink
   *in*k

Inland
   *in*lnd

Inlay
   *in*la

Inlet
   *in*lt

Inmate
   *in*mt

Inmost
   *in*mst

Inner
   *in*r

Innocent
   *in*snt

Innovate
   *in*o-v

Innuendo
   *in*ndo

Inoculate
   in-o

Inordinate		**Intellect**
inrdnt		intl-c
Inquest		**Intend**
inqst		intnd
Inquire		**Intense**
iqur		intns
Inroad		**Intent**
inrd		intnt
Insert		**Inter**
insrt		inter
Insipid		**Interest**
inspd		intrst
Insist		**Interfere**
insst		intrfr
Insnare		**Interim**
insnr		intrm
Insobriety		**Interior**
insbr-t		intrr
Insolent		**Interline**
inslnt		intrln
Inspire		**Intermit**
inspr		intrmt
Install		**Internal**
instl		intrnl
Instant		**Interpolate**
instnt		intrp-l
Instep		**Interpose**
instp		intrpos
Instill		**Interpret**
instl		intrprt
Instinct		**Interrogate**
instnct		introgt
Institute		**Interrupt**
inst-t		intr-u
Instruct		**Intersect**
in-str		intrsct
Insular		**Intersperse**
inslr		intrsprs
Insult		**Interval**
inslt		intrvl
Insure		**Intervene**
inshur		intrvn
Intaglio (tal)		**Intestate**
intlyo		intstt
Integer		**Intestine**
intjr		intstn
Integrate		**Intimate**
int-gr		intmt

Into int		**Invidious** invds	
Intoxicate intxct		**Invite** invt	
Intrench intrnch		**Invocate** inv-c	
Intrepid intrpd		**Invoice** invs	
Intricate intrct		**Invoke** invc	
Intrigue intrg		**Involve** volv	
Intrinsic intrnsk		**Iota** iota	
Introduce intrds		**Irascible** irsbl	
Introvert intrvrt		**Ire** ir	
Intrude intrud		**Iris** iris	
Intrust intrust		**Irish** irsh	
Intuitive intu-t		**Irksome** irksm	
Intwine intwn		**Iron** irn	
Inundate inn-d		**Irrigate** irgt	
Inure inur		**Irritate** ir-t	
Invade invd		**Isinglass** isngls	
Invalid invld		**Island (i)** i/nd	
Invalid' invld		**Isolate** iso-l.	
Invasion in-v		**Israelite** isrlit	
Invective inv-e		**Issue** isu	
Invent invnt		**Isthmus (is)** isms	
Inverse invrs		**It** it	
Invest invst		**Italian** itlyn	
Inveterate invtrat		**Itch** ich	

Item *itm*	**Jasper** *jaspr*
Iterate *itrat*	**Jaundice** *jaunds*
Itinerate *itnrat*	**Jaunt** *jaunt*
Itself *itsl*	**Javelin** *javln*
Ivory *ivry*	**Jaw** *jaw*
Ivy *ivy*	**Jay** *ja*
	Jealous *jels*
J.	**Jean** *jen*
Jabber *jabr*	**Jeer** *jer*
Jacinth *jasnth*	**Jehovah** *jeova*
Jack *jac*	**Jejune** *jejn*
Jackal *jacl*	**Jelly** *jely*
Jade *jad*	**Jeopard** *jeprd*
Jag *jag*	**Jerk** *jerk*
Jaguar *jagur*	**Jessamine** *jesmn*
Jail *jal*	**Jest** *jest*
Jalap *jalap*	**Jesuit** *jesut*
Jam *jam*	**Jet** *jet*
Jangle *jangl*	**Jewel** *jewl*
Janitor *jantr*	**Jewish** *jewsh*
January *jan*	**Jib** *jib*
Jar *jar*	**Jig** *jig*
Japan *japn*	**Jiff** *jif*
Jargon *jargn*	**Jingle** *jingl*
Jasmine *jasmn*	

Job	job
Jockey	jocy
Jocose	jocos
Jog	jog
Join	join
Joint	joint
Joist	joist
Joke	joc
Jolly	joly
Jostle (I)	jesl
Journal	jurnl
Journey	jurny
Joust	joust
Jovial	jovl
Jowl	jowl
Joy	joy
Jubilee	juble
Judaism	judism
Judge	juj
Judicature	jud-c
Judicial	judshl
Judicious	judshs
Jug	jug
Juggle	jugl

Juice	jus
Julep	julp
July	july
Jumble	jumbl
Jump	jump
Junction	juncshn
June	jun
Jungle	jungl
Junior	junr
Juniper	junpr
Junk	junc
Junket	junct
Junto	junto
Juridical	jurdcl
Jurisdiction	jurs-d
Jurisprudence	jurs-pr
Jurist	jurst
Juror	jurr
Jury	jur
Just	just
Justice	justs
Justify	justf
Jut	jut
Juvenescent	juvnsnt

Juvenile
juvnl

Juxtaposition
juxtshn

K.

Kale
cal

Kaleidoscope
caldskop

Kangaroo
cangroo

Kedge
cej

Keel
cel

Keen
cen

Keep
cep

Keg
ceg

Kelp
celp

Ken
cen

Kennel
cenl

Kept
cept

Kerchief
cerchf

Kernel
cernl

Kersey
cersy

Kettle
cetl

Key
ce

Kick
cic

Kid
cid

Kidnap
cidnp

Kidney
cidny

Kilderkin
cildren

Kill
cil

Kiln
cil

Kilt
cilt

Kimbo
cimbo

Kin
cin

Kind
cind

Kindle
cindl

Kindred
cindrd

Kine
cin

King
cing

Kink
cinc

Kinsman
cinsmn

Kipskin
cipskin

Kirk
circ

Kirtle
cirtl

Kiss
cis

Kit
cit

Kitchen
cichn

Kite
cit

Kitten
citn

Knack
nac

Knapsack
napsc

Knave
nav

Knead
ned

Knee
ne

Kneel
nel

Knell
nel

Knew
new

Knife (nif)
nif

Knight (nit)
nit

Knit (nit)
nit

Knob (nob)
nob

Knock (nok)
noc

Knoll (nol)
nol

Knot (not)
not

Know (no)
no

Knowledge (nolej)
nol

Knuckle (nukl)
nucl

Knurl (nurl)
nurl

Koran
coran

L.

La
la

Label
labl

Labial
labal

Labor
labr

Laboratory
labr-tr

Labyrinth
labrnth

Lac
lac

Lace
las

Lacerate
lasrt

Lachrymal
lacrml

Lack
lac

Lackadaisical
lac-d

Lackey
lacy

Laconic
lacn-i

Lacquer (laker)
lacr

Lacteal
lactl

Lad
lad

Ladder
ladr

Lade
lad

Ladle
ladl

Lady
lady

Lag
lag

Lagoon
lagoon

Laic
la-i

Laid
lad

Lain
lan

Lair
lar

Laird
lard

Laity
laty

Lake
lac

Lamb (lam) lam		**Lapse** laps	
Lambent lambnt		**Lapstone** lapstn	
Lame lam		**Larboard** larbrd	
Lamellate lamlat		**Larceny** larsny	
Lament lamnt		**Larch** larch	
Lamina lamna		**Lard** lard	
Lamp lamp		**Large** larj, larg	
Lampoon lampn		**Lark** larc	
Lamprey lampry		**Larva** larva	
Lance lans		**Larynx** larnx	
Lanch lanch		**Lascivious** lasvs	
Landau lando		**Lash** lash	
Landed landd		**Lass** las	
Landing land-ing		**Lassitude** las-t	
Lane lan		**Lasso** laso	
Language lang		**Last** last	
Languid langd		**Latch** lach	
Lank lanc		**Late** lat	
Lantern lantrn		**Latent** latnt	
Lanyard lanrd		**Lateral** latrl	
Lap lap		**Lath** lath	
Lapel lapl		**Lathe** lath	
Lapidary lapdry		**Lather** lathr	
Lappet lapt		**Latin** latin	

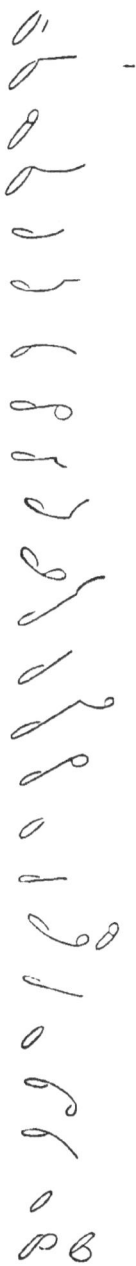

Latitude lat-t		**Lead** led
Latten latn		**Lead'** led
Latter latr		**Leaf** lef
Lattice lats		**League** leg
Laud laud		**Leak** lec
Laudanum laudnm		**Lean** len
Laugh (laf) laf		**Leap** lep
Launch lanch		**Learn** lern
Laundry landry		**Lease** les
Laureate laureat		**Leash** lesh
Laurel laurel		**Least** lest
Lava lava		**Leather** lethr
Lave lav		**Leave** lev
Lavender lavndr		**Leaven** levn
Lavish lavsh		**Leaves** levs
Law law		**Lecher** lechr
Lawn lawn		**Lection** lecshn
Lawyer lawyr		**Lecture** lectr
Lax lax		**Led** led
Lay la		**Ledge** lej
Lazar lazr		**Ledger** lejr
Lazy laz		**Leech** lech
Lea le		**Leek** lek
Leach lech		**Leer** ler

Lees les		**Leopard** lcprd	
Leeward lewrd		**Leper** lcpr	
Left left		**Lesion** lcshn	
Leg leg		**Less** les	
Legacy leg-s		**Lessor** lesr	
Legal legl		**Lest** lest	
Legate legt		**Let** let	
Legator legtr		**Lethargy** lethrj	
Legend lcjnd		**Lethe** lethe	
Leggin legn		**Letter** lctr	
Legible lejbl		**Lettuce** letus	
Legion lcjn		**Levant** lcvnt	
Legislate lcjslt		**Levee** lcve	
Legitimate lcjtmt		**Leveret** lcvret	
Legume legm		**Level** lcvl	
Leisure leshr		**Lever** levr	
Lemon lcmn		**Leviathan** lcvthn	
Lend lend		**Levigate** lcvgt	
Length lenth		**Levite** lcvt	
Lenient lenynt		**Levy** lcvy	
Lens lcns		**Lewd (lud)** lud	
Lent lcnt		**Lexicography** lcx-gr	
Lentil lcntl		**Lexicon** lcxcn	
Leonine lcnn		**Liable** liabl	

Liar
  l*i*r
Libation
  l*i*-b
Libel
  l*i*bl
Liberal
  l*i*brl
Liberate
  l*i*brat
Liberty
  l*i*br-t
Library
  l*i*brry
Librate
  l*i*brat
License
  l*i*sns
Licentious
  l*i*snshs
Lichen
  l*i*cn
Lick
  l*i*c
Lickerish
  l*i*crsh
Licorice
  l*i*cris
Lid
  l*i*d
Lie
  l*i*
Lief
  lcf
Liege
  lej
Lien (len)
  lcn
Lieu
  lew
Lieutenant
  lutnnt
Lieve
  lev
Life
  l*i*f
Lift
  l*i*ft

Ligament
  l*i*gmnt
Light
  l*i*t
Ligneous
  l*i*gnus
Lignumvitæ
  l*i*gnmvta
Like
  l*i*k
Lilac
  l*i*lc
Lily
  l*i*ly
Limb
  l*i*m
Lime
  l*i*m
Limit
  l*i*mt
Limn
  l*i*mn
Limp
  l*i*mp
Limpet
  l*i*mpt
Limpsy
  l*i*mp-s
Linch-pin
  l*i*nchpn
Linden
  l*i*ndn
Line
  l*i*n
Lineage
  l*i*n-a
Linen
  l*i*nn
Linger
  l*i*ngr
Linguist
  l*i*ngst
Lining
  l*i*ning
Link
  l*i*nk
Linnet
  l*i*net

Linseed
lmsd

Lint
lint

Lintel
lintl

Lion
lion

Lip
lip

Liquefy
liqf

Liquidate
liqdt

Liquor
licr

Lisp
lisp

List
list

Litany
litny

Literal
litrl

Literary
litry

Litharge
lithrj

Lithe
lith

Lithograph
lith g

Lithotomy
lithotmy

Litigate
lit g

Litigant
lit-g

Litter
litr

Little
li

Liturgy
litrj

Live
liv

Lives
liv

Liver
livr

Livid
livd

Lizard
lizrd

Lo
lo

Load
lod

Loaf
lof

Loam
lom

Loath
loth

Loaves
lovs

Lobe
lob

Lobby
loby

Lobster
lobstr

Local
locl

Locate
loct

Loch
loc

Lock
loc

Locomotion
loc-m

Locust
locst

Lode
lod

Lodge
loj

Loft
loft

Log
log

Logic
loj-i

Logomachy
logmcy

Loin
loin

Loiter
loitr

Loll
lol

Lone
lon

Long
long

Longitude
lonj-t

Loo
loo

Look
look

Loom
loom

Loon
loon

Loop
loop

Loose
loos

Lop
lop

Loquacious
lo-q

Lord
lord

Lore
lor

Lose
looz

Loss
los

Lot
lot

Lotion
loshn

Lottery
lotry

Loud
loud

Lough (lok)
loc

Lounge
lounj

Lout
lout

Love
luv

Low
lo

Lower
lor

Loyal
loyl

Lozenge
loznj

Lubber
lubr

Lubricate
lubr-c

Lucid
lusid

Luck
luc

Lucrative
lucr-t

Lucre
lucr

Lucubrate
lu-br

Luculent
luclnt

Ludicrous
luders

Luff
luf

Lug
lug

Luggage
lugj

Lukewarm
lucwrm

Lull
lul

Lumbago
lumbgo

Lumber
lumbr

Luminary
lumnry

Lump
lump

Lunacy lun-s	**Lye** ly
Lunar lunr	**Lymph** lymf
Lunch lunch	**Lynx** lynx
Lunette lunct	**Lyre** lyr
Lung lung	
Lunge lunj	## M.
Lupine lupn	**Macadamize** macdmis
Lurch lurch	**Macaroni** macrny
Lure lur	**Maccaboy** macby
Lured lurd	**Macaw** macaw
Lurid lurid	**Mace** mas
Lurk lurc	**Macerate** masrat
Luscious lushs	**Machinate** mac-n
Lust lust	**Machine** mashn
Luster lustr	**Mackerel** macrl
Lustrate lus-tr	**Macrocosm** macr-c
Lustrous lustrus	**Mad** mad
Lusty lus-t	**Madam** madm
Lute lut	**Madcap** madcp
Lutheran luthran	**Madder** madr
Luthern luthrn	**Made** mad
Luxate luxat	**Madeira** madra
Luxury luxry	**Madonna** madna
Lyceum lysm	**Madrepore** madrpr
	Madrigal madrgl

Magazine magzn	
Maggot magt	
Magi maji	
Magic maj-i	
Magistrate mags-tr	
Magna magna	
Magnanimity magnm-t	
Magnate magnat	
Magnet magnt	
Magnificent magnsnt	
Magnify magnf	
Magniloquent magnl-q	
Magnitude magn-t	
Magnolia magnla	
Magpie magpi	
Mahogany mahogny	
Mahometan mahmtn	
Maid mad	
Mail mal	
Maim mam	
Main man	
Maintain mantn	
Maize maz	
Majesty majst	
Major majr	
Make mak	
Maladministration maldmn-str	
Malady maldy	
Malapert malaprt	
Malaria malra	
Malcontent malcntnt	
Male mal	
Malediction mal-dc	
Malefactor malfctr	
Malevolent malvlnt	
Malfeasance malfsns	
Malice malis	
Malign maln	
Malison (zn) malzn	
Mall mal	
Malleable malbl	
Mallet malet	
Malmsey malmsy	
Malt malt	
Mamma mama	
Mammal maml	
Mammon mamn	
Mammoth mamth	

Man
man

Manacle
mancl

Manage
manj

Mandamus
mandms

Mandarin
mandrn

Mandate
mandt

Mandible
mandbl

Mandrel
mandrl

Mane
man

Manege (nazh)
manzh

Manes
manes

Maneuver
manvr

Manful
manfl

Manganese
mangnes

Mange
manj

Mangelwurzel
manglwrzl

Manger
manjr

Mangle
mangl

Mango
mango

Mangrove
mangrv

Mangy
manjy

Mania
manya

Manifest
manfst

Manifold
manfld

Manikin
mancn

Maniac
man-a

Manipulate
manplat

Mankind
mancnd

Manly
manly

Manner
manr

Manoeuvre (nu)
manvr

Manor
manor

Manse
mans

Mansion
manshn

Mantel
mantl

Mantua
mantua

Manual
manl

Manufacture
manfctr

Manumit
manmt

Manure
manur

Manuscript
manscrt

Many (meny)
meny

Map
map

Maple
mapl

Mar
mar

Maranatha
marntha

Marasmus
marsms

Maraud
maraud

Marble
marbl

March
march

Marchioness
marshnes

Mare
mar

Margin
marjn

Marigold
margld

Marine
marn

Mariner
marnr

Marital
marital

Marjoram
marjrm

Mark
marc

Market
marct

Marl
marl

Marline
marln

Marmalade
marmld

Marmorean
marmrn

Marmoset
· marmset

Maroon
marn

Marque
marc

Marquee (ke)
marce

Marquetry
marqtry

Marquis
marqs

Marriage
marj

Marrow
maro

Marry
mary

Marsh
marsh

Marshal
marshl

Mart
mart

Marten
martn

Martial
marshl

Martin
martn

Martinet
martnt

Martinmas
martnms

Martingal
martngl

Martlet
martlt

Martyr
martr

Marvel
marvl

Masculine
mascln

Mash
mash

Mask
masc

Maslin
masln

Mason
masn

Masquerade
masqrad

Mass
mas

Massacre
mascr

Massive
ma-s

Mast
mast

Master
mastr

Masticate	mastct	
Mastic	mastc	
Mastiff	mastf	
Mastodon	mastdn	
Mat	mat	
Match	mach	
Mate	mat	
Material	matrl	
Maternal	matrnl	
Mathematics	math-m	
Matin	matn	
Matrass	matrs	
Matrix	matrx	
Matricide	matrsid	
Matriculate	matrc-l	
Matron	matrn	
Matter	matr	
Matting	mat-ing	
Mattock	mat-o	
Mattress	matrs	
Mature	matur	
Maudlin	maudln	
Maul	maul	
Maunder	maundr	

Mausoleum	mauslm
Mavis	mavis
Maw	maw
Mawkish	mawcsh
Maxiliary	maxlry
Maxim	maxm
Maximum	maxmm
May	ma
Mayor	mar
Mazarine	mazrn
Mazard	mazrd
Maze	maz
Me	me
Mead	med
Meadow	medo
Meager	megr
Meal	mel
Mean	men
Meander	meandr
Meaning	mening
Meanly	menly
Meant	ment
Measles (zlz)	mesls
Measure	meshr

Mechanic mecnc	**Melody** meldy
Medal medl	**Melon** meln
Meddle medl	**Member** membr
Mediæval medevl	**Membrane** membrn
Medial medl	**Memento** memnto
Mediate medat	**Memoir** memr
Mediate medat	**Memory** memry
Medical medcl	**Men** men
Medicine medsn	**Menace** menas
Meditate med-t	**Menagerie** menjry
Medium medm	**Mend** mend
Medlar medlr	**Mendacious** men-d
Medley medly	**Mendicant** mendcnt
Medullar medulr	**Menial** menl
Meed med	**Menstruum** menstrm
Meek mec	**Mensuration** mens-r
Meerschaum mershm	**Mental** mentl
Meet met	**Mention** menshn
Meeting meting	**Mephitis** mefts
Melancholy melncly	**Mercantile** mercntl
Meliorate melrat	**Mercenary** mersnry
Mellifluent melflnt	**Mercer** mersr
Mellow melo	**Merchant** merchnt
Melodrame melodrm	**Merciful** mersfl

Mercury
mercry

Mercy
mer-s

Mere
mer

Meretricious
mer-tr

Merge
merj

Meridian
meridyn

Merino
merino

Merit
merit

Mermaid
mermad

Merman
mermn

Merry
mery

Mesh
mesh

Mesmerism
mesmrism

Mess
mes

Message
mesj

Messenger
mesnjr

Messiah
mesia

Messuage (swej)
meswj

Met
met

Metal
metl

Metamorphose
metmrfos

Metaphor
metfr

Metaphysics
met-fs

Mete
met

Meteor
metor

Meter
metr

Methinks
methnks

Method
methd

Metonomy
metnmy

Metrical
metrcl

Metropolis
metrpls

Mettle
metl

Mew
mew

Mewl
mewl

Mezzotinto
meztnto

Miasm
miasm

Mica
mica

Mice
mis

Michaelmas
miclms

Microcosm
micrcsm

Microscope
micrscp

Mid
mid

Midday
midd

Middle
midl

Midge
mij

Midland
midlnd

Midnight
midnt

Midriff
midrf

Midshipman
midshpmn

Midst
midst

Midway
midw

Mien
men

Miff
mif

Might
mit

Mignonette
minynt

Migrate
migrt

Milch
milch

Mild
mild

Mile
mil

Militant
miltnt

Militia (lisha)
mi-l

Milk
milk

Mill
mil

Millennium
milnym

Miller
milr

Millet
milet

Milliner
milnr

Million
milyn

Milt
milt

Mime
mim

Mimic
mim-i

Minaret
minrt

Mince
mins

Mind
mind

Mine
min

Mineral
minrl

Mingle
mingl

Miniature
mintur

Minim
minm

Minimum
minmm

Minion
minyn

Minister
ministr

Mink
mink

Minnow
mino

Minor
minr

Minotaur
minotaur

Minster
minstr

Minstrel
minstrl

Mint
mint

Minuend
minund

Minuet
minet

Minute (minit)
mint

Minute
minut

Minx
minx

Miracle
mircl

Mire
mir

Mirror mirr	**Mission** mishn
Mirth mirth	**Missive** mis
Miry miry	**Mist** mist
Misanthrope misnthrp	**Mistle** misl
Misapply mispli	**Mistress** mistrs
Misapprehend misprnd	**Misty** misty
Misbecome misbecm	**Mite** mit
Misbehave misbhv	**Mitigate** mit-g
Misbelief misblf	**Mitten** mitn
Miscalculate misclclt	**Mix** mix
Miscall miscl	**Mizzen** mizn
Miscarry miscry	**Mizzle** mizl
Miscellaneous mislns	**Mnemonics (ne)** nemn-i
Mischance mischns	**Moan** mon
Mischief mischf	**Moat** mot
Mischoose mischs	**Mob** mob
Miscite missit	**Mobility** moblt
Miscreant miscrnt	**Moccasin** mocsn
Miser misr	**Mock** moc
Misery misry	**Modal** modl
Misle misl	**Mode** mod
Miss mis	**Model** modl
Missal misl	**Moderate** modrt
Missile misl	**Modern** modrn

Modest modst	**Monarch** monrc
Modicum medcm	**Monastery** monastry
Modify modf	**Monday** mond
Modish modsh	**Money** mony
Modiste smodst	**Mongrel** mongrl
Modulate mod-l	**Monitor** montr
Mohair mohr	**Monk** monc
Mohammedan mohmdn	**Monkey** moncy
Moiety moi-t	**Monody** monody
Moil moil	**Monogamy** mongmy
Moist moist	**Monogram** mon-gr
Molar molr	**Monologue** mon-l
Molasses molss	**Monomaniac** monmn a
Mole mol	**Monopoly** monply
Molecule molcl	**Monosyllable** monslbl
Molest molst	**Monotheism** monthsm
Mollify molfy	**Monotone** montn
Molt molt	**Monotony** montny
Molten moltn	**Monsoon** monsn
Moment momnt	**Monster** monstr
Momentous momnts	**Month** month
Momentum momntm	**Monument** monmnt
Monachism moncsm	**Mood** mood
Monad monad	**Moon** moon

Moor	
moor	
Moose	
moos	
Moot	
moot	
Mop	
mop	
Mope	
mop	
Moral	
morl	
Morbid	
morbd	
Mordant	
mordnt	
More	
mor	
Moreen	
moren	
Moresque	
morsc	
Morn	
morn	
Morocco	
morc	
Morose	
moros	
Morris	
moris	
Morrow	
moro	
Morse	
mors	
Morsel	
morsl	
Mortal	
mortl	
Mortar	
mortr	
Mortgage (morgej)	
morgj	
Mortify	
mortf	
Mortise	
morts	
Mortmain	
mortmn	

Mosaic	
mosa-i	
Mosque (mosk)	
mosc	
Mosquito (ke)	
moscto	
Moss	
mos	
Most	
most	
Mote	
mot	
Moth	
moth	
Mother	
mothr	
Motion	
moshn	
Motive	
mo-t	
Motley	
motly	
Motor	
motr	
Motto	
moto	
Mould	
mold	
Moult	
molt	
Mound	
mound	
Mount	
mount	
Mourn	
morn	
Mouse	
mous	
Mouth	
mouth	
Move	
mov	
Mow	
mo	
Mow (mou)	
mow	
Much	
much	

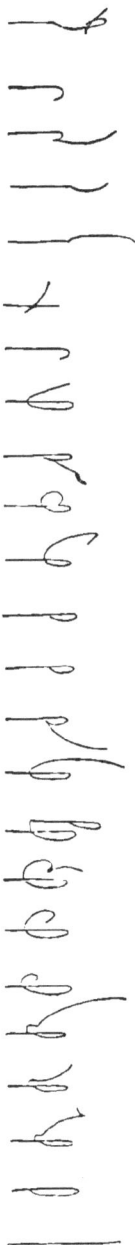

Mucilage	**Mumble**
muslꞏa	mʉmbl
Muck	**Mummer**
mʉc	'mʉmr
Mucus	**Mummy**
mʉcs	mʉmy
Mud	**Mumpish**
mʉd	mʉmpsh
Muff	**Mumps**
mʉf	mʉmps
Mufti	**Munch**
mʉfti	mʉnch
Mug	**Mundane**
mʉg	mʉndn
Mulatto	**Municipal**
mʉlto	mʉnspl
Mulberry	**Munificence**
mʉlbry	mʉnfsns
Mulch	**Muniment**
mʉlch	mʉnmnt
Mulet	**Munition**
mʉlct	mʉ-n
Mule	**Mural**
mʉl	mʉrl
Mull	**Murder**
mʉl	mʉrdr
Mullion	**Muriatic**
mʉlyn	mʉr-a
Multiform	**Murky**
mʉlfrm	mʉrky
Multinomial	**Murmur**
mʉltnml	mʉrmr
Multipartite	**Murrain**
mʉltprt	mʉran
Multiped	**Muscle**
mʉltpd	mʉsl
Multiple	**Muscovado**
mʉltpl	mʉsc-v
Multiplicand	**Muscular**
mʉltplcn	mʉsclr
Multiply	**Muse**
mʉltply	mʉs
Multiplication	**Museum**
mʉltpl-c	mʉsm
Multitude	**Mush**
mʉltd	mʉsh
Mum	**Mushroom**
mum	mshrm

Music
mus-i

Musk
musc

Musket
musct

Must
must

Mustache
mustsh

Mustard
mustrd

Muster
mustr

Musty
musty

Mutable
mutbl

Mute
mut

Mutilate
mut-l

Mutiny
mutny

Mutter
mutr

Mutton
mutn

Mutual
mutl

Muzzle
musl

My
my

Myriad
myrd

Myrrh (mer)
mer

Myrtle (mertl)
mertl

Mystery
mys-tr

Mystic
mystc

Mystify
mystf

Myth
myth

Mythology
myth-o

N.

Nab
nab

Nabob
nabb

Nacre
nacr

Nadir
nadr

Nag
nag

Naiad
naad

Nail
nal

Naked
nacd

Name
nam

Nankeen
nancn

Nap
nap

Nape
nap

Naphtha (nap)
napth

Napkin
napcn

Narcotic
narct-i

Narrate
narat

Narrow
naro

Narwhal
narwhl

Nasal
nasl

Nasty
nas-t

Natal
natl

Nation
nashn

Native na-t	**Nectary** nectry
Nature natr	**Need** ned
Naught (nawt) nawt	**Needle** nedl
Naughty naw-t	**Ne'er** ner
Nausea nausea	**Nefarious** ne-f
Nautical nautcl	**Negative** neg-t
Nautilus nautls	**Neglect** neg-l
Naval navl	**Negotiate** ne-go
Nave nav	**Negress** negrs
Navel navl	**Negro** negro
Navigate nav-g	**Negus** negus
Navy navy	**Neigh (na)** na
Nag nag	**Neighbor** nabr
Neap nep	**Neither** nethr
Near ner	**Neology** ne-o
Neat net	**Neophyte** nefit
Nebula nebla	**Nephew (nefyu)** nefu
Necessary nesry	**Nephritic** nefrtc
Necessity nesst	**Nepotism** neptism
Neck nec	**Nereid** nereid
Necrology necr-o	**Nerve** nerv
Necromancy necrmn-s	**Nescience** nesshns
Nectar nectr	**Nest** nest
Nectarine nectrn	**Net** net

Nether nethr	**Nimble** n*i*mbl
Netting neting	**Nimbus** n*i*mbs
Nettle netl	**Nine** n*i*n
Neuralgia neurlj	**Ninny** n*i*ny
Neuter nutr	**Nip** n*i*p
Never nevr	**Nipple** n*i*pl
New new	**Nit** n*i*t
News news	**Nitid** n*i*td
Newt (nut) newt	**Niter** n*i*tr
Next nex	**Nitrate** n*i*trat
Nib n*i*b	**Nitrogen** n*i*trjn
Nice n*i*s	**No** no
Niche n*i*ch	**Noble** nobl
Nick n*i*c	**Nobleman** noblmn
Nickel n*i*cl	**Nobody** nobd
Nick-nacks nicncs	**Nocturnal** noctrnl
Nickname nicnm	**Nod** nod
Nictate nict-t	**Noddle** nodl
Niece nes	**Noddy** nody
Niggard nigrd	**Node** nod
Nigh (ni) ni	**Nodule** nodul
Night (nit) nit	**Nog** nog
Nightingale nitngl	**Noise** nos
Nihility nihl-t	**Noisome** nosm

Nomad	
nomad	
Nomenclature	
nomncltr	
Nominal	
nomnl	
Nominate	
nom-n	
Nominee	
nome	
Nonage	
nonj	
Nondescript	
nond-scr	
None	
nun	
Nonentity	
nonn-t	
Nones	
nons	
Nonpareil	
nonprl	
Nonplus	
nonpls	
Nook	
nook	
Noon	
noon	
Noose	
noos	
Noose'	
noos	
Nor	
nor	
Normal	
norml	
North	
north	
Nose	
nos	
Nosology	
nos-o	
Nostril	
nostrl	
Nostrum	
nostrm	
Not	
not	

Notable	
notbl	
Notary	
not-ry	
Notation	
no-t	
Notch	
noch	
Note	
not	
Noted	
notd	
Nothing	
nuth-ing	
Notice	
notis	
Notify	
notf	
Notion	
noshn	
Notorious	
notors	
Notwithstanding	
notstnd-ing	
Nought (nawt)	
nawt	
Noun	
noun	
Nourish	
nursh	
Novel	
novl	
November	
nov	
Novice	
novs	
Now	
now	
Noxious (nokshus)	
nocshs	
Nozzle	
nozl	
Nucleus	
nucls	
Nude	
nud	
Nugatory	
nugtry	

Nugget		**O.**	
n*u*gt			
Nuisance		**O**	
n*u*sns			*o*
Null		**Oak**	
n*u*l		o*c*	
Numb		**Oar**	
n*u*m		o*r*	
Number		**Oasis**	
n*u*mbr		o*s*s	
Numerator		**Oat**	
n*u*mratr		o*t*	
Numerous		**Oath**	
n*u*nrs		o*th*	
Numismatics		**Obdurate**	
n*u*ms-m		o*b*drt	
Nun		**Obedience**	
n*u*n		o*b*dns	
Nuncio (shi)		**Obeisance**	
n*u*nsho		o*b*sns	
Nuncupative		**Obelisk**	
n*u*ncp-t		o*b*lsk	
Nunnery		**Obese**	
n*u*nry		o*b*s	
Nuptial		**Obey**	
n*u*pshl		o*b*a	
Nurse		**Obfuscation**	
n*u*rs		o*b*fs-c	
Nurture		**Obituary**	
n*u*rtr		o*b*try	
Nut		**Object**	
n*u*t		o*b*j	
Nutation		**Objurgatory**	
n*u*-t		o*b*jr-g	
Nut-gall		**Obligate**	
n*u*tgl		o*b*l-g	
Nutmeg		**Oblige**	
n*u*tmg		o*b*lj	
Nutriment		**Oblique**	
n*u*trmnt		o*b*lc	
Nymph		**Obliterate**	
nimf		o*b*ltrat	
Nys		**Oblivious**	
nys		o*b*lvs	
Nyssa		**Oblong**	
nysa		o*b*lng	
Nystagmus		**Obloquy**	
nystgms		o*b*lq	

Obnoxious
obncshs

Oboe
obo

Obovate
obvt

Obscene
obsn

Obscure
obscr

Obsequies
obsqs

Obsequious
obsqs

Observe
obsrv

Obsession
ob-s

Obsolescent
obslsnt

Obsolete
obslt

Obstacle
obstcl

Obstetrics
obsttr-i

Obstinate
obstnt

Obstreperous
obstrprs

Obstruct
ob-str

Obtain
obtn

Obtest
obtst

Obtrude
ob-tr

Obtuse
obtus

Obverse
obvrs

Obvert
obvrt

Obviate
obvat

Obvious
obvs

Occasion
oc-c

Occident
ocsdnt

Occiput
ocspt

Occlusion
oc-cl

Occult
oclt

Occupy
ocp

Occur
ocr

Ocean
oshn

Ocher
ocr

Octachord
octcrd

Octagon
octgn

Octahedral
octhdrl

Octangular
octnglr

Octave
octv

Octavo
octvo

October
oct

Octogenarian
octj-n

Ocular
oclr

Oculist
oclst

Odd
od

Odds
ods

Ode
od

Odeon
odn

Odium
odym

Word	Shorthand	Word	Shorthand
Odor odr		**Olfactory** olfctry	
O'er or		**Olibanum** olbnm	
Of (ov) ov		**Oligarchy** olgrcy	
Off of		**Olio** olio	
Offal ofl		**Olive** olv	
Offence o/ns		**Olympiad** olmpd	
Offer ofr		**Omega** omga	
Office o/s		**Omelet** omlet	
Officer ofsr		**Omen** omn	
Official of-f		**Omission** o-m	
Offing of-ing		**Omnibus** omnbs	
Offscouring ofscr-ng		**Omit** o-m	
Offset ofst		**Omnipotent** omnp-tnt	
Offspring ofspring		**Omnipresent** omni-prsnt	
Oft oft		**Omniscient** omns-nt	
Often (ofn) ofn		**Omnivorous** omnv-ors	
Ogee oje		**On** on	
Ogle ogl		**One (wun)** wun	
Ogre ogr		**Once** wuns	
Oh oh		**Onerary** onrary	
Oil oil		**Onion** onyn	
Oint oint		**Only** only	
Old old		**Onset** onst	
Oleaginous olagns		**Onslaught** onslt	

Ontology ont-o	
Onward onrd	
Onyx onx	
Ooze ooz	
Opacity opast	
Opal opl	
Open opn	
Opera opra	
Operate oprat	
Operose ofros	
Ophicleide ofclid	
Ophthalmy ofthlmy	
Opiate opat	
Opinion opnn	
Opium ofm	
Opodeldoc opdldc	
Opossum ofsm	
Opponent ofnnt	
Opportune oprtn	
Oppose ops	
Oppress ofrs	
Opprobrium oprobrum	
Oppugn opun	
Optative opt-t	

Optic optc	
Optimism optmism	
Option opshn	
Opulent oplnt	
Or or	
Oracle orcl	
Oral orl	
Orange ornj	
Orang-outang orngtng	
Oration o-r	
Orb orb	
Orbicular orbclr	
Orbit orbt	
Orchard orchrd	
Orchestra orcstr	
Orchis (kis) orcs	
Ordain ordn	
Ordeal ordl	
Order ordr	
Ordinal ordnl	
Ordinary ordnry	
Ordination ord-n	
Ordnance ordnns	
Ore or	

Organ		Osculate
orgn		osclt
Organism		Osier
orgnism		osr
Orgies		Osprey
orjs		ospry
Oriel		Osseous
orel		osus
Orient		Ossify
ornt		osf
Orifice		Ossivorous
orfs		osvrs
Origin		Ostensible
orjn		ostnsbl
Oriole		Ostentation
orol		ostn-t
Orion		Osteology
orin		oste-o
Orison		Ostiary
orsn		ostary
Orlop		Ostracism
orlp		ostrssm
Ormolu		Ostrich
ormlu		ostrch
Ornament		Other
ornmnt		ohr
Ornate		Otter
orn		ofr
Ornithology		Ottoman
ornth-o		otmn
Orology		Ouch
or-o		ouch
Orphan		Ought (awt)
orfn		awt
Orphie		Ounce
orfc		ouns
Orrery		Ours
orrry		ours
Orthodox		Ourselves
orthdx		oursl
Orthoepy		Oust
orthp		oust
Orthography		Out
orth-gr		out
Ortolan		Outward
ortln		ourd
Oscillate		Oval
os-l		ovl

Ovary		**Padlock**	
o*r*ry		p*a*dlc	
Ovate		**Pæan**	
o*r*at		p*æ*an	
Ovation		**Pagan**	
o-v		p*a*gn	
Oven		**Page**	
u*r*n		p*a*j	
Over		**Pageant**	
o*r*r		p*a*jnt	
Overt		**Pagoda**	
o*r*rt		p*a*god	
Oviform		**Paid**	
o*r*frm		p*a*d	
Oviparous		**Pail**	
o*r*prs		p*a*l	
Owe		**Pain**	
o*r*e		p*a*n	
Owl		**Paint**	
ow*l*		p*a*nt	
Own		**Pair**	
ow*n*		p*a*r	
Owner		**Palace**	
ow*n*r		p*a*ls	
Ox		**Paladin**	
o*c*s		p*a*ladn	
Oxide		**Palanquin (keen)**	
o*c*sid		p*a*lncn	
Oxygen		**Palatable**	
o*c*sjn		p*a*ltbl	
Oyer		**Palate**	
oy*r*		p*a*lat	
Oyster		**Palatine**	
oy*s*tr		p*a*latn	

P.

Pace		**Palaver**	
p*a*s		p*a*lvr	
Pacha		**Pale**	
p*a*sha		p*a*l	
Pacific		**Paleography**	
p*a*sfc		p*a*lo-gr	
Pack		**Paleology**	
p*a*c		p*a*le-o	
Pact		**Palette**	
p*a*ct		p*a*let	
Pad		**Palfrey**	
p*a*d		p*a*lfry	
		Paling	
		p*a*l ing	

Palisade palsad	**Pander** pandr
Pall pal	**Pane** pan
Palladium paladym	**Panegyric** panjr-i
Pallet palet	**Panel** panel
Palliate palat	**Pang** pang
Pallid palid	**Panic** pan-i
Palm (pam) pam	**Pannier (yer)** panyr
Palmated palmtd	**Panoply** panoply
Palmetto palmto	**Panorama** panrma
Palmistry pamstry	**Pansy** pansy
Palmy pamy	**Pantalets** pantlts
Palpable palpbl	**Pantaloons** pantlns
Palpitate palp-t	**Pantheism** panthism
Palsy palsy	**Pantheon** panthn
Palter paltr	**Panther** panthr
Paltry pal-tr	**Pantograph** pant-gr
Pamper pampr	**Pantomime** pantmm
Pamphlet pamflt	**Pantry** pantry
Pan pan	**Pap** pap
Panacea pansea	**Papa** papa
Pancake pancc	**Papacy** pap-s
Pancreas pancras	**Paper** papr
Pandect pandct	**Papilionaceous** paplo-n
Pandemonium pandmnm	**Papillary** paplry

Papist
papst

Pappoose
papoos

Pappy
papy

Papyrus
paprus

Par
par

Parable
parbl

Parabola
parbla

Parachute (shoot)
parsht

Paraclete
parclt

Parade
parad

Paradigm (dim)
pæradm

Paradise
pardis

Paradox
pardx

Paragogic
pargj-i

Paragon
pargn

Paragraph
pargrf

Parallax
parlx

Parallel
parl

Paralysis
parlss

Paramount
parmnt

Paramour
parmr

Parapet
parapt

Paraphernalia
parfrnla

Paraphrase
parfrs

Parasite
parsit

Parasol
parsol

Parboil
parbl

Parcel
parsl

Parch
parch

Parchment
parchmnt

Pard
pard

Pardon
pardn

Pare
par

Paregoric
pargr-i

Parent
parnt

Parenthesis
parnthss

Parhelion
parhlyn

Pariah
parla

Paring
par-ing

Parish
parsh

Parity
pari-t

Park
parc

Parlance
parlns

Parley
parly

Parliament
parlmnt

Parlor
parlr

Parochial
parocl

Parody
parody

Parol
parol

Paronym
paronm

Paronymous
paronms

Paroquet (ket)
parocet

Parotid
parotd

Paroxysm
parxm

Parquet (ka)
parca

Parricide
parsid

Parrot
parot

Parry
pary

Parse
pars

Parsimony
parsmny

Parsley
parsly

Parsnip
parsnp

Parson
parsn

Part
part

Partake
partc

Parterre (ter)
partr

Partial
parshl

Participant
partspnt

Participle
partspl

Particle
partcl

Particular
partclr

Partisan
partsn

Partition
par-t

Partitive
part-t

Partly
partly

Partner
partnr

Partook
partc

Partridge
partrj

Party
party

Paschal
pascl

Pasha
pasha

Pasquinade
pasqnad

Pass
pas

Passage
pasj

Passenger
pasnjr

Passion
pashn

Passive
pa-s

Passover
pasvr

Passport
pasprt

Past
past

Paste
past

Pastern
pastrn

Pastille
pastl

Pastime
pastm

Pastor
pastr

Pastry
pastry

Pasture
pastur

Pasty
pasty

Pat
pat

Patch
pach

Pate
pat

Patent
patnt

Paternal
patrnl

Paternity
patrn-t

Path
path

Pathetic
patht-i

Pathless
pathls

Pathologic
path-o

Pathos
pathos

Patience
pashns

Patient
pashnt

Patriarch
patrrc

Patrician
pa-tr

Patrimony
patrmny

Patriot
patrt

Patristic
patrst-i

Patrol
patrl

Patron
patrn

Patronymic
patrnm-i

Patten
patn

Patter
patr

Pattern
patrn

Patty
paty

Paucity
paus-t

Paunch
paunch

Pauper
paupr

Pause
paus

Pave
pav

Pavilion
pavln

Paw
paw

Pawn
pawn

Pay
pa

Pea
pe

Peace
pes

Peach
pech

Peak
pec

Peal
pel

Pean
pean

Pear
par

Pearl
perl

Peasant
pesnt

Pease
pes

Peat
pet

Pebble
pebl

Pecan pecn	**Pelican** pelcn
Peccable pecbl	**Pelisse** pelis
Peccadillo pecdl	**Pell** pel
Peek pec	**Pellet** pelet
Pectoral pectrl	**Pell-mell** pelml
Peculate pec-l	**Pellucid** pelusd
Peculiar peclr	**Pelt** pelt
Pecuniary pecnry	**Pelvis** pelvs
Pedagogue pedgg	**Pemmican** pemcn
Pedal pedl	**Pen** pen
Pedant pednt	**Penal** penl
Peddle pedl	**Penalty** penlt
Pedestal pedstl	**Penance** penns
Pedestrian pedstrn	**Pencil** pensl
Pedigree pedgre	**Pendant** pendnt
Pediment pedmnt	**Pendent** pendnt
Pedobaptist pedbptst	**Pendulous** pendls
Peduncle pedncl	**Pendulum** pendlm
Peel pel	**Penetrable** pentrbl
Peep pep	**Penguin** pengwn
Peer per	**Peninsula** pennsla
Peevish pevsh	**Penitence** pentns
Peg peg	**Penitentiary** pentnshry
Pelf pelf	**Pence** pens

Penknife (nif)
penf

Penmanship
penmnshp

Pennant
pennt

Pennate
penat

Penny
peny

Pensile
pensl

Pension
penshn

Pensive
pen-s

Pent
pent

Pentagon
pentgn

Pentagraph
pent gr

Pentahedron
penthdrn

Pentameter
pentmtr

Pentateuch
penttc

Pentecost
pentcst

Penult
penlt

Penumbra
penmbra

Penurious
penrs

Penury
penry

Peon
peon

Peony
peony

Peonage
pen-a

People
pepl

Peradventure
pervntr

Perambulate
permblat

Perceive
persv

Percentage
persntj

Perceptible
per-sp

Perception
per-sp

Perch
perch

Perchance
perchns

Percolate
perclt

Percussion
percshn

Perdition
per-d

Perdu
perdu

Peregrination
pergr-n

Peremptory
permp-tr

Perennial
pernl

Perfect
perfct

Perfidy
perfdy

Peri
peri

Pericardium
percrdm

Pericarp
percrp

Perigee
perje

Perihelion
perhlyn

Peril
perl

Perimeter
permtr

Period
perd

Periodical perodcl		**Persimmon** persmn		
Periphery perfry		**Persist** persst		
Periphrase perfras		**Person** persn		
Perish persh		**Perspective** perspc-t		
Peristaltic perstlt-i		**Perspicuity** perspc-i		
Peristyle perstl		**Perspire** perspr		
Periwig perwg		**Persuade** perswd		
Periwinkle perwncl		**Pert** pert		
Perjure perjr		**Pertain** pertn		
Perk perc		**Pertinent** pertnnt		
Permanent permnt		**Pertly** pertly		
Permeate permat		**Perturb** pertrb		
Permission per-m		**Peruke** peruc		
Permit permt		**Peruse** perus		
Permutation perm-t		**Pervade** pervd		
Pernicious per-n		**Perverse** pervrs		
Peroration pero-r		**Pervert** pervrt		
Perpendicular perpndclr		**Pervious** pervs		
Perpetrate prp-tr		**Pest** pest		
Perpetual perptl		**Pestle** pesl		
Perplex perplx		**Pet** pet		
Perquisite perqst		**Petal** petl		
Persecute persct		**Petard** petrd		
Persevere persvr		**Petiole** petol		

Petiolule petlul	
Petit (y) pety	
Petition pe-t	
Petrel petrl	
Petrify petrf	
Petroleum petrlm	
Petticoat petct	
Pettifogger petfgr	
Pettish petsh	
Pettitoes pettos	
Petty pety	
Petulant petlnt	
Pew (pu) pew	
Pewit pewt	
Pewter pewtr	
Phaeton fatn	
Phalanx falnx	
Phantasm fantsm	
Phantom fantm	
Pharisee farse	
Pharmacy farm-s	
Pharos faros	
Pharynx farnx	
Phase fas	

Phenix fenx	
Phenomenon fenmnn	
Phial (vi) vil	
Philanthropy filnthrp	
Philippic filpc	
Philology fil-o	
Philomel filml	
Philoprogenitive- filprjn-t [ness	
Philosopher filsfr	
Philter filtr	
Phiz fiz	
Phlebotomy flebtmy	
Phlegm flem	
Phœnix fenx	
Phonetic fon-e	
Phonography fon-gr	
Phonology fon-o	
Phosphorus fosfrs	
Photograph fot-gr	
Phrase fras	
Phrenology fren-o	
Phrensy frensy	
Phthisic (tizik) tsc	
Phylactery filctry	

Pierce p*e*rs	**Pink** p*i*nk
Piety p*ie*-t	**Pinnace** p*i*nas
Pig p*i*g	**Pinnacle** p*i*ncl
Pigeon (pijun) p*i*jn	**Pint** p*i*nt
Pigment p*i*gmnt	**Pintle** p*i*ntl
Pigmy p*i*gmy	**Pioneer** p*i*nr
Pike p*i*c	**Piony** p*i*ony
Pilaster p*i*lstr	**Pious** p*i*us
Pilchard p*i*lchrd	**Pip** p*i*p
Pile p*i*l	**Pipe** p*i*p
Pilgrim p*i*lgrm	**Pipkin** p*i*pkn
Pill p*i*l	**Pippin** p*i*pn
Pillage p*i*lj	**Piquant** p*e*cnt
Pillar p*i*lr	**Pique** p*e*c
Pillion p*i*lyn	**Piquet (ket)** p*i*cet
Pillow p*i*lo	**Pirate** p*i*rt
Pilot p*i*lt	**Piscatory** p*i*sctry
Pimple p*i*mpl	**Pish** p*i*sh
Pin p*i*n	**Pistachio** p*i*stsho
Pinch p*i*nch	**Pistareen** p*i*strn
Pincers p*i*nsrs	**Pistil** p*i*stl
Pine p*i*n	**Pistol** p*i*stl
Pinfold p*i*nfld	**Pistole** p*i*stl
Pinion p*i*nyn	**Piston** p*i*stn

Pit		**Planet**
p*i*t		pl*a*net
Pitch		**Planish**
p*i*ch		pl*a*nsh
Pitcher		**Plank**
p*i*chr		pl*a*nk
Piteous		**Plant**
p*i*tus		pl*a*nt
Pitfall		**Plantain**
p*i*tfl		pl*a*ntn
Pith		**Plantation**
p*i*th		pl*a*n-t
Pitiful		**Planter**
p*i*tyfl		pl*a*ntr
Pittance		**Plantigrade**
p*i*tns		pl*a*ntgrd
Pity		**Plash**
p*i*ty		pl*a*sh
Pivot		**Plaster**
p*i*vt		pl*a*str
Placable		**Plastic**
pl*a*cbl		pl*a*stc
Placard		**Plat**
pl*a*crd		pl*a*t
Place		**Plate**
pl*a*s		pl*a*t
Placid		**Plateau (to)**
pl*a*sid		pl*a*to
Plagiary		**Platen**
pl*a*jry		pl*a*tn
Plague		**Platform**
pl*a*g		pl*a*tfrm
Plaice		**Platinum**
pl*a*s		pl*a*tnm
Plaid		**Platitude**
pl*a*d		pl*a*t-t
Plain		**Platonic**
pl*a*n		pl*a*tnc
Plaint		**Platoon**
pl*a*nt		pl*a*tn
Plaintiff		**Platter**
plf		pl*a*tr
Plait		**Plaudit**
pl*a*t		pl*au*dt
Plan		**Plausible**
pl*a*n		pl*au*sbl
Plane		**Play**
pl*a*n		pl*a*

Plea	
ple	
Plead	
pled	
Pleasant	
plesnt	
Please	
ples	
Pleasure	
pleshr	
Plebeian	
plebn	
Pledge	
plej	
Pledget	
plejet	
Pleiades (ya)	
pledes	
Plenary	
plenry	
Plenipotent	
plenptnt	
Plenitude	
plen-t	
Plenty	
plen-t	
Pleonasm	
plensm	
Plethora	
plethra	
Pleurisy	
plursy	
Pleuro-pneumonia	
pleurnmny	
Plexiform	
plexfrn:	
Pliable	
pliatl	
Pliers	
plirs	
Plight (plit)	
plit	
Plinth	
plinth	
Plod	
plod	
Plot	
plot	

Plover
plovr
Plow
plow
Pluck
pluc
Plug
plug
Plum
plum:
Plumage
plumj
Plumb
plum:
Plumbago
plumbgo
Plume
plum
Plummet
plumet
Plump
plump
Plunder
plundr
Plunge
plunj
Plural
plurl
Plus
plus
Plush
plush
Pluvial
pluvl
Ply
ply
Pneumatic
neumatc
Pneumonia
neumony
Poach
poch
Pock
poc
Pod
pod
Poem
pom

Poesy
poe-s

Poet
poet

Poh
po

Poignant (poin)
poinnt

Point
point

Poise
pois

Poison
poisn

Poke
pok

Polar
polr

Pole
pol

Polemic
polmc

Police
poles

Policy
polsy

Polish
polsh

Polite
polit

Politics
poltx

Polity
polty

Polka
polca

Poll
pol

Pollard
polrd

Pollen
poln

Pollock
pol-o

Poll-tax
poltx

Pollute
polut

Poltroon
poltrn

Polyanthus
polanths

Polygamy
poligmy

Polyglot
poliglt

Polygon
polign

Polygraph
poli-gr

Polyhedron
polihdrn

Polynomial
poli-n

Polyp
polip

Polypus
polips

Polyscope
poliscp

Polysyllable
polislbl

Polytechnic
politcnc

Polytheism
polthsm

Pomace
pomas

Pomade
pomad

Pomatum
pomtm

Pomegranate
pomgrnt

Pommel
poml

Pommelion
pomlyn

Pomology
pom-o

Pomp
pomp

Pond
pond

Ponder
pondr

Pongee	Porridge
penj	porj
Poniard (yard)	**Porringer**
ponrd	pornjr
Pontiff	**Port**
pontf	port
Pontoon	**Portable**
pontn	portbl
Pony	**Portage**
pony	portj
Poodle	**Portal**
poodl	portl
Pool	**Portcullis**
pool	portclis
Poor	**Porte**
poor	port
Pop	**Porte-monnaie**
pop	portmna
Pope	**Portend**
pop	portnd
Poplar	**Portent**
poplr	portnt
Poplin	**Porter**
popln	portr
Populace	**Portfolio**
popls	portflo
Populate	**Portico**
poplt	portco
Popular	**Portion**
poplr	porshn
Porcelain	**Portly**
porsln	portly
Porch	**Portmanteau (to)**
porch	portmnto
Porcine	**Portrait**
porsn	portrt
Porcupine	**Pose**
porcpn	pos
Pore	**Poser**
por	posr
Pork	**Position**
porc	pos-s
Porous	**Positive**
porus	postv
Porphyry	**Possess**
porfry	poss
Porpoise	**Posset**
porps	poset

Possible posbl	**Pound** pound
Post post	**Pour** por
Postage postj	**Pout** pout
Posterior postrr	**Poverty** povrt
Postern postrn	**Powder** powdr
Postfix postfx	**Power** power
Postillion postlyn	**Pox** pox
Posture postur	**Practice** practs
Posy posy	**Pragmatic** pragmtc
Pot pot	**Prairie** prary
Potable potbl	**Praise** pras
Potash potsh	**Prance** prans
Potato potato	**Prank** pranc
Potent potnt	**Prate** prat
Potentate potntat	**Prattle** pratl
Potential potnshl	**Prawn** prawn
Pother pothr	**Pray** pra
Potion poshn	**Prayer** prar
Potsherd potshrd	**Preach** prch
Pottage potj	**Preamble** prembl
Potter potr	**Prebend** prebnd
Pouch pouch	**Precarious** precrs
Poultry poltry	**Precaution** pre-c
Pounce pouns	**Precede** presd

Precentor presntr	
Precept prespt	
Precinct presnct	
Precious preshs	
Precipice presps	
Precipitate presp-t	
Precise press	
Preclude precld	
Precocity precost	
Predaceous pre-d	
Predatory pred-tr	
Predestinate predstnt	
Predetermine predtrmn	
Predial predl	
Predicate predct	
Predict pred-i	
Pre-emption premshn	
Preface prefs	
Prefect prefct	
Prefer prefr	
Prefigure prefgr	
Pregnant pregnnt	
Prehension prehnshn	
Prejudice prejds	

Prelate prelat	
Prelection preleshn	
Preliminary prelmnry	
Prelude prelud	
Premature premtur	
Premeditate premd-t	
Premier premr	
Premise premis	
Premises premss	
Premium premm	
Premonish premnsh	
Prepare prepr	
Prepay prepa	
Prepense prepns	
Preposition prep-s	
Preposterous prepstrs	
Prerogative prergtv	
Presage presj	
Presbyter presbtr	
Presbyterian presbtrn	
Prescience (shi) preshns	
Present presnt	
Present' presnt	
Preserve presrv	

Preside
  presid

President
  pres

Press
  pres

Presume
  presm

Pretend
  pretnd

Pretense
  pretns

Preterit
  pretrit

Pretext
  pretxt

Pretor
  pretr

Pretty
  prity

Prevail
  prevl

Prevaricate
  prevrct

Prevent
  prevnt

Previous
  prevs

Prey
  pra

Price
  pris

Prick
  pric

Pride
  prid

Priest
  prest

Prig
  prig

Prim
  prim

Primage
  primj

Primary
  primry

Primate
  primat

Prime
  prim

Primer
  primr

Primeval
  primvl

Priming
  prim-ing

Primitive
  prim-t

Primogeniture
  primjntr

Primordial
  primrdl

Primrose
  primros

Prince
  prins

Principal
  prinspl

Principle
  prinspl

Prink
  princ

Print
  print

Prior
  prior

Priory
  prory

Prism
  prism

Prison
  prisn

Pristine
  pristn

Prithee
  prithe

Private
  privt

Privation
  pri-v

Privet
  privet

Privilege
  privlj

Prize
  priz

Probable probbl		**Prognosis** prognoss	
Probate pro-b		**Program** progrm	
Probation pro-b		**Progress** progrs	
Probe prob		**Progress'** progrs	
Problem problm		**Prohibit** prohbt	
Proboscis probss		**Project** pro-j	
Proceed prosd		**Project'** pro-j	
Process pross		**Prolate** pro-l	
Proclaim proclm		**Prolicide** prolisd	
Proclivity proclv-t		**Prolific** prolfc	
Proconsul procnsl		**Prolix** prolx	
Procrastinate procrstnt		**Prolocutor** prolctr	
Profane profn		**Prologue (log)** prolg	
Profess profs		**Prolong** prolng	
Proffer profr		**Promenade** promnd	
Proficient pro-f		**Prominent** premnnt	
Profile profl		**Promiscuous** promscs	
Profit proft		**Promise** premse	
Profligate profl-g		**Promissory** promsry	
Profound profnd		**Promote** pro-m	
Profundity profnd-t		**Prompt** promt	
Profuse profus		**Promulgate** proml-g	
Prog prog		**Prone** pron	
Progeny projny		**Prong** prong	

Pronoun pronn	**Proscribe** proscrb
Pronounce pronns	**Prose** pros
Proof proof	**Prosecute** pros-c
Prop prop	**Proselyte** proslit
Propagate prop-g	**Prosody** prosdy
Propel propl	**Prospect** prospt
Propense propns	**Prosper** prospr
Proper propr	**Prostitute** prost t
Property propr-t	**Prostrate** pros-tr
Prophecy prof-s	**Prostyle** prostl
Prophet proft	**Prosy** pro-s
Propinquity propnqt	**Protect** protct
Propitiate pro-p	**Protege (tazha)** protsha
Propitious pro-p	**Protest** protst
Propolis propolis	**Protestant** protstnt
Proportion pro-pr	**Prothonotary** prothn-tr
Propose propos	**Protocol** protcl
Propound propnd	**Prototype** prottp
Proprietor propritr	**Protract** protrct
Propriety propri-t	**Protrude** protrud
Propulsion pro-pl	**Protuberance** protbrns
Prorogue prorg	**Proud** proud
Prosaic prosa-i	**Prove** prev
Proscenium prosnm	**Provender** provndr

Proverb
provrb

Provide
provid

Providence
provdns

Provision
pro-v

Proviso
provso

Provoke
prov-o

Provost
provo

Provost-marshal
provomrshl

Prow
prow

Prowess
prows

Prowl
prowl

Proximate
proxmat

Proximity
proxmt

Proximo
prox

Proxy
proxy

Prude
prud

Prudence
prudns

Prudish
prudsh

Prune
prun

Prunella
prunla

Prurience
prurns

Prussic
prus-i

Pry
pri

Psalm (sam)
sam

Psalter (sawl)
saltr

Pshaw (shaw)
shaw

Psychology (si)
siclj

Ptolemaic (tol)
tolma

Puberty
pubrt

Public
publc

Publish
publsh

Pucker
pucr

Pudding
pud-ing

Puddle
pudl

Puerile
puril

Puerperal
purprl

Pug
pug

Pugilist
pujlst

Pugnacious
pug n

Puisne (pune)
pune

Puissance
pusns

Puke
puc

Pule
pul

Pull
pul

Pullet
pult

Pulley
puly

Pulp
pulp

Pulpit
pulpt

Pulpy
pulpy

Pulsate
pulsat

Pulverize
pulvrs

Pulverulent
pulvrlnt

Pumice
pumis

Pump
pump

Pumpkin
pumcn

Punch
punch

Puncheon (un)
punchn

Punchinello
punchnlo

Punctilio
punctlo

Puncto
puncto

Punctual
punctl

Punctuate
punctat

Puncture
punctr

Pundit
pundt

Pungent
punjnt

Punic
pun-i

Punish
punsh

Punk
punc

Punt
punt

Puny
puny

Pup
pup

Pupa
pupa

Pupil
pupl

Puppet
pupt

Purblind
purblnd

Purchase
purchs

Pure
pur

Purge
purj

Purify
purf

Purism
purism

Puritan
purtn

Purity
purt

Purl
purl

Purlieu (lu)
perlu

Purlin
perln

Purloin
purln

Purple
purpl

Purport
purprt

Purpose
purps

Purse
purs

Pursue
pursu

Pursuivant (swi)
purswvnt

Pursy
pursy

Purulence
purlns

Purvey
purva

Purview
purveu

Pus
pus

Push
push

Pusillanimous
puslnms

Puss
pus

Pustule
pustul

Put
put

Putative
put-t

Putrefy
putrf

Putrid
putrid

Putty
puty

Puzzle
puzl

Pygmy
pigmy

Pyramid
pirmd

Pyre
pir

Pyriform
pirfrm

Pyrites
pirites

Pyroligneous
pirolgnes

Pyrometer
pirmtr

Pyrotechnics
pirotcn-i

Pyrotechnist
pirotcnst

Pyx
pix

Q.

Quack
qac

Quadragesima
q-jsma

Quadrangle
q-rngl

Quadrant
q-nt

Quadrat
q-t

Quadrate
q-t

Quadrennial
q-ns

Quadrille (dril)
q-l

Quadripartite
q prtt

Quadrumanous
q-mns

Quadruped
q-pd

Quadruple
q-pl

Quaff
qaf

Quagmire
qagmr

Quaggy
qagy

Quail
qal

Quaint
qant

Quake
qac

Quaker
qacr

Qualify
qalf

Quality
qalt

Qualm (kwam)
qam

Quandary
qandry

Quantity
qanty

Quarantine
qarntn

Quarrel
qarl

Quarry	
q*a*ry	
Quart	
q*a*rt	
Quartan	
q*a*rtn	
Quarter	
q*a*rtr	
Quartet	
q*a*rtt	
Quarto	
q*a*rto	
Quartz	
q*a*rtz	
Quash	
q*a*sh	
Quassation	
q*a*s-s	
Quassia	
q*a*sa	
Quaternion	
q*a*trnn	
Quaver	
q*a*vr	
Quay (ke)	
c*e*	
Quean	
q*e*n	
Queasy	
q*e*-s	
Queen	
q*e*n	
Queer	
q*e*r	
Quell	
q*e*l	
Quench	
q*e*nch	
Querist	
q*e*rst	
Quern	
q*e*rn	
Querulous	
q*e*rls	
Query	
q*e*ry	
Quest	
q*e*st	

Question	
q	
Questioned	
qd	
Quibble	
q*i*bl	
Quick	
q*i*c	
Quicksilver	
q*i*cslr	
Quiddity	
q*i*d-t	
Quidnunc	
q*i*dnnc	
Quiescence	
q*i*sns	
Quiet	
q*i*t	
Quietus	
q*i*ts	
Quill	
q*i*l	
Quilt	
q*i*lt	
Quinary	
q*i*nry	
Quince	
q*i*ns	
Quinine	
q*i*nn	
Quinquagesima	
qu*i*ncjsm	
Quinquangular	
q*i*nqanglr	
Quinquennial	
q*i*nqnl	
Quinsy	
q*i*nsy	
Quintal	
q*i*ntl	
Quintan	
q*i*ntn	
Quintessence	
q*i*ntsns	
Quintuple	
q*i*ntpl	
Quip	
q*i*p	

Quire
qir

Quirk
qirc

Quit
qit

Quite
qit

Quiver
qivr

Quixotism
qicstsm

Quiz
qiz

Quoin (kwoin)
qoin

Quoit
qoit

Quondam
qondm

Quorum
qorm

Quota
qota

Quoth
qoth

Quotidian
qotdn

Quotient
qoshnt

R.

Rabbet
rabt

Rabbi
rabi

Rabbit
rabt

Rabble
rabl

Rabid
rabd

Raccoon
racn

Race
ras

Raceme
rasm

Rack
rac

Racy
rasy

Radiance
radns

Radiate
radat

Radical
radcl

Radicle
radcl

Radish
radsh

Radius
radus

Raff
raf

Raffle
rafl

Raft
raft

Rafter
raftr

Rag
rag

Rage
raj

Ragout (goo)
ragoo

Rail
ral

Railing
ral-ing

Railroad
ralrd

Railway
ralw

Raiment
ramnt

Rainbow
ranbo

Rainy
rany

Raise
ras

Raisin
rasn

Rake	**Rape**
rac	rap
Rally	**Rapid**
raly	rapd
Ram	**Rapier**
ram	raper
Ramble	**Rapine**
rambl	rapn
Ramify	**Rappee**
ramf	rape
Rammer	**Rapt**
ramr	rapt
Ramose	**Rapture**
ramos	raptur
Rampant	**Rare**
rampnt	rar
Ramrod	**Rarefy**
ramrd	rarf
Ran	**Rarity**
ran	rarty
Rancho	**Rascal**
rantsho	rascl
Ranch	**Rase**
ranch	ras
Ranchero (cha)	**Rash**
rantsharo	rash
Rancid	**Rasp**
ransd	rasp
Rancor	**Rasure**
rancr	rasur
Random	**Rat**
randm	rat
Rang	**Ratchet**
rang	rachet
Range	**Rate**
ranj	rat
Rank	**Rather**
ranc	rathr
Ransack	**Ratify**
ransc	ratf
Ransom	**Ratio**
ransm	rasho
Rant	**Ratiocination**
rant	rashosh-n
Rap	**Ratsbane**
rap	ratsbn
Rapacity	**Rattan**
raps-t	ratn

Ratting rat-ing		**Reap** rep	
Rattle ratl		**Reappear** reapr	
Raucity raus-t		**Reappoint** reapnt	
Ravage ravj		**Rear** rer	
Rave rav		**Reason** resn	
Ravel ravl		**Reassume** reasm	
Raven ravn		**Reassure** reasur	
Ravine ravn		**Rebate** rebt	
Ravish ravsh		**Rebec** rebc	
Raw raw		**Rebel** rebl	
Ray ra		**Rebel** rebl	
Raze ras		**Rebound** rebnd	
Razee rase		**Rebuff** rebf	
Razor razr		**Rebuke** rebc	
Reach rech		**Rebus** rebs	
React react		**Rebut** rebt	
Read red		**Recall** recl	
Readmit readmt		**Recant** recnt	
Ready redy		**Recaption** recpshn	
Real rel		**Recapture** recptr	
Realize relis		**Recast** recst	
Realm relm		**Recede** resed	
Ream rem		**Receipt** reset	
Reanimate rean-m		**Receive** resv	

Recency
  resn-s

Recent
  resnt

Recension
  resnshn

Receptacle
  resptcl

Reception
  respshn

Recess
  rcss

Recession
  rc-s

Recharge
  rcchrg

Recherche (rusbar-
  rushrsha   sha)

Recipe
  rcsp

Recipient
  respnt

Reciprocal
  resprcl

Reciprocation
  respr-c

Recital
  resitl

Recitative
  rcsi-t

Recite
  rcsit

Reckless
  rccls

Reckon
  rccn

Reclaim
  rcclm

Recline
  rccln

Recluse
  rcclus

Recognize
  rccgns

Recoil
  rccl

Recollect
  rcclct

Recommend
  rccmnd

Recommit
  rccmit

Recompense
  rccmpns

Recompose
  rccmpos

Reconcile
  rccnsl

Recondite
  rccndt

Reconnoissance
  rccnsns

Reconnoiter
  rccntr

Reconquer
  rccncr

Reconsider
  rccnsdr

Record
  rccrd

Record'
  rccrd

Recount
  rccnt

Recourse
  rccrs

Recover
  rccvr

Recreant
  rccrnt

Recreate
  rccrat

Recrement
  rccrmnt

Recriminate
  rccrm-n

Recruit
  rccrut

Rectangle
  rctngl

Rectify
  rctf

Rectilinear
  rctlnr

Rectitude
  rct-t

Rector rectr		**Refine** refn
Rectum rectm		**Refit** reft
Recumbent recmbnt		**Reflect** refl·c
Recuperate recprat		**Reflex** reflx
Recur recr		**Reflux** reflx
Recusant recsnt		**Reform** refrm
Red red		**Refract** refrct
Redan redan		**Refragable** refrgbl
Redeem redm		**Refrain** refrn
Redintegrate rednt·gr		**Refresh** refrsh
Redolence redlns		**Refrigerate** refrjrat
Redouble redbl		**Refuge** refj
Redoubt redout		**Refugee** refje
Redound redound		**Refulgent** refljnt
Redress redrs		**Refund** refnd
Reduce redus		**Refuse** refs
Redundant redndnt		**Refuse'** refs
Reedy redy		**Refute** reft
Reef ref		**Regain** regu
Reek rec		**Regal** regl
Reel rel		**Regale** regl
Reeve rev		**Regalia** reglya
Refection re-fc		**Regard** regrd
Refer refr		**Regatta** regta

Regency regn-s		**Rejuvenate** rejv-n	
Regenerate rejnrat		**Relate** relt	
Regent rejnt		**Relative** reltv	
Regicide rejsid		**Relax** relx	
Regime (razheem) razhm		**Relay** rela	
Regimen rejmn		**Release** reles	
Regiment rejmnt		**Relent** relnt	
Region rejn		**Relevant** relvnt	
Register rejstr		**Reliance** relins	
Registry rejstry		**Relic** relc	
Regnant regnnt		**Relict** relct	
Regret regret		**Relief** relf	
Regular reglr		**Relieve** relv	
Regulate reglt		**Relievo** relvo	
Regurgitate regrj-t		**Religion** reljn	
Rehabilitate rehabl-t		**Relinquish** relnqsh	
Rehearse rehrs		**Reliquary** relqry	
Reign (ran) ran		**Relish** relsh	
Reindeer randr		**Reluctant** relctnt	
Reins rans		**Rely** reli	
Reiterate reitrat		**Remain** reman	
Reject rejct		**Remand** remand	
Rejoice rejs		**Remark** remarc	
Rejoin rejn		**Remarkable** remarcbl	

Remedial
remedl

Remedy
remdy

Remember
remembr

Remind
remind

Remiss
remis

Remit
remit

Remnant
remnnt

Remonstrate
remonstrt

Remorse
remors

Remote
remot

Remove
remov

Remunerate
remunrat

Renal
renl

Renard
renrd

Renascent
renasnt

Rend
rend

Render
rendr

Rendezvous (de- **voo)**
rendv

Rendition
ren-d

Renegade
rengd

Renew
renu

Rennet
renet

Renounce
renouns

Renovate
ren-v

Renown
renown

Rent
rent

Repair
repr

Repartee
reprt

Repast
repst

Repeal
repl

Repeat
rept

Repel
repl

Repent
repnt

Repertory
reprtry

Repetend
reptnd

Repetition
rep-t

Repine
repin

Replete
replt

Replevin
replvn

Replication
repl c

Reply
repli, pli

Report
reprt

Repose
repos

Reposit
reposit

Reprehend
reprnd

Represent
reprsnt

Repress
reprs

Reprieve
reprv

Reprimand
reprmnd

Reprisal
reprsl

Reproach
reprch

Reprobate
reprbt

Reproof
reprf

Reprove
reprv

Reptile
reptl

Republic
repblc

Repudiate
repdat

Repugnant
repgnnt

Repulse
repls

Reputable
reptbl

Repute
rept

Request
reqst

Requiem
reqm

Require
reqr

Requisite
reqsit

Requite
reqt

Rescind
resind

Rescript
rescrpt

Rescue
rescu

Research
resrch

Resemble
resembl

Resent
resent

Reserve
reserv

Reservoir (vwor)
reservr

Reset
reset

Reside
resid

Residue
resdu

Resign (zin)
resin

Resilience
resilns

Resin
resn

Resist
resst

Resolute
reslt

Resolve
reslv

Resonant
resnnt

Resort
resort

Resound
resound

Resource
resors

Respect
respt

Respire
respr

Respite
respt

Resplendent
resplnnt

Respond
respnd

Rest
rest

Restaurant (to)
restrnt

Restive
rest

Restitution
rest-t

Restless restls		**Revere** rever	
Restore restr		**Reverie** revry	
Restrain restrn		**Reverse** revers	
Restrict restrct		**Revert** revert	
Result result		**Review (vu)** revu	
Resume resum		**Revile** revil	
Resume (razuma) razma		**Revise** revis	
Resurrection resr-c		**Revive** reviv	
Resuscitate ress-t		**Revoke** revoc	
Retail retal		**Revolt** revolt	
Retain retan		**Revolution** revo-l	
Retake retac		**Revolve** revolv	
Retreat retrct		**Revulsion** revulshn	
Retrench retrench		**Reward** rewrd	
Retribution retri-b		**Rhapsody (rap)** rapsdy	
Retrieve retrcv		**Rhenish** rensh	
Retrocession retro-s		**Rhetoric** retrc	
Retrograde retrogrd		**Rheum (rum)** rum	
Retrospect retro-sp		**Rheumatism** rumtsm	
Reveal revel		**Rhinoceros** rinosros	
Revel revl		**Rhomb (romb)** romb	
Revenge revnj		**Rhubarb (ru)** rubrb	
Revenue revnu		**Rhyme (rim)** rim	
Reverberate reverbrt		**Rhythm** rithm	

Rib
rıb

Ribald
rıbld

Ribbed
rıbd

Ribbon
rıbn

Rice
rıs

Rich
rıch

Rick
rıc

Rickets
rıcts

Ricochet
rıccha

Rid
rıd

Riddle
rıdl

Ride
rıd

Ridge
rıj

Ridicule
rıdcl

Rife
rıf

Riffraff
rıfrf

Rifle
rıfl

Rift
rıft

Rig
rıg

Right
rıt

Righteous (richus)
rıchs

Rigid
rıjd

Rigor
rıgr

Rill
rıl

Rim
rım

Rime
rım

Rind
rınd

Ring
rıng

Rinse
rıns

Riot
rıot

Rip
rıp

Ripe
rıp

Ripple
rıpl

Rise
rız

Risk
rısc

Rite
rıt

Ritual
rıtul

Rival
rıvl

Rive
rıv

River
rıvr

Rivet
rıvt

Rivulet
rıvlt

Rix-dollar
rıxdlr

Roach
roch

Road
rod

Roam
rom

Roan
ron

Roar
ror

Roast
rost

Rob
rob

Robe
rob

Robin
robn

Robust
robst

Rochet
rochet

Rock
roc

Rocket
roct

Rod
rod

Rode
rod

Rodent
rodnt

Rodomontade
rodmntad

Roe
ro

Roebuck
robc

Rogation
ro-g

Rogue
rog

Roil
roil

Roll
rol

Roman
romn

Romance
romns

Romp
romp

Rood
rood

Roof
roof

Rook
rooc

Room
room

Roost
roost

Root
root

Rope
rop

**Roquelaur (roke-
lor)**
roclr

Rosary
rozry

Rose
roz

Rosemary
rosmry

Rosette
rozet

Rosin
rozn

Roster
rostr

Rostrum
rostrm

Rot
rot

Rotate
rotat

Rote
rot

Rotten
rotn

Rotunda
rotnda

Rouge (roozh)
roozh

Rough (ruf)
ruf

Roulette
rulet

Rounce
rouns

Round
round

Roundelay
roundla

Rouse
rouz

Rout
rout

Route (root)
root

Routine
rootn

Rove
rov

Row
ro

Row'
ro

Rowel
rowel

Rowen
rowen

Royal
royl

Rub
rub

Rubbish
rubsh

Rubicund
rubcnd

Ruble
rubl

Rubric
rubrc

Ruby
ruby

Ruddy
rudy

Rude
rud

Rue
ru

Ruff
ruf

Ruffian
rufn

Ruffle
rufl

Rufous
rufs

Rug
rug

Rugged
rugd

Ruin
run

Rule
rul

Rum
rum

Rumble
rumbl

Ruminate
rum n

Rummage
rumj

Rumor
rumr

Rump
rump

Rumple
rumbl

Run
run

Runagate
rungt

Rundle
rundl

Rung
rung

Runlet
runlt

Runner
runr

Runnet
runet

Rupee
rupe

Rupture
ruptr

Rural
rurl

Ruse
ruz

Rush
rush

Rusk
rusk

Russ
rus

Russet
ruset

Russian
rushn

Rust
rust

Rustic
rustc

Rustle (l)
rusl

Rut
rut

Rutabaga
rutbga

Ruth
ruth

Ruthless
ruthls

Rye (ri)
ri

S.

Sabaoth
sabath

Sabbatarian
sabtrn

Sabbath
sabth

Saber
sabr

Sable
sabl

Sac
sac

Saccharine
sacrn

Sacerdotal
sasrdtl

Sachem
sachm

Sack
sac

Sacrament
sacrmnt

Sacred
sacrd

Sacrifice
sacrfs

Sacrilege
sacrlj

Sacristan
sacrstn

Sacristy
sacrst

Sad
sad

Saddle
sadl

Sadducee
sadsc

Sad-iron (urn)
sadrn

Safe
saf

Saffron
safrn

Sag
sag

Sagacity
sags-t

Sagamore
sagmr

Sage
saj

Sagittal
sagitl

Sago
sago

Said (sed)
sed

Sail
sal

Sailor
salr

Saint
sant

Sake
sac

Salable
salbl

Salacious
sa l

Salad
sald

Salamander
salmndr

Salary
salry

Sale
sal

Saleratus
salrts

Salic
sal i

Salient
salynt

Salify
salfy

Saline
saln

Saliva
salva

Sallow
salo

Sally
saly

Salmagundi
salmgndy

Salmon (samun)
samn

Saloon
salu

Salsify
salsfi

Salt
salt

Saltation
sal-t

Salt-cellar
saltslr

Saltpeter
saltptr

Salt-rheum (rum)
saltrm

Salubrity
salbr-t

Salutation
sal t

Salutatorian
saltutrn

Salute
salut

Salvable
salvbl

Salvage
salvj

Salvation
sal v

Salve (sav)
sav

Salver
savr

Salvo
savo

Same
sam

Samiel
saml

Samp
samp

Samphire
samfr

Sample
sampl

Sanative
san-t

Sanctify
sanctf

Sanctimony
sanctmny

Sanction
sancshn

Sanctity
sanct-t

Sanctuary
sanctry

Sanctum
sanctm

Sand
sand

Sandal
sandl

Sandiver
sandvr

Sandstone
sandstn

Sandwich
sanwch

Sandy
sandy

Sane
san

Sangaree
sangre

Sangfroid (song-
sangfrau frwa)

Sanguiferous
sangfrs

Sanguine
sangn

Sanhedrim
sanhdrm

Sanious
sanius

Sanitary
san-tr

Sanity
sen-t

Sank
sanc

Sanskrit
sanscrt

Sap
sap

Sapid
sapid

Sapience
sapns

Saponaceous
sap-n

Saponify
sapnl

Sapor
sapor

Sapphic
saf-i

Sapphire
safr

Saraband
sarbnd

Sarcasm
sar-c

Sarcenet
sarsnt

Sarcophagus
sarcfgs

Sardius
sardus

Sardonic
sardn-i

Sardonyx
sardnx

Sarsaparilla
sarsprla

Sash
sash

Sassafras
sasfrs

Sat
sat

Satan
satn

Satchel
sachl

Sate
sat

Satellite
satlit

Satiate (shi)
sa-sh

Satin
satn

Satinet
satnt

Satire
satr

Satisfy
st-f

Satrap
satrp

Saturate
saturt

Saturday
satrd

Saturn
satrn

Saturnine
satrnn

Satyr
satr

Saucer
sausr

Saucy
sau-s

Saunter
sauntr

Saurian
saurn

Sausage
sausj

Savable	**Scaly**
savbl	scaly
Savage	**Scammony**
savj	scamny
Savanna	**Scamp**
savna	scamp
Savant (savong)	**Scamper**
savng	scampr
Save	**Scan**
sav	scan
Savor	**Scandal**
savr	scandl
Savior	**Scansorial**
savyr	scansrl
Saw	**Scant**
saw	scant
Saxifrage	**Scantling**
saxfrj	scantlng
Saxon	**Scape**
saxn	scap
Say	**Scapula**
sa	scapla
Scab	**Scar**
scab	scar
Scabbard	**Scaree**
scabrd	scars
Scabrous	**Scare**
scabrs	scar
Scaffold	**Scarf**
scafld	scarf
Scagliola (sklyo)	**Scarify**
scalyo	scarfi
Scalade	**Scarlatina**
scalad	scarltna
Scald	**Scarlet**
scald	scarlt
Scald'	**Scarp**
scald	scarp
Scale	**Scath**
scal	scath
Scalene	**Scatter**
scaln	scatr
Scallion	**Scavenger**
scalyn	scavnjr
Scallop	**Scene**
scalop	scn
Scalp	**Scenography**
scalp	scn-gr

Scent	sent		**Scoop**	scoop
Scepter	septr		**Scope**	scop
Schedule (sked)	scedl		**Scorbutic**	scorbt-i
Scheme	scem		**Scorch**	scorch
Schism (sism)	sism		**Score**	scor
Scholar	scolr		**Scoria**	scoria
Scholastic	scolstc		**Scorn**	scorn
Scholiast	scolst		**Scorpion**	scorpn
Scholium	scolm		**Scot**	scot
School	scool		**Scotch**	scoch
Schooner	scoonr		**Scoundrel**	scoundrl
Sciatica	siatc		**Scour**	scour
Science	sins		**Scourge**	scurj
Scintillate	sintlt		**Scout**	scout
Sciolism	silism		**Scow**	scow
Scion	sion		**Scowl**	scowl
Scirrhosity	scirost		**Scrabble**	scrabl
Scirrhous	scirous		**Scrag**	scrag
Scirrhus	scirus		**Scrap**	scrap
Scissors	sisrs		**Scrape**	scrap
Sclerotic	scler-o		**Scratch**	scrach
Scoff	scof		**Scrawl**	scrawl
Scold	scold		**Scrawny**	scrawny
Sconce	scons		**Screak**	screc

Scream
scrēm

Screech
screch

Screed
scrĕd

Screen
scrēn

Screw (skru)
screw

Scribe
scrīb

Scrimp
scrimp

Scrip
scrip

Script
script

Scripture
scriptr

Scrivener
scrivnr

Scrofula
scrofla

Scroll
scrŏl

Scrub
scrŭb

Scruple
scrŭpl

Scrutiny
scrŭtny

Scrutoire (twor)
scrŭtwr

Scud
scŭd

Scuffle
scŭfl

Scull
scŭl

Scullery
scŭlry

Sculpture
scŭlptr

Scum
scŭm

Scupper
scŭpr

Scurf
scurf

Scurrilous
scurls

Scurvy
scurvy

Scutcheon
scuchn

Scutiform
scutfrm

Scuttle
scutl

Scymetar
simtr

Scythe
sīth

Sea
sē

Seal
sēl

Seam
sēm

Sear
sēr

Search
serch

Season
sēsn

Seat
sēt

Sebaceous
sē-b

Secant
sēcnt

Secede
sēsd

Seckel
sēcl

Seclude
sēclud

Second
sēcnd

Secret
sēcrt

Secretary
sēctry

Secrete
sēcrt

Sect
sect

Sectarian
sectrn

Sectile
sectl

Section
secshn

Sector
sectr

Secular
seclr

Secure
secr

Sedan
sedn

Sedate
sedt

Sedative
sed-t

Sedge
sej

Sediment
sedmnt

Seduce
sedus

Sedition
se-d

Sedulity
sedlt

See
se

Seed
sed

Seek
sec

Seem
sem

Seen
sen

Seer
ser

Seethe
seth

Segment
segmnt

Segregate
segr-g

Seigneurial
senurl

Seignior (seen-
senyr **yur)**

Seine
san

Seize
sez

Seizin
sezn

Seldom
seldm

Select
sel-e

Self
self

Sell
sel

Selvage
selvj

Selves
selvs

Semblance
semblns

Seminal
semnl

Seminary
semnry

Sempiternal
semptrnl

Senate
senat

Senator
senatr

Send
send

Senescence
sensns

Senile
senl

Senior
senyr

Senna
sena

Sennight
sennit

Sensation
sen-s

Sense sens		**Seraphine** scrfn
Sensible sensbl		**Seraphim** scrfm
Sensitive sens-t		**Serenade** scrnd
Sensual sensl		**Serene** scrn
Sent sent		**Serf** scrf
Sentence sentns		**Serge** scrj
Sentient sentnt		**Sergeant (sar)** sarjnt
Sentiment sentmnt		**Serial** scryl
Sentinel sentnl		**Series** scres
Sentry sen-tr		**Serious** scrius
Separate seprat		**Sermon** scrmn
Sepoy sepoy		**Seroon** scroon
September sept		**Serous** scrus
Septennial septnl		**Serpent** scrpnt
Septic septc		**Serrate** scrat
Septuagint septjnt		**Serum** scrm
Septuple septpl		**Serve** scrv
Sepulcher seplcr		**Session** scshn
Sequacious se-q		**Sess-pool** scspl
Sequel seql		**Set** sct
Sequester seqstr		**Setaceous** se-t
Sequin seqn		**Set-off** scto
Seraglio (ralyo) serlyo		**Seton** sctn
Seraph serf		**Setose** sctos

Settee sete		**Shade** shad	
Settle setl		**Shaft** shaft	
Set-to sett		**Shag** shag	
Seven sevn		**Shagreen** shagrn	
Seventeen sevntn		**Shah** sha	
Seventy sevn-t		**Shake** shak	
Sever sevr		**Shale** shal	
Several sevrl		**Shall** shal	
Severe sever		**Shalloon** shaln	
Sew (so) so		**Shallop** shalp	
Sewer (suer) sewr		**Shallow** shalo	
Sex sex		**Shalt** shalt	
Sexagenarian sexg-n		**Sham** sham	
Sexagesima sexjsma		**Shamble** shambl	
Sexennial sexnl		**Shame** sham	
Sextant sextnt		**Shampoo** shampo	
Sextile sextl		**Shamrock** shamrc	
Sexton sextn		**Shank** shanc	
Sextuple sextpl		**Shanty** shan-t	
Sexual sexl		**Shape** shap	
Shab shab		**Shard** shard	
Shabby shaby		**Share** shar	
Shackle shacl		**Shark** sharc	
Shad shad		**Sharp** sharp	

Shatter
shatr

Shave
shav

Shawl
shawl

Shawm
shawm

She
she

Sheaf
shef

Shear
sher

Sheath
sheth

Sheathe
sheth

Sheave
shev

Shed
shed

Sheen
shen

Sheep
shep

Sheer
sher

Sheet
shet

Shekel
shecl

Sheldrake
sheldrc

Shelf
shelf

Shell
shel

Shelter
sheltr

Shelve
shelv

Shepherd
sheprd

Sherbert
sherbrt

Sheriff
sherf

Sherry
shery

Shibboleth
shiblth

Shield
sheld

Shift
shift

Shilling
shilng

Shin
shin

Shine
shin

Shingle
shingl

Shining
shin-ing

Ship
ship

Shire
sher

Shirk
shirk

Shirt
shirt

Shive
shiv

Shiver
shivr

Shoal
shol

Shock
shoc

Shod
shod

Shoe
shu

Shone
shon

Shook
shooc

Shoot
shoot

Shop
shop

Shore
shor

Short short		**Shrug** shrug	
Shortened shortnd		**Shrunk** shrunc	
Shorthand shortnd		**Shuck** shuc	
Shot shot		**Shudder** shudr	
Shote shot		**Shuffle** shufl	
Should shud		**Shun** shun	
Shoulder sholdr		**Shunt** shunt	
Shout shout		**Shut** shut	
Shove shuv		**Shy** shy	
Shovel shuvl		**Sibilation** sib-l	
Show sho		**Sibyl** sibl	
Shower shower		**Sick** sic	
Shred shr.d		**Side** sid	
Shrew (shru) shrew		**Sidereal** sidrl	
Shriek shrec		**Sidle** sidl	
Shrike shric		**Siege** scj	
Shrill shril		**Siesta** scesta	
Shrimp shrimp		**Sieve** siv	
Shrine shrin		**Sift** sift	
Shrink shrinc		**Sigh (si)** si	
Shrivel shrivl		**Sight** sit	
Shroud shroud		**Sign** sin	
Shrove tide shrovtid		**Signal** signl	
Shrub shrub		**Signature** signtr	

Signatures
signtrs

Signer (sin)
sinr

Signet
signt

Signify
sinf

Silence
silns

Silent
silnt

Silica
silca

Silk
silc

Sill
sil

Sillabub
silbb

Silly
sily

Silt
silt

Silver
silr

Similar
similr

Simile
simly

Simmer
simr

Simony
simny

Simoon
simoon

Simper
simpr

Simple
simpl

Simulate
simlt

Simultaneous
siml-t

Sin
sin

Sinapism
sinpsm

Since
sins

Sincere
sinsr

Sine
sin

Sinecure
sincr

Sinew (yu)
sinew

Sing
sing

Singe
sinj

Single
singl

Singular
singlr

Sinister
sinistr

Sinistrous
sinistrs

Sink
sinc

Sinuation
sin-w

Sip
sip

Siphon
sifn

Sir
sir

Sire
sir

Siren
sirn

Sirloin
sirln

Sirocco
sir-o

Sirrah
sira

Sirup
sirp

Sister
sistr

Sit
sit

Site		**Skull**
s*i*t		sc*u*l
Situation		**Skunk**
s*i*t-w		sc*u*nc
Six		**Sky**
s*i*x		sc*y*
Sixteen		**Slab**
s*i*xtn		sl*a*b
Sixty		**Slack**
s*i*x-t		sl*a*c
Size		**Slag**
s*i*z		sl*a*g
Skate		**Slain**
sc*a*t		sl*a*n
Skein		**Slake**
sc*a*n		sl*a*c
Skeleton		**Slam**
sc*e*ltn		sl*a*m
Skeptic		**Slander**
sc*e*ptc		sl*a*ndr
Sketch		**Slang**
sc*e*ch		sl*a*ng
Skewer (sku)		**Slant**
sc*u*r		sl*a*nt
Skid		**Slap**
sc*i*d		sl*a*p
Skiff		**Slash**
sc*i*f		sl*a*sh
Skill		**Slat**
sc*i*l		sl*a*t
Skillet		**Slate**
sc*i*let		sl*a*t
Skim		**Slattern**
sc*i*m		sl*a*trn
Skin		**Slaughter**
sc*i*n		sl*au*tr
Skip		**Slave**
sc*i*p		sl*a*v
Skirmish		**Slay**
sc*i*rmsh		sl*a*
Skirt		**Sleazy**
sc*i*rt		sl*e*z
Skittish		**Sled**
sc*i*tsh		sl*e*d
Skittles		**Sledge**
sc*i*tls		sl*e*j
Skulk		**Sleek**
sc*u*lc		sl*e*c

Sleep slep		**Slop** slop	
Sleet slet		**Slope** slop	
Sleeve slev		**Slot** slot	
Sleigh sla		**Sloth** sloth	
Sleight slit		**Slouch** slouch	
Slender slendr		**Slough (slou)** slou	
Slept slept		**Slough (sluf)** sluf	
Slew slu		**Sloven** slovn	
Sley sla		**Slow** slo	
Slice slis		**Slue** slu	
Slide slid		**Sluggard** slugrd	
Slight slit		**Sluice** slus	
Slily slily		**Slumber** slumr	
Slim slim		**Slump** slump	
Slime slim		**Slung** slung	
Sling sling		**Slunk** slunc	
Slink slinc		**Slur** slur	
Slip slip		**Slut** slut	
Slipper slipr		**Sly** sly	
Slit slit		**Smack** smac	
Sliver slivr		**Small** smal	
Slobber slobr		**Smalt** smalt	
Sloe slo		**Smart** smart	
Sloop sloop		**Smash** smash	

Smatter
smatr

Smear
smer

Smell
smel

Smelt
smelt

Smile
smil

Smirch
smirch

Smirk
smirc

Smite
smit

Smith
smith

Smock
smoc

Smoke
smoc

Smolder
smoldr

Smooth
smooth

Smote
smot

Smother
smothr

Smuggle
smugl

Smut
smut

Smutch
smuch

Snack
snac

Snaffle
snafl

Snag
snag

Snail
snal

Snake
snac

Snap
snap

Snare
snar

Snarl
snarl

Snatch
snach

Snath
snath

Sneak
snec

Sneer
sner

Sneeze
snez

Sniff
snif

Snicker
snicr

Snip
snip

Snipe
snip

Snivel
snivl

Snob
snob

Snooze
snooz

Snore
snor

Snort
snort

Snot
snot

Snout
snout

Snow
sno

Snub
snub

Snuff
snuf

Snug
snug

So
so

Soak
sok

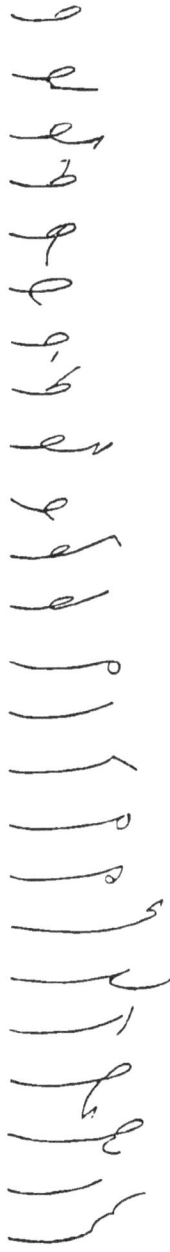

Soap sop		**Sole** sol	
Soar sor		**Solecism** sclssm	
Sob sob		**Solicit** solst	
Sober sobr		**Solid** solid	
Sobriquet (breka) sobrca		**Soliloquy** sollq	
Sociability sosh-b		**Solitary** soltry	
Society sos-t		**Solitude** sol-t	
Socinian sosnn		**Solo** solo	
Sock soc		**Solstice** solsts	
Socket soct		**Soluble** solbl	
Sod sod		**Solvable** solvbl	
Soda soda		**Solve** solv	
Solder sodr		**Somber** sombr	
Sofa sofa		**Some** smm	
Soffit sofit		**Somebody** smmbd	
Soft soft		**Somehow** smmh	
Soggy sogy		**Somewhat** smmwht	
Soil soil		**Somnambulist** scmnmblst	
Soiree (swara) swara		**Somniferous** somnfrs	
Sojourn sojrn		**Somnific** somn-i	
Sol sol		**Somniloquist** somnlqst	
Solace solas		**Somnolence** somnlns	
Sold sold		**Son** son	
Soldier soldr		**Sonata** sonata	

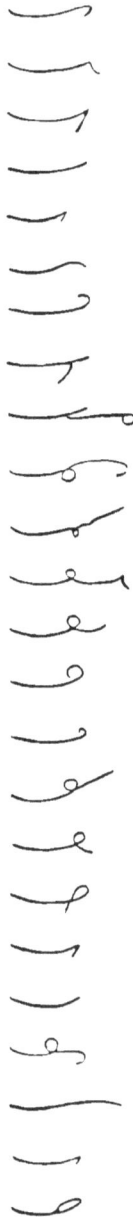

Song
  song

Sonnet
  sonet

Sonorous
  sonors

Soon
  soon

Soot
  soot

Sooth
  sooth

Sop
  sop

Sophist
  sofist

Sophomore
  sofmr

Soporific
  soprfc

Soprano
  soprano

Sorcery
  sorsry

Sordid
  sordd

Sore
  sor

Sorrel
  sorl

Sorrow
  soro

Sorry
  sory

Sort
  sort

Sot
  sot

Sou
  soo

Souchong
  soochng

Sough (suf)
  suf

Sought
  sout

Soul
  sol

Sound
  sound

Soup
  sup

Sour
  sour

Source
  sors

South
  south

Souvenir (soov-
  suvnr   **neer)**

Sovereign (in)
  suvrn

Sow
  so

Soy
  soy

Spa
  spa

Space
  spas

Spade
  spad

Span
  span

Spangle
  spangl

Spaniard
  spanrd

Spaniel
  spanl

Spank
  spanc

Spar
  spar

Spare
  spar

Spark
  sparc

Sparse
  spars

Spartan
  spartn

Spasm
  spasm

Spatter
  spatr

Spatula spatula		**Spelt** spelt	
Spavin spavn		**Spelter** speltr	
Spawn spawn		**Spencer** spcnsr	
Spay spay		**Spend** spend	
Speak spec		**Sperm** sperm	
Spear sper		**Spermaceti** spcrmse-t	
Special speshl		**Spew** spew	
Specie (shy) speshy		**Sphere** sfer	
Specifie spcsfc		**Sphinx** sfinx	
Specify spcsf		**Spice** spis	
Specimen spcsmn		**Spicular** spiclr	
Specious spcshs		**Spider** spidr	
Speck spec		**Spigot** spigt	
Spectacle spcctcl		**Spike** spic	
Spectator spec-t		**Spikenard** spicnrd	
Specter spcctr		**Spile** spil	
Spectrum spcctrm		**Spin** spin	
Specular spcclr		**Spinach (ej)** spinj	
Speculate spcclt		**Spinal** spinl	
Speculum spcclm		**Spindle** spindl	
Sped spcd		**Spine** spin	
Speech spcch		**Spinel** spinl	
Speed spcd		**Spinet** spinet	
Spell spcl		**Spinosity** spinost	

Spinster
spinstr

Spiral
spirl

Spire
spir

Spirit
spirt

Spirt
spirt

Spissitude
spis -t

Spit
spit

Spite
spit

Splash
splash

Spleen
splen

Splendid
splendd

Splice
splis

Splint
splint

Split
split

Spoil
spoil

Spoke
spoc

Spondaic
sponda-i

Spondee
sponde

Sponge
sponj

Sponsor
spensr

Spontaneity
spentn-t

Spontoon
spontn

Spool
spool

Spoon
spoon

Spoonful
spoonfl

Sporadic
spord-i

Sport
sport

Spot
spot

Spouse
spous

Spout
spout

Sprain
spran

Sprang
sprang

Sprat
sprat

Sprawl
sprawl

Spray
spra

Spread
spred

Spree
spre

Sprig
sprig

Spright
sprit

Sprightly
spritly

Spring
spring

Springe
sprinj

Sprinkle
sprincl

Sprite
sprit

Sprout
sprout

Spruce
sprus

Sprung
sprung

Spry
spry

Spryness	spr*i*ns	**Squeamish**	sq*c*msh
Sprume	spr*u*m	**Squeeze**	sq*e*z
Spumous	sp*u*mous	**Squib**	sq*i*b
Spun	sp*u*n	**Squill**	sq*i*l
Spunk	sp*u*nc	**Squint**	sq*i*nt
Spur	sp*u*r	**Squire**	sq*i*r
Spurge	sp*u*rj	**Squirm**	sq*u*rm
Spurious	sp*u*rus	**Squirrel**	sq*i*rl
Spurn	sp*u*rn	**Squirt**	sq*i*rt
Spurt	sp*u*rt	**Stab**	st*a*b
Sputter	sp*u*tr	**Stable**	st*a*bl
Spy	spy	**Stack**	st*a*c
Squab	sq*a*b	**Staddle**	st*a*dl
Squad	sq*a*d	**Staff**	st*a*f
Squadron	sq*a*drn	**Stag**	st*a*g
Squalid	sq*a*lid	**Stage**	st*a*j
Squall	sq*a*l	**Stagger**	st*a*gr
Squalor	sq*a*lr	**Stagnate**	st*a*gnt
Squander	sq*a*ndr	**Staid**	st*a*d
Square	sq*a*r	**Stain**	st*a*n
Squash	sq*a*sh	**Stair**	st*a*r
Squat	sq*a*t	**Stake**	st*a*c
Squeak	sq*e*c	**Stalactite**	st*a*lctt
Squeal	sq*e*l	**Stalagmite**	st*a*lgmt

Stale
stal

Stalk
stac

Stall
stal

Stallion
stalyn

Stalwart
stalwrt

Stamen
stamn

Stammer
stamr

Stamp
stamp

Stampede
stampd

Stanch
stanch

Stanchion
stanchn

Stand
stand

Standard
standrd

Standing
stand-ing

Standish
standsh

Stanza
stan-s

Staple
stapl

Star
star

Starch
starch

Stare
star

Stark
starc

Start
start

Starve
starv

State
stat

Static
stat-i

Station
stashn

Stationery
stashnry

Statistics
statst-i

Statue
statu

Stature
statur

Statute
statut

Stave
stav

Stay
sta

Stead
sted

Steak
stac

Steal
stel

Steam
stem

Steatite
stea-t

Steed
sted

Steel
stel

Steep
step

Steeple
stepl

Steer
ster

Stellar
stelr

Stem
stem

Stench
stnch

Stencil
stnsl

Stenography
stn-gr

Stentorian	
stentrn	
Step	
step	
Steppe	
stepe	
Stereoscope	
sterscp	
Stereotype	
stertp	
Sterile	
sterl	
Sterling	
sterlng	
Stern	
stern	
Sternutation	
stern-t	
Stertorous	
stertrs	
Stethoscope	
stethscp	
Stevedore	
stevdr	
Stew	
stew	
Stick	
stic	
Stickle	
sticl	
Stiff	
stif	
Stifle	
stifl	
Stigma	
stigma	
Stiletto	
stilto	
Still	
stil	
Stilt	
stilt	
Stimulate	
stimlt	
Stimulus	
stimlus	
Sting	
sting	

Stingy	
stinj	
Stink	
stinc	
Stint	
stint	
Stipend	
stipnd	
Stipple	
stipl	
Stipulate	
stip-l	
Stir	
stir	
Stirrup	
stirp	
Stitch	
stich	
Stive	
stiv	
Stiver	
stivr	
Stoat	
stot	
Stock	
stoc	
Stoic	
sto-i	
Stole	
stol	
Stolid	
stolid	
Stomach	
stumc	
Stone	
ston	
Stood	
stood	
Stool	
stool	
Stoop	
stoop	
Stop	
stop	
Stopple	
stopl	
Storage	
storj	

Store	
st*o*r	
Stork	
st*o*rc	
Storm	
st*o*rm	
Stoup	
st*u*p	
Story	
st*o*ry	
Stout	
st*ou*t	
Stove	
st*o*v	
Stow	
st*o*	
Strabismus	
str*a*bsms	
Straddle	
str*a*dl	
Straggle	
str*a*gl	
Straight	
str*a*t	
Strain	
str*a*n	
Strait	
str*a*t	
Strake	
str*a*c	
Strand	
str*a*nd	
Strange	
str*a*nj	
Strangle	
str*a*ngl	
Strangury	
str*a*ngry	
Strap	
str*a*p	
Strata	
str*a*ta	
Stratagem	
str*a*tjm	
Strategy	
str*a*tj	
Stratify	
str*a*tf	

Stratum	
str*a*tm	
Straw	
str*aw*	
Strawberry	
str*aw*bry	
Stray	
str*a*	
Streak	
str*e*c	
Stream	
str*e*m	
Street	
str*e*t	
Strength	
str*e*nth	
Strenuous	
str*e*nus	
Stress	
str*e*s	
Stretch	
str*e*ch	
Strew (strn)	
str*ew*	
Striated	
str*i*atd	
Stricken	
str*i*cn	
Strict	
str*i*ct	
Stride	
str*i*d	
Strife	
strif	
Strike	
str*i*c	
String	
str*i*ng	
Stringent	
str*i*ngnt	
Strip	
str*i*p	
Stripe	
str*i*p	
Strive	
str*i*v	
Stroke	
str*o*c	

Stroll
  strol

Strong
  strorg

Strop
  strop

Strophe
  strofe

Strove
  strov

Strow
  stro

Struck
  struc

Structure
  structr

Struggle
  strugl

Strumous
  strums

Strumpet
  strumpt

Strung
  strung

Strut
  strut

Strychnine
  stricnn

Stub
  stub

Stubble
  stubl

Stubborn
  stubrn

Stucco
  stuco

Stuck
  stuc

Stud
  stud

Student
  studnt

Studied
  studd

Studio
  studo

Study
  study

Stuff
  stuf

Stultify
  stultf

Stumble
  stumbl

Stump
  stump

Stun
  stun

Stung
  stung

Stunt
  stunt

Stupefy
  stupf

Stupendous
  stupnds

Stupid
  stupd

Stupor
  stupr

Sturdy
  sturdy

Sturgeon
  sturjn

Stutter
  stutr

Sty
  sty

Stygian
  styjn

Stylar
  stylr

Style
  styl

Styptic
  styptc

Suasion (swa)
  swashn

Suavity
  swav-t

Subaltern
  subltrn

Subdue
  subdu

Subject
  sub

Subjoin		**Substantiate**
*su*bjn		*su*bstnsht
Subjugate		**Substitute**
*su*bj-g		*su*b-st
Subjunctive		**Substratum**
*su*bjnctv		*su*b-str
Sublet		**Substruction**
*su*blt		*su*b-strc
Sublime		**Subtend**
*su*blm		*su*btnd
Sublunary		**Subtense**
*su*blnry		*su*btns
Submarine		**Subterfuge**
*su*bmrn		*su*btrfj
Submerse		**Subterranean**
*su*bmrs		*su*btrrnn
Sublimity		**Subtile**
*su*blm-t		*su*btl
Sublingual		**Subtle (sutl)**
*su*blngl		*su*tl
Submerge		**Subtract**
*su*bmrj		*su*b-tr
Submissive		**Subtrahend**
*su*bm-s		*su*btrhnd
Submit		**Suburbs**
*su*bmt		*su*brbs
Subordinate		**Subvert**
*su*brdnt		*su*bvrt
Suborn		**Succeed**
*su*brn		*su*csd
Subscribe		**Success**
*su*scrb		*su*css
Subsequence		**Succession**
*su*bs-q		*su*c-s
Subserve		**Succinct**
*su*bsrv		*su*csnct
Subside		**Succor**
*su*bsd		*su*cr
Subsidiary		**Succotash**
*su*bsdry		*su*ctsh
Subsidy		**Succulent**
*su*bsdy		*su*clnt
Subsist		**Succumb**
*su*bsst		*su*cm
Substance		**Such**
*su*bstns		*su*ch
Substantial		**Suck**
*su*bstnshl		*su*c

Sudden
sudn

Suds
suds

Sue
su

Suet
suet

Suffer
sufr

Suffice (fiz)
sufis

Sufficient
su-f

Suffix
sufx

Suffocate
sufct

Suffragan
sufrgn

Suffrage
sufrj

Suffuse
sufus

Sugar (shug)
shugr

Suggest
sujst

Suicide
susd

Suitable
sutbl

Suite (sweet)
swet

Suitor
sutr

Sulky
sulcy

Sullen
suln

Sully
suly

Sulphate
sulft

Sulphur
sulfr

Sultan
sultn

Sultry
sul-tr

Sum
sum

Sumac
sumc

Summary
sumry

Summer
sumr

Summit
sumit

Summon
sumn

Sumpter
sumptr

Sumptuous
sumpts

Sun
sun

Sunday
sund

Sunder
sundr

Sundry
sundry

Sung
sung

Sunk
sunc

Sup
sup

Superannuate
supran-w

Superb
suprb

Supercilious
suprslus

Supererogation
suprro-g

Superficial
supr-f

Superfluous
suprfls

Superior
suprr

Superlative
suprl-t

Supernal
suprnl

Supersede
suprsd

Superstition
supr-st

Supervene
suprvn

Supervise
suprvs

Supine
supin

Supine
supin

Supper
supr

Supplant
suplnt

Supple
supl

Supplement
suplmnt

Suppliant
suplnt

Supplicate
suplct

Supply
supl, spli

Support
suprt

Suppose
spos

Suppress
suprs

Suppurate
suprat

Supreme
suprm

Surcharge
surchrj

Surcingle
sursngl

Surd
surd

Sure
shur

Surf
surf

Surface
surfs

Surfeit
surft

Surge
surj

Surgeon
surjn

Surloin
surln

Surly
surly

Surmise
surmis

Surmount
surmnt

Surname
surnm

Surpass
surps

Surplus
surpls

Surprise
surprs

Surrender
surndr

Surreptitious
surep t

Surrogate
suro-g

Surround
surnd

Surtout (toot)
surtut

Survey
surv

Survey
surv

Survive
survv

Susceptible
sus-c

Suspect
suspt

Suspend
suspnd

Suspicion
sus-p

Sustain		**Sweet**
sustn		swet
Sustenance		**Swell**
sustnns		swel
Sutler		**Swelter**
sutlr		sweltr
Suttee		**Swept**
sute		swept
Suture		**Swerve**
sutur		swerv
Swab		**Swift**
swab		swift
Swaddle		**Swig**
swadl		swig
Swag		**Swill**
swag		swil
Swain		**Swim**
swan		swim
Swale		**Swindle**
swal		swindl
Swallow		**Swine**
swalo		swin
Swam		**Swing**
swam		swing
Swamp		**Swinge**
swamp		swinj
Swan		**Swingle**
swan		swingl
Swap		**Swipe**
swap		swip
Sward		**Swiss**
sward		swis
Swarm		**Switch**
swarm		swich
Swarthy		**Swivel**
swarthy		swivl
Swath		**Swollen**
swath		swoln
Swathe		**Swoon**
swath		swoon
Sway		**Swoop**
swa		swoop
Swear		**Swop**
swer		swop
Sweat		**Sword (sord)**
swet		sord
Sweep		**Swore**
swep		swor

Swung sw*u*ng	**Synopsis** synopss
Sycamore sycmr	**Syntax** syntx
Sycophant sycfnt	**Synthesis** synthss
Syenite s*i*nit	**Syphilis** syfls
Syllable sylbl	**Syriac** syr–a
Syllabub sylbb	**Syringa** syrnga
Syllabus sylbs	**Syringe** syrnj
Syllogism syljsm	**System** systm
Sylph sylf	**Systole** systl
Sylvan sylvn	T.
Symbol symbl	**Tab** tab
Symmetry sym-tr	**Tabby** taby
Sympathy sympth	**Tabernacle** tabrncl
Symphony symſny	**Tablature** tabltr
Symptom symptm	**Table** tabl
Syneresis synrss	**Tableau (lo)** tablo
Synagogue (gog) syngg	**Tablet** tablt
Synchronal syncrnl	**Taboo** taboo
Syncopate syncpt	**Tabor** tabr
Syncope syncp	**Tacit** tasit
Syndic syndc	**Tack** tack
Synechdoche synecdc	**Tackle** tacl
Synod synd	**Tact** tact
Synonym synnm	**Tactics** tact-i

Tactual		**Tampion**	
tactul		tampn	
Tadpole		**Tan**	
tadpl		tan	
Taffrail		**Tandem**	
tafrl		tandm	
Taffeta		**Tang**	
tafta		tang	
Tag		**Tangent**	
tag		tanjnt	
Tail		**Tangible**	
tal		tanjbl	
Tailor		**Tangle**	
talr		tangl	
Taint		**Tank**	
tant		tanc	
Take		**Tankard**	
tac		tancrd	
Tale (o)		**Tanner**	
tolc		tanr	
Tale		**Tannin**	
tal		tann	
Talent		**Tansy**	
talnt		tan-s	
Talisman		**Tantalize**	
talsmn		tantlis	
Talk		**Tantamount**	
tak		tantmnt	
Tall		**Tap**	
tal		tap	
Tallow		**Tape**	
talo		tap	
Tally		**Taper**	
taly		tapr	
Talmud		**Tapestry**	
talmd		tapstry	
Talon		**Tapioca**	
taln		tapi-o	
Tamarind		**Tap-house**	
tamrnd		tapous	
Tambour		**Tap-root**	
tambr		taprut	
Tame		**Tapster**	
tam		tapstr	
Tammy		**Tarantula**	
tamy		tarntula	
Tamp		**Tardy**	
tamp		tardy	

Tare		**Tax**	
tar		tax	
Target		**Taxidermy**	
targt		taxdrmy	
Tariff		**Tea**	
tarf		te	
Tarlatan		**Teach**	
tarltn		tech	
Tarnish		**Teal**	
tarnsh		tel	
Tarpaulin		**Team**	
tarpln		tem	
Tarry		**Tear**	
tary		ter	
Tart		**Tease**	
tart		tes	
Tartan		**Teat**	
tartn		tet	
Tartarean		**Technical**	
tartrn		tecncl	
Tartareous		**Technology**	
tartrs		tecn-o	
Task		**Techy**	
task		tecy	
Tassel		**Tectonic**	
tasl		tectn-i	
Taste		**Tedder**	
tast		tedr	
Tatter		**Te Deum**	
tatr		tedm	
Tatterdemalion		**Tedious**	
tatrdmln		tedus	
Tattle		**Teem**	
tatl		tem	
Tattoo		**Teens**	
tatoo		tens	
Taught		**Teeter**	
taut		tetr	
Taunt		**Teeth**	
taunt		teth	
Taut		**Teetotal**	
taut		tettl	
Tautology		**Teetotum**	
taut-o		tettm	
Tavern		**Tegument**	
tavrn		tegumnt	
Tawdry		**Telegram**	
tawdry		tel-gr	

Telescope telscp	**Tent** tent
Tell tel	**Tentacle** tentcl
Temerity temr-t	**Tentative** tent-t
Temper tempr	**Tenter** tentr
Temperature temprtr	**Tenth** tenth
Tempest tempst	**Tenuity** tenu-t
Templar templr	**Tenure** tenur
Temple templ	**Tepefaction** tep-fc
Templet templt	**Tepid** tepd
Temporal temprl	**Teraphim** terfm
Temporary tempry	**Terebinth** terbnth
Temporize tempris	**Tergiversation** tergvr-s
Tempt temt	**Term** term
Tenable tenabl	**Termagant** termgnt
Tenant tennt	**Terminate** term-n
Tend tend	**Terminus** termns
Tender tendr	**Terminology** termn-o
Tendon tendn	**Termite** termt
Tendril tendrl	**Ternary** ternry
Tenement tenmnt	**Terrace** teras
Tenet tenet	**Terra cotta** tercta
Tennis tenis	**Terrapin** terpn
Tenon tenn	**Terraqueous** tera-q
Tenor tenr	**Terrene** tern

Terrible terbl	Teutonic tutnc
Terrier teryr	Text text
Terrify terf	Textile textl
Territory tertry	Textual textul
Terror terr	Than than
Terse ters	Thane than
Tertian tershn	Thank thanc
Tesselation tes-l	Thatch thach
Test test	Thaw thaw
Testacean tes-t	The the
Testament testmnt	Theater theatr
Testator tes-tator	Theft theft
Testatrix testrx	Their ther
Tester testr	Theist thest
Testify testf	Them them
Testily testly	Theme them
Testimony testmny	Then then
Tetanus tetns	Thence thens
Tete-a-tete (tat-a-tat) tatatt	Theocracy the-or
Tether tethr	Theodolite theodlt
Tetragon tetrgn	Theology the-o
Tetrahedron tetrhdrn	Theorbo therbo
Tetrameter tetrmtr	Theorem therm
Tetrarch tetrrc	Theory thery

There
ther

Thermal
therml

Thermometer
thermmtr

Thereat
therat

Thereby
therb

Therefore
therfr

Therein
therin

Thereof
thero

Thereon
theron

Thereupon
therpn

Therewith
therw

Thesaurus
thesrs

These
thes

Thesis
thess

They
tha

Thick
thic

Thief
thef

Thieve
thev

Thigh
thi

Thills
thils

Thimble
thimbl

Thin
thin

Thine
thin

Thing
thing

Think
thinc

Third
third

Thirst
thirst

Thirteen
thirtn

Thirty
thir-t

Thistle
thisl

Thither
thithr

Thole
thol

Thong
thong

Thorax
thorx

Thorn
thorn

Thorough
thoro

Those
thos

Though (tho)
tho

Thought
thot

Thousand
thousn

Thralldom
thraldm

Thrash
thrash

Thread
thred

Threat
thret

Three
thre

Thresh
thresh

Threshold
threshold

Threw
threw

Thrice
thris

Thrid
thrid

Thrift
thrift

Thrill
thril

Thrive
thriv

Throat
throt

Throb
throb

Throe
thro

Throne
thron

Throng
throng

Throttle
throtl

Through (thro)
throo

Throve
throv

Throw
thro

Thrum
thrum

Thrust
thrust

Thrush
thrush

Thug
thug

Thumb
thum

Thump
thump

Thunder
thunr

Thursday
thursd

Thus
thus

Thwack
thwac

Thwart
thwart

Thy
thy

Thyme (tim)
tim

Thyself
thysl

Tiara
tiara

Tick
tic

Ticket
tict

Tickle
ticl

Tide
tid

Tidings
tid-s

Tidy
tidy

Tie
ti

Tier
ter

Tierce
ters

Tiff
tif

Tiffany
tifny

Tiger
tigr

Tight
tit

Tilbury
tilbry

Tile
til

Till
til

Tilt
tilt

Tilt-hammer
tilthmr

Timber
timbr

Time		**Tit**		
tim		tit		
Timid		**Titbit**		
timd		titbt		
Tin		**Tithe**		
tin		tith		
Tincal		**Titillate**		
tincl		tit-l		
Tincture		**Title**		
tinctr		titl		
Tinder		**To**		
tindr		to		
Tine		**Toad**		
tin		tod		
Tin-foil		**Toast**		
tinfl		tost		
Ting		**Tobacco**		
ting		tobco		
Tinge		**Tocsin**		
tinj		tocsn		
Tingle		**Tod**		
tingl		tod		
Tinker		**To-day**		
tincr		tod		
Tinny		**Toddle**		
tiny		todl		
Tinsel		**Toddy**		
tinsl		tody		
Tint		**Toe**		
tint		to		
Tiny		**Together**		
tiny		togtr		
Tip		**Toil**		
tip		toil		
Tippet		**Toilet**		
tipt		toilet		
Tipple		**Tokay**		
tipl		toca		
Tipstaff		**Token**		
tipstf		tocn		
Tipsy		**Told**		
tip-s		told		
Tirade		**Tole**		
tirad		tol		
Tire		**Tolerable**		
tir		tolrbl		
Tissue		**Tolerate**		
tisu		tolrat		

Toll
tol

Tomahawk
tomhc

Tomato
tomto

Tomb (toom)
toom

Tomboy
tomboy

Tome
tom

To-morrow
tomro

Ton
ton

Ton'
tun

Tongs
tongs

Tongue (tung)
tung

Tonic
ton-i

To-night
tont

Tonnage
tonj

Tonsil
tonsl

Tonsure
tonshr

Tontine
tontn

Too
too

Took
tooc

Tool
tool

Toot
toot

Tooth
tooth

Top
top

Topaz
topz

Toper
topr

Tophet
toft

Topic
topc

Topography
top-gr

Topple
topl

Torch
torch

Tore
tor

Torment
tormnt

Torn
torn

Tornado
torndo

Torpedo
torpdo

Torpid
torpd

Torpor
torpr

Torrefy
torf

Torrent
tornt

Torrid
torid

Torsion
torshn

Tort
tort

Tortoise
torts

Tortuous
tortus

Torture
tortur

Tory
tory

Toss
tos

Total
totl

Totter		**Traduce**	
totr		tradus	
Touch		**Traffic**	
tuch		trafc	
Tough (tuf)		**Tragedy**	
tuf		trajdy	
Toupee		**Trail**	
tupe		tral	
Tour		**Train**	
tur		tran	
Tournament		**Traipse**	
turnmnt		traps	
Tourniquet		**Trait**	
turncet		trat	
Touse		**Traitor**	
tous		tratr	
Tow		**Traject**	
to		tra-j	
Toward		**Tram**	
tord		tram	
Towel		**Trammel**	
towel		traml	
Tower		**Tramontane**	
tower		tramntn	
Tow-line		**Tramp**	
tolin		tramp	
Town		**Trample**	
town		trampl	
Toxicology		**Trance**	
toxc-o		tranc	
Toy		**Tranquil**	
toy		tranql	
Trace		**Transact**	
tras		trans-a	
Trachea		**Transalpine**	
traca		translpn	
Track		**Transcend**	
trac		t-nd	
Tract		**Transcript**	
tract		t-crpt	
Tractate		**Transept**	
tractat		t-cpt	
Tractile		**Transfer**	
tractl		t-fr	
Trade		**Transfigure**	
trad		t-fgr	
Tradition		**Transfix**	
tra d		t-fx	

Transfuse t-fs	**Travail** travl
Transgress grs	**Travel** travl
Transient t-nt	**Traverse** travrs
Transit t-it	**Travesty** travs-t
Transitory t-try	**Tray** tra
Translate t-lt	**Treachery** trechry
Translucent t-lsnt	**Treacle** trecl
Transmit t-mt	**Tread** tred
Transmute t-mut	**Treason** tresn
Transom t-m	**Treasure** tresr
Transparent t-prnt	**Treat** tret
Transpire t-pr	**Treble** trebl
Transplant t-plnt	**Tree** tre
Transport t-prt	**Trefoil** trefl
Transpose t-pos	**Trellis** trelis
Transubstantiation t-bstnshn	**Tremble** trembl
Transude t-ud	**Tremendous** tremnds
Transverse t-vrs	**Tremor** tremr
Trap trap	**Trench** trench
Trapan trapn	**Trend** trend
Trapezium trapzm	**Trepan** trepn
Trapezoid trapzd	**Trephine** trefn
Trappings trap-s	**Trepidation** trep-d
Trash trash	**Trespass** tresps

Tress tres	
Trestle (tresl) tresl	
Tret tret	
Trevet trevet	
Trey tra	
Triad triad	
Triangle triangl	
Tribe trib	
Tribulation trib-l	
Tribune tribn	
Tribute tribut	
Trice tris	
Trick tric	
Trickle tricl	
Trident tridnt	
Triennial trinl	
Trier trir	
Trifid trifid	
Trifle trifl	
Trig trig	
Trigger trigr	
Triglyph triglf	
Trigonometry trignm-tr	
Trigraph tri-gr	

Trihedral trihdrl	
Trihedron trihdrn	
Trilateral trilatrl	
Triliteral trilitrl	
Trill tril	
Trillion trilyn	
Trim trim	
Trine trin	
Trinity trin-t	
Trinket trinct	
Trinomial trinml	
Trio trio	
Trip trip	
Tripartite triprtt	
Tripe trip	
Triphthong tripthng	
Triple tripl	
Triplet triplt	
Triplicate tripl-c	
Tripod tripd	
Trisyllable trislbl	
Trite trit	
Tritheism trithism	
Triturate tritrat	

Triumph triumf	**Trover** trovr
Triumphant triumfnt	**Trow** tro
Triumvir triumvr	**Trowel** trowel
Triune triun	**Troy-weight** troywt
Trivet trivt	**Truant** trunt
Trivial trivl	**Truce** trus
Trocar trocr	**Truck** truc
Trod trod	**Truculence** truclns
Troll trol	**Trudge** truj
Trollop trolop	**True** tru
Trombone trombn	**Truffle** trufl
Troop troop	**Truism** truism
Trope trop	**Trull** trul
Trophy trofy	**Trump** trump
Tropic tropc	**Truncate** trunct
Trot trot	**Truncheon (shun)** trunshn
Troth troth	**Trundle** trundl
Trotter trotr	**Trunk** trunc
Trouble trubl	**Trunnion** trunyn
Trough trof	**Truss** trus
Trounce trouns	**Trust** trust
Trowsers trowsrs	**Trustee** truste
Trousseau (trooso) trooso	**Truth** truth
Trout trout	**Try** try

Tub
tub

Tube
tub

Tubercle
tubrcl

Tuberose
tubros

Tubular
tublr

Tuck
tuc

Tuesday
tusd

Tuft
tuft

Tug
tug

Tuition
tu-i

Tulip
tulip

Tumble
tumbl

Tumbrel
tumbrl

Tumefy
tumf

Tumid
tumd

Tumor
tumr

Tumulous
tumlus

Tumult
tumlt

Tun
tun

Tune
tun

Tunic
tun-i

Tunicle
tuncl

Tunnel
tunl

Turban
turbn

Turbid
turbd

Turbulent
turblnt

Tureen
turen

Turf
turf

Turgid
turjd

Turkey
turcy

Turkois (koiz)
turcois

Tumerie
turmrc

Turmoil
turml

Turn
turn

Turnip
turnp

Turnkey
turnce

Turnsole
turnsl

Turnstile
turnstl

Turpentine
turpntn

Turpitude
turptd

Turquoise
turcois

Turret
turet

Turtle
turtl

Tuscan
tuscn

Tusk
tusc

Tussle
tusl

Tutelar
tutlr

Tutor
tutr

Twaddle twadl	**Tympan** tympn
Twain twan	**Tympanum** tympnm
Twang twang	**Type** typ
Twattle twatl	**Typhoid** tyfd
Tweak twec	**Typhoon** tyfn
Tweedle twedl	**Typhus** tyfs
Tweeds tweds	**Typify** typf
Tweezers twezrs	**Typography** tipo-gr
Twelve twelv	**Tyranny** tyrny
Twenty twen-t	**Tyrant** tyrnt
Twice twis	**Tyro** tyro
Twig twig	**U.**
Twilight twilit	**Ubiquity** ubqt
Twill twil	**Udder** udr
Twine twin	**Ugly** ugly
Twinge twinj	**Ulcer** ulsr
Twinkle twincl	**Ullage** ulj
Twirl twirl	**Ulterior** ultrr
Twist twist	**Ultimate** ultmt
Twit twit	**Ultra** ultra
Twitch twich	**Umbel** umbl
Twitter twitr	**Umber** umbr
Two (too) to	**Umbilical** umblcl
Tymbal tymbl	**Umbles** umbls

Umbrage umbrj	**Up** up
Umbrella umbrla	**Upon** upn
Umpire umpr	**Upper** upr
Un un	**Upward** uprd
Unable unabl	**Uranium** urnm
Unanimous unnms	**Uranus** urans
Uncle uncl	**Urban** urbn
Uncouth uncth	**Urbane** urban
Unction uncshn	**Urchin** urchn
Under undr	**Urge** urj
Undulate undult	**Urn** urn
Unguent (gwent) ungwnt	**Us** us
Unicorn uncrn	**Usage** usj
Unify unf	**Use** us
Union unn	**Usher** ushr
Uniparous unprs	**Usquebaugh** usqbau
Unique (neek) unc	**Usual** usl
Unison unsn	**Usufruct** usfrct
Unit unt	**Usurp** usrp
Unitarian untrn	**Usury** usry
Unite unit	**Utensil** utnsl
Unity un-t	**Uterine** utrn
Universe unvrs	**Utility** u/lt
Unto unt	**Utmost** utmst

Utopian
u*t*pn

Utter
u*t*r

Uveous
u*r*us

Uxorious
u*c*sors

V.

Vacant
v*a*cnt

Vaccinate
v*a*cs-n

Vaccine
v*a*csn

Vacillate
v*a*s-l

Vacuity
v*a*cu-t

Vagabond
v*a*gbn

Vagary
v*a*gry

Vagrant
v*a*grnt

Vague
v*a*g

Vail
v*a*l

Vain
v*a*n

Valance
v*a*lns

Valediction
v*a*l-dc

Valentine
v*a*lntn

Valerian
v*a*lryn

Valet
v*a*ly

Valetudinary
v*a*ltdnry

Valiant
v*a*lnt

Valid
v*a*ld

Valise
v*a*lis

Vallation
v*a*l-l

Valley
v*a*ly

Valor
v*a*lr

Value
v*a*lu

Valve
v*a*lv

Vamp
v*a*mp

Vampire
v*a*mpr

Vandal
v*a*ndl

Vandyke
v*a*ndc

Vane
v*a*n

Vanilla
v*a*nla

Vanish
v*a*nsh

Vanity
v*a*n-t

Vanquish
v*a*nqsh

Vantage
v*a*ntj

Vapid
v*a*pd

Vapor
v*a*pr

Varicose
v*a*rcs

Variety
v*a*rt

Varlet
v*a*lt

Varnish
v*a*rnsh

Vary
v*a*ry

Vascular
v*a*sclr

Vase
vas

Vast
vast

Vastation
vas-t

Vat
vat

Vaticinate
vats-n

Vault
vault

Vaunt
vaunt

Veal
vel

Vedette
vedt

Veer
ver

Vegetable
vejtbl

Vehement
vehmnt

Vehicle
vehcl

Veil
val

Vein
van

Vellum
velm

Velocipede
velospd

Velocity
velosty

Velvet
velvt

Venal
venl

Vend
vend

Vendue
vendu

Veneer
venr

Venerate
venrat

Venereal
venral

Venesection
ven-sc

Vengeance
venjns

Vengeful
venjfl

Venial
venyl

Venison
vensn

Venom
venm

Venous
vens

Vent
vent

Ventilate
vent-l

Ventral
ventrl

Ventrical
ventrcl

Ventriloquist
ventrl-q

Venture
ventr

Venue
venue

Venus
venus

Veracity
verst

Veranda
vernda

Verb
verb

Verbatim
ver-b

Verbiage
verbj

Verbose
verbos

Verdant
verdnt

Verdict
verd-i

Verdigris verdgrs		**Vervain** vervn
Verdure verdr		**Very** very
Verge verj		**Vesicate** ves-c
Verify verf		**Vesicle** vescl
Verity vert		**Vesper** vespr
Verjuice verjus		**Vessel** vesl
Vermicelli vermsli		**Vest** vest
Vermiculation vermc-l		**Vestal** vestl
Vermifuge vermfj		**Vested** vestd
Vermilion vermln		**Vestibule** vestbl
Vermin vermn		**Vestige** vestj
Vermiparous ver-mp		**Vestment** vestmnt
Vermivorous ver-mv		**Vestry** vestry
Vernacular vernclr		**Vesture** vestr
Vernal vernl		**Vetch** vech
Versatile verstl		**Veteran** vetrn
Verse vers		**Veterinary** vetrnry
Versify versf		**Veto** veto
Version vershn		**Vex** vex
Vertebra vertbr		**Vexation** vexshn
Vertebre vertbre		**Viable** vibl
Vertex vertx		**Viaduct** vidct
Vertical vertcl		**Vial** vil
Vertigo vertgo		**Viands** vinds

Vibrate	**Vinaceous**
v*i*brt	v*i*-n
Vicar	**Vindicate**
v*i*cr	v*i*nd-c
Vice	**Vindictive**
v*i*s	v*i*ndc-t
Vice'	**Vine**
v*i*s	v*i*n
Vicinage	**Vinegar**
v*i*snj	v*i*ngr
Vicinity	**Vinous**
v*i*sn-t	v*i*nus
Vicious	**Viol**
v*i*shs	v*i*l
Vicissitude	**Viola**
v*i*sstd	v*i*la
Victim	**Violable**
v*i*ctm	v*i*labl
Victor	**Violaceous**
v*i*ctr	v*i*olashs
Victual	**Violation**
v*i*tl	v*i*-l
Videlicet	**Violent**
v*i*dlst	v*i*lnt
Vie	**Violet**
v*i*	v*i*lt
View (vu)	**Violin**
v*u*	v*i*ln
Vigil	**Viper**
v*i*jl	v*i*pr
Vignette (vinyet)	**Virago**
v*i*nyt	v*i*rago
Vigor	**Virgin**
v*i*gr	v*i*rjn
Vile	**Viridity**
v*i*l	v*i*rid-t
Vilify	**Virile '**
v*i*lf	v*i*rl
Villa	**Virtu**
v*i*la	v*i*ru
Village	**Virtual**
v*i*lj	v*i*rtul
Villain	**Virtuoso**
v*i*ln	v*i*rtuso
Villous	**Virulence**
v*i*lus	v*i*rulns
Vimineous	**Virus**
v*i*mnes	v*i*rus

Visage visj		**Vocation** vo-c	
Viscera visra		**Vocative** voc-t	
Viscid visid		**Vociferate** vosf-r	
Viscount (vi) vicount		**Vogue** vog	
Viscous viscs		**Voice** vois	
Visible visbl		**Void** void	
Vision vishn, visn		**Volatile** voltl	
Visit visit		**Volcano** volcno	
Visor visr		**Volition** vo-l	
Vista vista		**Volley** voly	
Visual visul		**Voluble** volbl	
Vital vitl		**Volume (yum)** volm	
Vitiate visht		**Voluntary** voln-tr	
Vitrifaction vitr-fc		**Voluptuous** vo-lpt	
Vitriol vitrl		**Volute** volut	
Vituperate vituprt		**Vomit** vomt	
Vivacity vivsty		**Voracity** vo-r	
Vivid vivd		**Vortex** vortx	
Viviparous vivprs		**Votary** vo-tr	
Vixen vixn		**Vote** vot	
Vizard vizrd		**Votive** vo-t	
Vizier vizr		**Vouch** vouch	
Vocable vocbl		**Vow** vow	
Vocal vocl		**Vowel** vowl	

Voyage
voyj

Vulcanize
vulcnis

Vulgar
vulgr

Vulgate
vulgt

Vulnerable
vulnrbl

Vulpine
vulpn

Vulture
vultr

W.

Wabble
wabl

Wad
wad

Waddle
wadl

Wade
wad

Wafer
wafr

Waffle
wafl

Waft
waft

Wag
wag

Wage
waj

Waggery
wagry

Wagon
wagn

Waif
waf

Wail
wal

Wain
wan

Waist
wast

Wait
wat

Waive
wav

Wake
wac

Wale
wal

Walk
wac, walc

Wall
wal

Wallet
walet

Wallop
walp

Wallow
walo

Walnut
walnt

Walrus
walrs

Waltz
waltz

Wampum
wampm

Wan
wan

Wand
wand

Wander
wandr

Wane
wan

Want
want

Wanton
wantn

War
war

Warble
warbl

Ward
ward

Ware
war

Warm
warm

Warn
warn

Warp warp		**Wear** war
Warrant warnt		**Weary** wery
Warren warn		**Weasand** wesnd
Warrior warr		**Weather** wethr
Wart wart		**Weave** wev
Wary wary		**Web** web
Was was		**Wed** wed
Wash wash		**Wedding** wed-ing
Wasp wasp		**Wedge** wej
Wassail wasl		**Wedlock** wedlc
Wast wast		**Wednesday** wensd
Waste wast		**Wee** we
Watch wach		**Weed** wed
Water watr		**Ween** wen
Wattle watl		**Weep** wep
Waul wal		**Weevil** wevl
Wave wav		**Weft** weft
Wax wax		**Weight (wat)** wat
Way way		**Weird** werd
We we		**Welcome** welcm
Weak wec		**Weld** weld
Weal wel		**Welfare** welfr
Wealth welth		**Welkin** welcn
Wean wen		**Well** wel

Welsh welsh		**Whey** wha	
Welt welt		**Which** which	
Wen wen		**Whiff** whif	
Wench wench		**Whig** whig	
Went went		**While** whil	
Wept wept		**Whim** whim	
Were wer		**Whin** whin	
West west		**Whine** whin	
Wet wet		**Whip** whip	
Wether wedhr		**Whir** whir	
Whale whal		**Whirl** whirl	
Wharf wharf		**Whisk** whisc	
What what		**Whisky** whiscy	
Wheat whet		**Whist** whist	
Wheel whel		**Whistle** whisl	
Wheeze whez		**Whit** whit	
Whelm whelm		**White** whit	
Whelp whelp		**Whither** whithr	
When when		**Whitlow** whitlo	
Whence whens		**Whiz** whiz	
Where wher		**Who (hoo)** hoo	
Wherry whery		**Whole (hol)** hol	
Whet whet		**Whom** hum	
Whether whethr		**Whoop** hup	

Whose hws	Win win
Whur whur	Wince wins
Why why	Winch winch
Wick wic	Wind wind
Wicked wiced	Wind' wind
Wicker wicr	Winding wind-ing
Wicket wict	Window windo
Wide wid	Wine win
Widgeon wijn	Wing wing
Widow wido	Wink winc
Width width	Winnow wino
Wield weld	Winter wintr
Wife wif	Wipe wip
Wig wig	Wire wir
Wight wit	Wisdom wisdm
Wigwam wigwm	Wise wis
Wild wild	Wish wish
Wilderness wildrns	Wisp wisp
Wile wil	Wit wit
Will wil	Witch wich
Willow wilo	With wi
Wilt wilt	Wither withr
Wily wily	Withers withrs
Wimble wimbl	Withy withy

Witless		**Worse**	
witls		wors	
Witness		**Worship**	
witns		worshp	
Witty		**Worst**	
wi-t		worst	
Wives		**Worsted**	
wivs		worstd	
Wizard		**Wort (wurt)**	
wizrd		wurt	
Wizen		**Worth**	
wizn		worth	
Woad		**Would**	
wod		wu	
Woe		**Wound**	
wo		wound	
Woful		**Wove**	
wofl		wov	
Wolf		**Wrangle (rangl)**	
wolf		rangl	
Woman		**Wrap (rap)**	
womn		rap	
Won		**Wrath (rath)**	
won		rath	
Wonder		**Wreak**	
wondr		rec	
Wont		**Wreath**	
wont		reth	
Woo		**Wreathe**	
woo		reth	
Wood		**Wreck**	
wood		rec	
Woof		**Wren**	
woof		ren	
Woolen		**Wrench**	
wooln		rench	
Word		**Wrest**	
word		rest	
Wore		**Wretch**	
wor		rech	
Work (wurk)		**Wriggle**	
wurc		rigl	
World		**Wright**	
world		rit	
Worm		**Wring**	
worm		ring	
Worry		**Wrinkle**	
wory		rincl	

Wrist
rist

Writ
rit

Write
rit

Writhe
rith

Wrong
rong

Wrote
rot

Wroth
roth

Wrought (rawt)
rawt

Wrung
rung

Wry
ry

X.

Xanthic
zanthc

Xanthid
zanthd

Xanthine
zanthn

Xanthite
zantht

Xanthium
zanthm

Xantho
zantho

Xanthous
zanths

Xanthoxylum
zantcslm

Xebec
zebc

Xenotime
zentm

Xerophagy
zerfgy

Xiphoid
zifoid

Xylography
zyl-gr

Y.

Yacht (yot)
yot

Yam
yam

Yankee
yance

Yard
yard

Yarn
yarn

Yarrow
yaro

Yaw
yaw

Yawl
yawl

Yawn
yawn

Ye
ye

Yea
ya

Yean
yen

Year
yer

Yearn
yern

Yeast
yest

Yelk
yelc

Yell
yel

Yellow
yelo

Yelp
yelp

Yeoman
yomn

Yerk
yerc

Yes
yes

Yester
yestr

Yesterday
yestrd

Yet
yct

Yew (yu)
yew

Yield
yeld

Yoke
yoc

Yolk
yolc

Yonder
yonr

Yore
yor

You
you

Young
ung

Your
your, ur

Yourself
ursl

Youth
uth

Yule
yul

Z.

Zaffer
zafr

Zany
zany

Zeal
zel

Zebra
zebr

Zenith
zenth

Zephyr
zefr

Zero
zero

Zest
zest

Zigzag
zigzg

Zinc
zinc

Zodiac
zodc

Zone
zon

Zoography
zo-gr

Zoology
zo-o

Zoonomy
zoonmy

Zoophyte
zoft

Zootomy
zootmy

Zouave
zouav

Zounds
zounds

Zoutch
zouch

Zuche
zuc

Zuffolo
zuflo

Zumbooruk
zumbre

Zumology
zum-o

Zumometer
zummtr

Zurlite
zurlt

Zygadite
zigdt

Zygapophysis
zigpfss

Zygodactyle
zigdctl

Zygoma
zigm

Zymology
zim-o

Zymosis
zimss

Zymotic
zym-o

SUPPLEMENT.

Pages 241 to 243, overlooked words.

Pages 244 to 246, shorthand equivalent of words found on pages 47 to 53, from coma to convulse, inclusive, written without the use of prefix sign for com, con, but with the *lengthened c*.

Admirable admrbl		**Cozen** cusn	
Adolescent adlsnt		**Cubit** cubt	
Adopt dɔpt		**Cuddle** cudl	
Ahead ahd		**Currier** curr	
Aid ad		**Decalogue** dec-l	
Agent ajnt		**Decrial** decril	
Alcaid alcd		**Defamation** def-m	
Alms ams		**Devious** devs	
Alum alm		**Devotee** devte	
Among amng		**Dictate** dic-t	
Appoint apnt		**Dine** din	
Ass as		**Discontinue** d-tn	
Attract atrct		**Diverse** divrs	
Augment augmnt		**Dote** dct	
Augur augr		**Egress** egrs	
Bathe bath		**Farewell** farwl	
Becloud bccloud		**Flit** flit	
Become bccm		**Fortune** fortn	
Bequest bc-q		**Frigid** frijd	
Cesura scsra		**Galloon** galn	
Chasm casm		**Glad** glad	
Chaste chast		**Grey** gra	
Clan clan		**Grip** grip	
Corporal corprl		**Groat** grot	

Guarantee garn-t	**Perforce** perfrs
Guise giz	**Perform** perfrm
Hail hal	**Perfume** perfum
Handle handl	**Perfunctory** perfnctry
Hart hart	**Perhaps** praps
Imperfect imprfct	**Pheasant** fesnt
Jacket jact	**Physic** fysc
Land land	**Physics** fyscs
Laver lavr	**Physiognomy** fys-og
Lumbar lumbr	**Physiology** fys-o
Meat met	**Pianoforte** pinfrt
Mold mold	**Piazza** piaza
Myrmidon myrmdn	**Piece** pes
Oakum ocm	**Pick** pic
Obit obt	**Picket** pict
Offset ofst	**Pickle** picl
Orgasm orgsm	**Picnic** pic-n
Paleontology palnt-o	**Pictorial** pictrl
Pant pant	**Picture** pictr
Peerage perj	**Pie** pi
Pellicle pelcl	**Piebald** pibld
Pendency pendnsy	**Pied** pid
Pepper pepr	**Pier** per
Perforate perfrat	**Pinafore** pinfr

Pry
pry

Puff
puf

Pulmonary
pulmnry

Pulse
puls

Pun
pun

Pur
pur

Quotation
qo-t

Quote
qot

Rampart
ramprt

Ration
rashn

Savior
savr

Slough
slo

Solemn
solm

Soothe
sooth

Spill
spil

Subjacent
sub-j

Tamper
tampr

Tardy
tardy

Tartar
tartr

Tawdry
tawdry

Teak
tek

Telegraph
tel-g

Ten
ten

Tense
tens

Tension
tenshn

Terrestrial
terstrl

Tetter
tetr

Thee
the

Therapeutic
therptc

Thou
thou

Tone
ton

Tuber
tubr

Turbine
turbn

Turbot
turbt

Twin
twin

Vale
val

Vassal
vasl

Vineyard
vinrd

Virtue
virtu

Weapon
wepn

Whittle
whitl

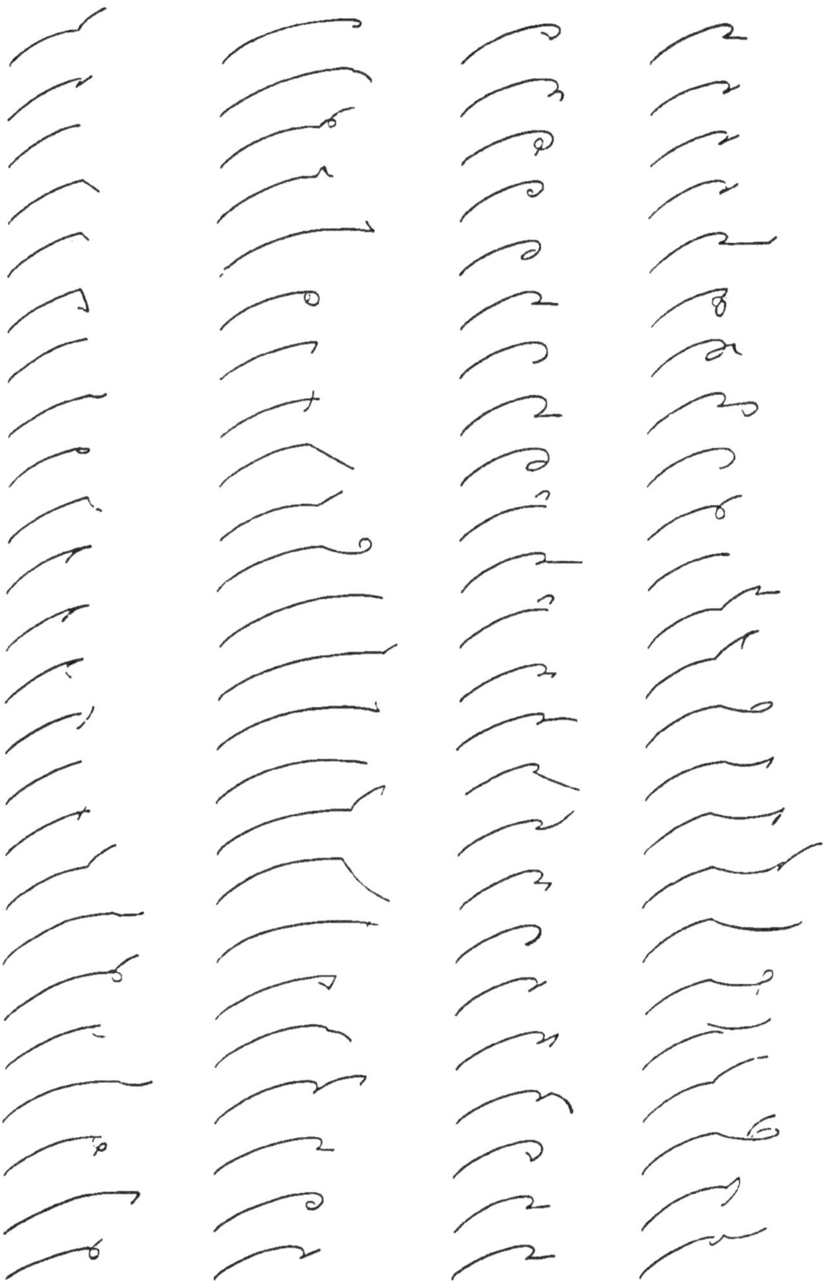

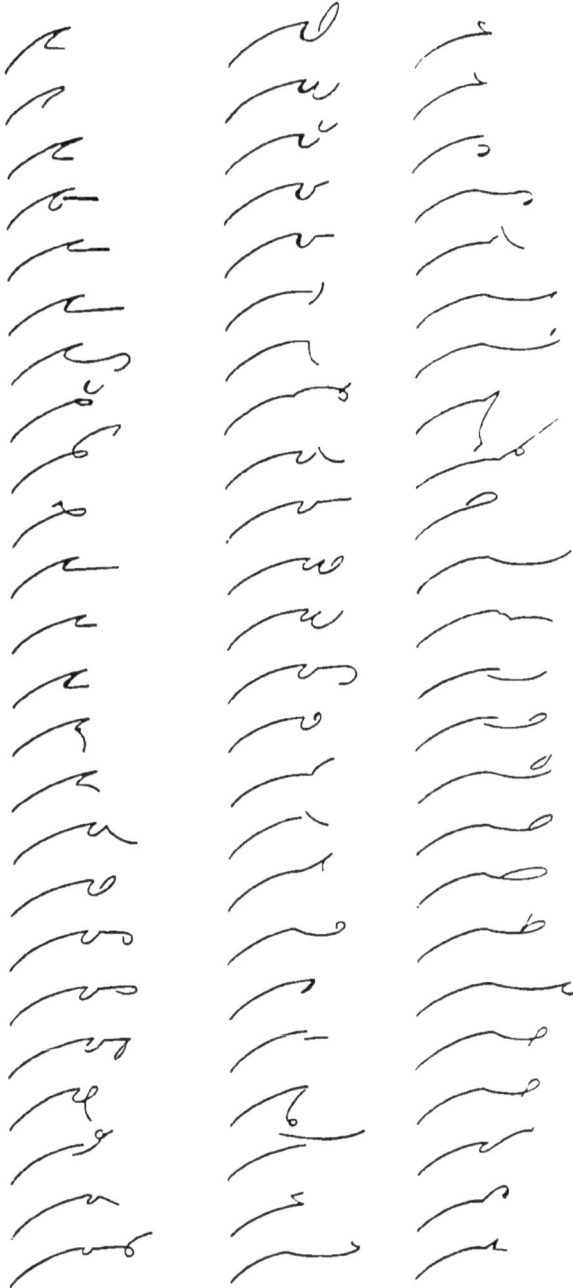

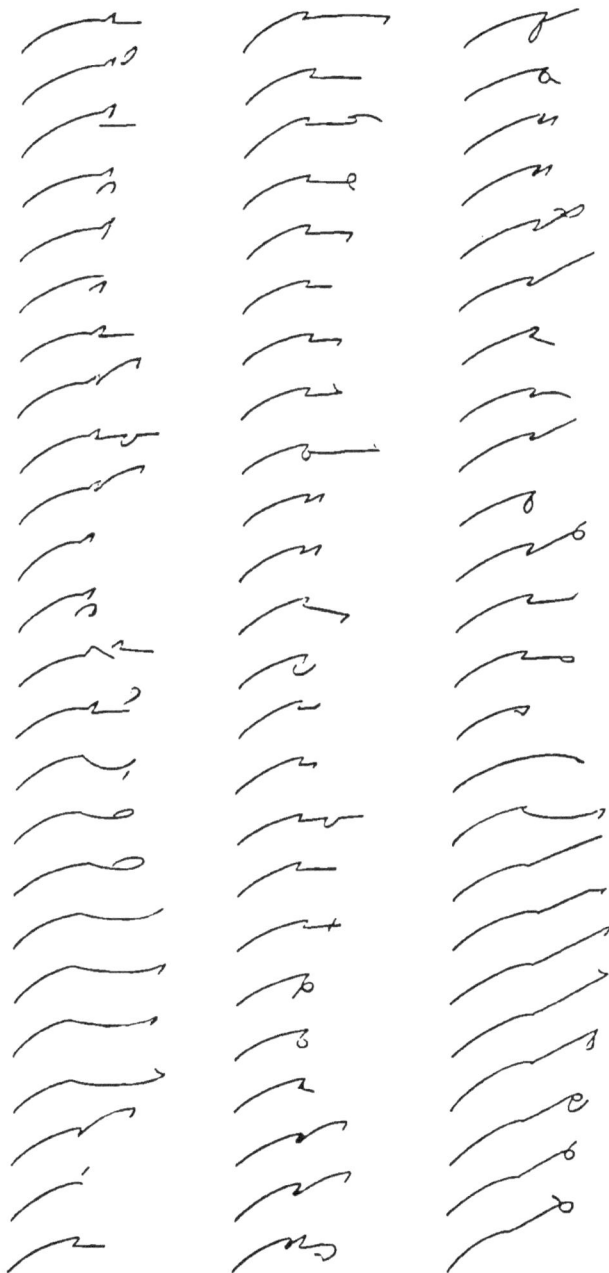

PREFIXES

These are treated of in two classes:

I.   Pages 249 to 263, inclusive, prefixes which are not expressed by arbitrary signs.

II.   Those arbitrarily represented, 264 to 271, inclusive.

Affable
a/bl

Affair
a/r

Affect
af-e

Affiant
a/int

Afflict
a/lct

Affirm
a/rm

Aggravate
agr-v

Aggregate
agr-g

Aggrieve
agrv

Agitate
a/-t

Agonize
agns

Agnostic
agnstc

Albeit
a/bet

Albino
a/bno

Alderman
a/drmn

Allege
a/ej

Alleviate
a/e-v

Always
a/ws

All-abandoned
a/bnnd

All-cheering
a/chrng

All-important
a/mprtnt

All-saints-day
a/sntsd

All-souls-day
a/slsd

Allspice
a/spis

Afterclap
a/trclp

Aftercrop
a/trcrp

Aftermath
a/trmth

Aftermost
a/trmst

Afternoon
a/trnn

Afterward
a/trwrd

Anagram
ana-gr

Analytic
anlt i

Anapest
anpst

Ancestor
ansstr

Angel
anjl

Anger
angr

Antechamber
antchmbr

Antedate
ant-d

Antelope
antlop

Antemeridian
antmrdn

Antenuptial
antnpshl

Antepast
antpst

Antichrist
antcrst

Anticlimax
antlcmx

Antidote
ant-d

Antinomian
antnmn

Antipapal
antppl

Antislavery
antslvry

Apathy
a/thy

Aperture
a/rtr

Apologue
a/-l

Appall
a/al

Appeal
a/l

Appellate
a/-l

Arbiter
arbtr

Arcade
arcd

Arcanum
arcnm

Architect
arctct

Argue
argu

Armada
armada

Archbishop
archbshp

Archdeacon
archdcn

Archduke
archdc

Archery
archry

Archfiend
archfnd

Archetype
archtyp

Asbestos
asbsts

Ascend
asnd

Ascribe
ascrb

Asperse
asprs

Aspires
asprs

Asphaltum
asfltm

Asphyxia
asfxa

Assails
asls

Atheneum
ath̃nem

Athletic
athltc

Athlete
athlt

Atlantic
atlnt i

Atlas
atls

Atmosphere
atmsfr

Attain
atan

Attempt
atmt

Attribute
atrbt

Astrological
astro-l

Astronomy
astrnmy

Astronomical
astrnmcl

Autocrat
autcrt

Autobiography
autb-gr

Autodafe
autdfa

Autograph
autc-gr

Automatic
autmt-i

Aphorism
afrsm

Aphorist
afrst

Apogee
afj

Apologue
af-l

Apoplexy
afplxy

Apothegm
afthm

Apotheosis
afthss

Aristocrat
arstcrt

Bedeck
bedc

Because
becs

Become
becm

Beget
begt

Beguile
begl

Behold
behld

Benefit
benft

Benefactor
benfctr

Benefice
benfs

Benediction
ben-dc

Benevolent
benvlnt

Bicephalous
bisfls

Biennial
binl

Biform
bifrm

Bifurcated
bifr-c

Bilingual
bilngl

Binocular
bin o

Biped
bipd

Biography
bi-gr

Biographer
bi-gr

Bibliographer
bibl gr

Bibliography bibl gr	
Bibliographical bibl gr	
Bibliomaniac biblmn-a	
By-end bynd	
By-law byla	
By-laws bylas	
By-path bypth	
By-passage bypsj	
By-stander bystndr	
By-way byw	
By-word bywrd	
Cisalpine sisalpn	
Cisatlantic sisatlntc	
Cispadane sispdn	
Century sentry	
Centennial sentnyl	
Centigrade sentgrd	
Centiped sentpd	
Centuplicate sentplct	
Co-operate cooprt	
Cohesion co-h	
Colaborer colbrr	
Coexist coxst	
Coextend coxtnd	

Cogitate coj-t	
Cognate cog-n	
Cognition cog-n	
Collate col-l	
Colleague coleg	
Collect col-c	
Collide colid	
Collocate col-c	
Colonize colnis	
Combat combt	
Combine combn	
Combustion combshn	
Comment comnt	
Commune comn	
Compact compct	
Concave concv	
Conceal consl	
Concern consrn	
Concise conss	
Concoct con-c	
Condign condn	
Corporal corprl	
Corporate corprt	
Corpulent corplnt	

Correlative	corl-t
Correspond	corspnd
Corroborate	corbrat
Contradict	contrdct
Contradistinction	contrstncshn
Contravallation	contr-vl
Contravention	contr-vn
Contraposition	contrp-s
Controvert	contrvrt
Controversy	contrvr-s
Controversial	contr-vr
Controvertible	contr-vrt
Contumacious	contu-m
Contumacy	contm-s
Contumely	contmly
Contusion	con-t
Counteract	countr-a
Countercurrent	countrcrnt
Counterfeit	countrft
Countermand	countrmnd
Countermarch	countrmrch
Countersign	countrsn
Catacomb	catcm
Catalepsy	catlp-s
Catalogue	cat-l
Catamount	cat-mnt
Cataplasm	catplsm
Cataract	catrct
Chorography	coro-gr
Chirography	ciro-gr
Chiromancy	ciromn-s
Chiropodist	ciropdst
Chronology	cron-o
Chronometer	cronmtr
Chronicle	croncl
Chronic	cron-i
Cosmography	cosm-gr
Cosmogony	cosmgny
Cosmopolite	cosmplt
Deduce	dedus
Degrade	degrd
Debark	debrc
Dejected	de-j
Defraud	defrd
Departure	deprtr
Diameter	dimtr
Diagonal	dignl
Diagram	digrm, di-g

Dialogue d*i*-l		**Emerge** emrj
Diapason d*i*psn		**Evade** evad
Diatribe d*i*trb		**Evict** evct
Diatonic d*i*tn-i		**Eccentric** x*c*ntrc
Different d*i*frnt		**Ecclesiastic** eclstc
Difficult d*i*fclt		**Eclectic** ec-lc
Diffident d*i*fdnt		**Ecstatic** ec-stt
Diffuse d*i*fus		**Ecumenical** ecmncl
Disarm dis*a*rm		**Efface** efas
Disaster dis*a*str		**Effectual** ef-fc
Disband disb*a*nd		**Effeminate** ef-fm
Disburse disb*u*rs		**Effervesce** efrvs
Discipline displ*i*n		**Effulgent** ef-fl
Dyspepsy disp*e*ps		**Effusive** efu-s
Duplicate d*u*pl-c		**Elegance** elgns
Duplicity d*u*pls-t		**Elegist** eljst
Durable d*u*rbl		**Element** elmnt
Durance d*u*rns		**Elevate** el-v
Duration d*u*-r		**Embody** embdy
Duodecimo d*u*dsmo		**Embolden** embldn
Duodenum d*u*dnm		**Embrace** embrs
Educe ed*u*s		**Embassador** embsdr
Elapse el*p*s		**Embroider** embrdr
Elect el-e		**Embroil** embrl

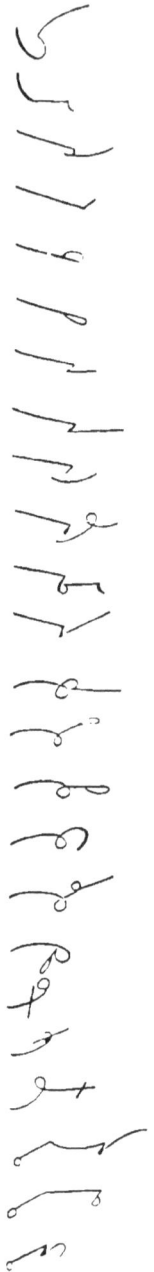

Enable		**Eupeptic**	
e*n*abl		eu*p*ptc	
Enact		**Euphony**	
e*n*ct		eu*f*ny	
Endorse		**Exclude**	
e*n*drs		xcl*u*d	
Enforce		**Excess**	
e*n*frs		x*c*s	
Engage		**Exhaust**	
e*n*gj		x*au*st	
Enjoy		**Exhale**	
e*n*joy, joy		x*a*l	
Envelop		**Extend**	
e*n*velp		xt*e*nd	
Epicure		**Extreme**	
e*p*cr		xtr*e*m	
Epidemic		**Extradition**	
e*p*dm-i		xtr*a*-d	
Epigram		**Extrajudicial**	
e*p*-gr		xtr*a*-jd	
Epilepsy		**Extraordinary**	
e*f*lp-s		xt*r*ornry	
Epilogue		**Extravagant**	
e*p*-l		xtr*a*v	
Episode		**Forearm**	
e*p*sd		forrm	
Equidistant		**Forecast**	
qu*i*dsnt		f*o*rcst	
Equilateral		**Foreknowledge**	
qu*i*ltrl		fornl	
Equilibrium		**Forepart**	
qu*i*lbrm		f*o*rprt	
Equisonance		**Foreshow**	
qu*i*snns		f*o*rsho	
Equivocal		**Foretell**	
qu*iv*cl		fortl	
Equivocate		**Geography**	
qu*iv*-c		j*e*o-gr	
Entomology		**Geology**	
e*n*tm-o		j*e*-o	
Entomolite		**Geometry**	
e*n*tmlit		j*e*m-tr	
Eucharist		**Heliocentric**	
eu*c*rst		h*e*losntrc	
Eulogize		**Heliometer**	
eu*l*js		h*e*lomtr	
Eupathy		**Heliotrope**	
eu*p*thy		h*e*lotrp	

Heptagon
heptgn

Heptarchy
heptrcy

Septennial
septnl

Septuple
septpl

Septangular
septnglr

Homogeneous
homjns

Homologous
homlgus

Hydrant
hydrnt

Hydrology
hydrlj

Hydrophobia
hydrfba

Hydropathy
hydrpthy

Hydrostatic
hydrsttc

Hyperbole
hiprbl

Hypercritical
hiprcrtcl

Hyperoxyd
hifrxd

Hypocrite
hifcrt

Hypothesis
hifthss

Hypochondria
hifcndry

Ichthyology
icth-o

Igneous
ignes

Ignite
ignt

Ignoble
ignbl

Ignominy
ignmny

Ignorant
ignrnt

Illation
il-l

Illegal
i/gl

Illegible
i/jbl

Illiberal
i/brl

Illegitimate
i/jtmt

Illuminate
i/m-n

Illustrate
i/strat

Imagine
majn

Imbibe
imbb

Imbosom
imbsm

Imitate
im-t

Immaterial
imtrl

Immeasurable
imshrbl

Inaugurate
in-au

Incarcerate
incrsrat

Incarnate
incrnt

Incident
insdnt

Inclusive
incl-s

Indecorus
indcrs

Intelligent
intljnt

Invalid
invld

Interchange
intrchnj

Interfere
intrfr

Intermix
intrmx

Interpose
intrpos

Interrupt
intr-u

Interval
intrvl

Introduce
intr-d

Introgression
intro-gr

Introversion
intro-vr

Inframundane
infrmndn

Infraposition
infrp-s

Irrational
ir-r

Irredeemable
irdmbl

Irreligion
irljn

Irreligious
irljs

Irreparable
irprbl

Irresolute
irslt

Irreverent
irvrnt

Jurisconsult
jursensit

Jurisdiction
jurs-dc

Jurisprudence
jursprdns

Juxtaposition
juxtp-s

Malcontent
malcntnt

Malediction
mal-dc

Malefactor
malfctr

Malpractice
malprcts

Maltreat
maltrt

Malfeasance
malfsns

Malleable
malabl

Malversation
malvr-s

Manual
manl

Manufactory
manfctry

Manumit
manmt

Manuscript
man-scr

Metabasis
metbass

Metamorphose
metmrfs

Metaphorical
metfrcl

Metaphysics
metfscs

Misanthropy
misnthrpy

Misapply
mispli

Misbecome
misbcm

Misbelieve
misblv

Misbehave
misbhv

Misemploy
mismploy

Misgive
misg

Necessity
nesst

Nefarious
nefars

Negation
ne-g

Negotiate
ne-g

Neology
ne-o

Nonentity
nen-en

Noctambulist
noctmblst

Noctivagant
noctvgnt

Nocturnal
noctrnl

Non-conformity
n-frm-t

Nondescript
nond-scr

Non-juror
nonjrr

Non-resistance
nonrsstns

Nonsense
nonsns

Obdurate
obdrt

Obelisk
oblsc

Object
obj

Obligation
obl-g

Obnoxious
obnxshs

Obtainable
obtnbl

Occur
ocr

Occupant
ocpnt

Occupy
ocp

Octagon
octgn

Octahedral
octhdrl

October
octbr

Octavo
octvo

Offer
ofr

Offense
ofns

Officious
ofshs

Omnibus
o-bs

Omnipotent
o-tnt

Omnipresent
o-prsnt

Omniscient
o-nt

Omnivorous
o-vrs

Opera
ofra

Operose
ofros

Opponent
ofnt

Opportune
ofrtn

Oppose
ofpos, ofs

Optical
oftcl

Orthodox
orthdx

Orthoepy
orthpy

Orthography
orth-gr

Orthology
orth-o

Ornithology
ornth-o

Osteogeny
ostogny

Osteology
ost-o

Outdo
outd

Outgo
outg

Outlaw
outla

Outreach
outrch

Outrun
outrn

Outwear
outwr

Outwork ou?wrc	
Overanxious ovranshs	
Overestimate o?rstmt	
Overflow o?rflo	
Overhead o?rhd	
Overhaul o?rhl	
Overjoy o?rjy	
Overland o?rlnd	
Perambulate permblt	
Percentage persntj	
Peremptory perm-tr	
Perfection perfcshn	
Periphrase perfras	
Permanent permnt	
Plenipotence plenptns	
Plenipotentiary plenptnshry	
Plenitude plen-t	
Postfix postfx	
Posthumous postums	
Postmeridian postmrdn	
Postpone pospn	
Postscript pos-scr	
Preliminary prelmnry	
Prelude prelud	

Premature premtr	
Premeditate premd-t	
Premonish premnsh	
Presumption presmshn	
Preterition pretr-i	
Preterlegal pretr-l	
Pretermit pretrmt	
Preternatural pretrntrl	
Primage primj	
Primary primry	
Primitive prim-t	
Primogenitor primjntr	
Primordial primrdl	
Paradox pardx	
Paragon pargn	
Parallel parall	
Paramount parmnt	
Pentachord pentcrd	
Pentagon pentgn	
Pentameter pentmtr	
Pentateuch pentc	
Perigee perje	
Perihelion perhlyn	
Period perd	

Periphery perfry		**Quadruplicate** q-plct	
Philological filo-l		**Re-enter** reentr	
Philologist filogst		**Recant** recant	
Philomath filomth		**Redeem** redem	
Philosophy filosfy		**Refresh** refresh	
Philanthropy filnthrp		**Remind** remind	
Philomel filml		**Renew** renew	
Physicologic fisc-l		**Renown** renown	
Physiognomy fis-og		**Resume** resum	
Physiologic fis-l		**Revive** reviv	
Physiology fis-o		**Retroaction** retro-a	
Polyanthus polnths		**Retrograde** retrogrd	
Polygamy polgmy		**Retropulsive** retroplsv	
Polygraph pol-gr		**Retrospection** retro-sp	
Polypus polpus		**Seclude** seclud	
Polysyllable pol-lbl		**Secure** secur	
Polytheism polthsm		**Seduce** sedus	
Pyroligneous pyrolgns		**Select** slct	
Pyrology pyr-o		**Senescence** snsns	
Pyrotechnics pyro-tc		**Sequester** sqstr	
Quadrangle q-rngl		**Sexagenarian** sex-j	
Quadrate q-rt		**Sexagesima** sex-js	
Quadrennial q-rnl		**Sexangular** sexnglr	
Quadruped q-pd		**Sexennial** sexnl	

Hexagon	**Succinct**
hexgn	susnct
Hexameter	**Succor**
hexmtr	sucr
Hexandrous	**Succulent**
hexandrs	suclnt
Semicircle	**Succumb**
semsrcl	sucm
Semicolon	**Suction**
semcln	sucshn
Semidiameter	**Suffer**
semdmtr	sufr
Semilunar	**Suffice**
semlnr	sufs
Semiquaver	**Sufficient**
semqvr	su-f
Semitone	**Suffix**
semtn	sufx
Sine cure	**Suffocate**
sincur	sufct
Sine die	**Suffrage**
sindi	sufrj
Solidarity	**Suffusion**
soldr-t	suf-f
Solitary	**Sugar**
sol-tr	shugr
Solitude	**Suggest**
sol-t	sujst
Soliloquy	**Supplant**
sollq	suplnt
Subacid	**Supplement**
subasd	suplmnt
Subaltern	**Suppliant**
subltrn	suplint
Subdivide	**Supplicate**
subd-v	supl-c
Subduct	**Support**
sub-d	suprt
Subjacent	**Suppress**
sub-j	suprs
Subject	**Suppurate**
sub	suprat
Subjugate	**Subterfuge**
sub-g	subtrfj
Succeed	**Subterraneous**
susd	subtrns
Successor	**Superannuate**
sucssr	supran-w

Superabundant *suprbnt*	**Syncopate** *syncpt*
Supercargo *suprcrg*	**Synod** *synod*
Supereminence *suprmns*	**Synonym** *synnm*
Superscribe *supr-scr*	**Syntax** *syntx*
Susceptible *sus-c*	**Synthesis** *synthss*
Suspect *suspt*	**Stenography** *sten-gr*
Suspend *suspnd*	**Stenotype** *stentp*
Suspense *suspns*	**Stereoscope** *sterscp*
Suspicion *sus-p*	**Stereotype** *stertp*
Sustain *sustn*	**Stereometry** *sterm-tr*
Sustentation *sustn-t*	**Triangle** *triangl*
Syllable *sylbl*	**Triennial** *trinyl*
Syllabub *sylbb*	**Tricolored** *triclrd*
Syllabus *sylbs*	**Triflorous** *triflors*
Syllogism *syl-j*	**Tripod** *tripod*
Sylvan *sylvn*	**Triumph** *triumf*
Symbolic *symblc*	**Triune** *triun*
Symmetry *symtr*	**Theology** *the-o*
Sympathize *sympths*	**Theocracy** *the-o*
Symphony *symfny*	**Theorem** *therm*
Synagogue *syngg*	**Theoretical** *ther-e*
Syneresis *synrss*	**Topography** *top-gr*
Synchronal *syncrnl*	**Typographic** *typo-gr*
Synchronism *syncrnism*	**Under-agent** *undrajnt*

Resolve reslv	**Undercurrent** undrcrnt
Resolved reslvd	**Underlet** undrlt
Resolves reslvs	**Under-officer** undrofsr
Resolving reslving	**Underpin** undrpn
Resolvent reslvnt	**Undersell** undrsl
Resolvable reslvbl	**Understand** undrstnd
Resolvedness reslvdns	**Uniform** unifrm
Resolver reslvr	**Unitarian** untrn
Pronounce pronns	**Unity** un-t
Pronounced pronnsd	**Univalve** unvlv
Pronouncing pronnsing	**Universe** unvrs
Pronounces pronnss	**Withdraw** widr
Pronounceable pronnsbl	**Withhold** wihld
Pronunciation pronun-sh	**Within** win
Pronunciamento pronnshmnto	**Without** wiout
Irritate ir-t	**Withstand** wistnd
Irritated ir-t	**Zoology** zo-o
Irritates ir-t	
Irritating ir-t	
Irritation ir-t	
Irritative ir-t	
Irritant ir-t	
Irritable ir-t	
Irritability ir-t	

Accommodate
a-dt

Accomplice
a-pls

Accomplish
a-plsh

Accompany
a-pny

Accountable
a-bl

Accountant
a-nt

Accumbent
a-bnt

Accumulate
a-lt

Accumulator
a-ltr

Administer
ad-tr

Administrate
ad-trt

Administration
ad-trshn

Administrative
ad-trv

Administrator
ad-trtr

Administratrix
ad-trx

Ambidexter
am-dxtr

Ambient
am-nt

Ambiguous
amg-us

Ambiguity
am-gt

Amphibious
am-bs

Amphibian
am-bn

Amphibology
am-b-o

Amphitheatre
am-thtr

Amplify
amplf

Amplitude
ampltd

Amplification
ampl-c

Amputation
amp-t

Amputate
amptt

Command
coma-nd

Commend
come-nd

Comminute
comi-nt

Community
comu-n-t

Company
compa-ny

Compend
compe-nd

Component
compo-nnt

Computed
compu-td

Complainant
compla-nnt

Complement
comple-mnt

Complicity
compli-st

Compulsory
compul-sry

Contagion
conta-jn

Contends
cont.-nds

Continent
conti-nnt

Contortion
contor-sn

Controversy
contro-vrs

Contusion
contu-sn

Consanguinity
consa-ngnt

Concentrate
consc-ntrt

Conceivable consc-vbl	**Distant** distnt
Consider consi-dr	**Distress** distrs
Consolatory conso-ltry	**Disrepute** disrput
Consummate consu-mt	**Disrespect** disrespt
Conflagration confla-grshn	**Disregard** disregrd
Conflicted confli-ctd	**Disreputable** disreptbl
Concomitance concom-tns	**Dissatisfied** dst-fd
Circumjacent sm-jsnt	**Dissatisfaction** dst-fshn
Circumlocution sml-q	**Distemper** distmpr
Circumnavigate sm-nv-g	**Distribute** distrbt
Circumpolar sm-plr	**Distrustful** distrstfl
Circumscribe sm-scrb	**Disturb** distrb
Circumspect sm-spt	**Discomfit** d-ft
Circumstance sm-tns	**Discommode** d-d
Circumvallation sm-vlshn	**Discomposure** d-posr
Circumvention sm-vnshn	**Disconcert** d-srt
Disclaim disclm	**Disconnect** d-ct
Disclose discls	**Discontinue** d-tn
Disburse disbrrs	**Discounted** d-td
Disastrous disastrs	**Discourage** dr-j
Disarm disarm	**Discouragement** dr-jmnt
Disorder disordr	**Discourtesy** dr-tsy
Dismay disma	**Equanimity** e-nmt
Disqualify disqli	**Equator** e-tr

Equiangular e-nglr		**Hypochondria** h-cndr	
Equidistant e-dstnt		**Hypochondriac** h-cndrc	
Equilateral e-ltrl		**Hypocrisy** h-crsy	
Equilibrity e-lbr-t		**Hypocrite** h-crt	
Equilibrium e-lbrm		**Hypocritical** h-crtcl	
Equinoctial e-ncshl		**Hypostatic** h-sttc	
Equipage e-pj		**Hypotenuse** h-tns	
Equipment ep-mnt		**Hypothecate** h-thct	
Equipoise e-ps		**Hypothecation** h-thcshn	
Equiponderant e-pndrnt		**Hypothesis** h-thss	
Equitably e-tbly		**Hypothetical** h-thtcl	
Equivocate ev-ct		**Hypothetically** h-thtcly	
Equivocation ev-cshn		**Indication** ind-c	
Equivoke e-vk		**Indicative** ind-c	
Governance g-ns		**Indicator** ind-c	
Governess g-cs		**Indiction** indction	
Government g-mnt		**Indigent** indjnt	
Governor g-or		**Indigestible** indjstbl	
Hyperbola h-bla		**Indigestion** indjshn	
Hyperbole h-bl		**Indignation** indg-n	
Hyperbolical h-blcl		**Indignity** indgn-t	
Hyperborean h-brn		**Indigo** indgo	
Hypercritical h-crtcl		**Indirect** indirct	
Hypercriticism h-crtssm		**Indirectly** indrcly	

Indiscernable i-rnbl	
Indiscretion i-crshn	
Indiscriminate i-crmnt	
Indiscriminately i-cimtly	
Indiscrimination i-crm-n	
Indispensible i-pnsbl	
Indispose i-pos	
Indisposition i-po-s	
Indisputable i-ptbl	
Indisputably i-ptbl	
Indissoluble i-slbl	
Indissolubly i-slbl	
Indissolvable i-slvbl	
Indistinct i-tinct	
Indistinguishable i-tnshbl	
Incombustible in-bstbl	
Incommensurate in-mensrat	
Incommensurable in-menshrbl	
Incommode in-md	
Incommodious in-mds	
Incommunicable in-mncbl	
Incomparable in-prbl	
Incomparably in-prbl	
Incompassionate in-pshnt	

Incompatible in-ptbl	
Incompatibility in-ptblt	
Incompetence in-ptns	
Incompetency in ptnsy	
Incompetent in-ptnt	
Incomplete in-plt	
Incomprehensible in-prnsbl	
Incomprehensibly in-prnsbly	
Incompressible in-prsbl	
Inconceivable in-svbl	
Misconceive m-sv	
Misconduct m-dct	
Misconjecture m-jctr	
Misconstrue m-stru	
Non-conductor n-dctr	
Non-conformist n-frmst	
Non-conformity n-frmt	
Omnibus o-bs	
Omnipotent o-ptnt	
Omnipresence o-prsns	
Omnipresent o-prsnt	
Omniscience o-sns	
Omniscient o-snt	
Omnivagant o-gnt	

Omnivorous
o-rs

Preconceive
p-sv

Preconception
p-spshn

Preconcert
p-srt

Preconcerted
p-srtd

Precontract
p-trct

Quadrangle
q-gl

Quadrangular
q-glr

Quadrature
q-tr

Quadrennial
q-yl

Quadrilateral
q-ltrl

Quadripartite
q-prtt

Quadrisyllable
q-slbl

Quadrivalve
q-vlv

Quadrumanous
q-mns

Quadruplicate
q-plct

Quadruplication
q-plcshn

React
r-act

Reality
r-alt

Realization
r-al-z

Reappear
r-a/r

Reappoint
r-a/nt

Rebound
r-bound

Rebut
r-but

Rebuke
r-buc

Rebellious
r-belys

Recast
r-cast

Receive
r-sev

Recent
r-sent

Recess
r-ses

Reciprocal
r-siprcl

Recital
r-srtl

Reclaim
r-clam

Recluse
r-clus

Recourse
r-cors

Recreant
r-crent

Recriminate
r-crim-n

Recurrence
r-curns

Reduce
r-dus

Re-elect
r-el-e

Re-embark
r-embrc

Re-enforce
r-enfrs

Re-enter
r-entr

Re-examine
r-xamn

Refine
r-fin

Refuse
r-fus

Refers
r-fers

Reflex
r-flex

Refresh
r-fresh

Regal
r-gal

Regard
r-gard

Regenerate
r-jenrt

Repass
r-pas

Repose
r-pos

Repulse
r-puls

Repeat
r-pet

Repine
r-pin

Reply
r-pli

Resent
r-sent

Respect
r-spet

Reinter
r-intr

Reiterate
r-itrat

Reorganize
r-orgnis

Reinsure
r-inshr

Rejoin
r-join

Rejuvenate
r-juv-n

Retailer
r-talr

Retails
r-tals

Return
r-turn

Retouch
r-tuch

Retake
r-tac ,

Retrieve
r-trev

Reunite
r-unt

Reunion
r-unn

Restrain
r-stran

Restore
r-stor

Reveal
r-vel

Revive
r-viv

Revives
re-vivs

Revulsion
r-vulshn

Revolve
r-volv

Revamp
r-vamp

Reward
r-ward

Rewrite
r-rit

Resound
r-sound

Recollect
r-ct

Recollection
r-cshn

Recognition
r-nshn

Recognizable
r-nsbl

Recommence
r-mns

Recommend
r mnd

Recommit
r-mt

Recompense
r-pns

Recompose
r-pos

Reconcile
r-sl

Recondite
r-dit

Reconnaissance
r-sns

Reconnoiter
r-oitr

Reconquer
r-qr

Self-conceit
s-cnset

Self-esteem
s-stm

Self-evident
s-evdnt

Self-existence
s-xstns

Self-love
s-lv

Self-same
s-sm

Self-will
s-wl

Satisfy
st-f

Satisfied
st-fd

Satisfaction
st-fshn

Satisfactory
st-fry

Transact
t-ct

Transatlantic
t-lntc

Transcend
t-nd

Transcribe
t-scrb

Transept
t-spt

Transfer
t-fr

Transfigure
t-fgr

Transfix
t-fx

Transform
t-frm

Transfuse
t-fs

Transgress
t-grs

Transit
t-st

Transient
t-nt

Transition
t-ishn

Transitive
t-tv

Translate
t-lt

Translucent
t-lsnt

Transmigrate
t-mgrt

Transmit
t-mt

Transmute
t-mut

Transparent
t-prnt

Transplant
t-plnt

Transport
t-prt

Transpose
t-pos

Transubstantiation
t-sb-stn

Transude
t-ud

Transverse
t-vrs

Uncomfortable
un-frbl

Uncommon
un-mn

Uncompromising
un-pr-msng

Unconcern
un-srn

Unconditional
un-dshnl

Unconquerable
un-qrbl

Unconscionable
un-shnbl

Unconstitutional un–st-t	
Uncontrollable un–trlbl	
Unconverted un–vrtd	
Undiscerning u–srn-ing	
Undisciplined u–plnd	
Undisclose u–cls	
Undiscrete u–crt	
Undisposed u–posd	
Undisputed u–ptd	
Undistinctive u–tnctv	
Excommunicate x–ct	
Excommunication x–cshn	
Unsatisfied un–fd	
Unsatisfaction un–fshn	
Unsatisfactory un–fry	
Give satisfaction gi–fshn	
No satisfaction no–fshn	
Good satisfaction good–fshn	
Not satisfactory not–fry	
Very satisfactory very–fry	
Am satisfied am–fid	
Well satisfied wel–fid	
Be satisfied be–fid	

Unreconciled unr–sld	
Unreconcilable unr–slbl	
Unreconcilably unr–slbly	
Vice-admiral visadmrl	
Vice-chancellor vischnslr	
Vicegerent visjrnt	
Vice-king viscng	
Vice-legate vislgt	
Vice-man vismn	
Vice-president visprs	
Viceroy visroy	
Withhold wihld	
Withholden wihldn	
Withholder wihldr	
Withholdment wihldmnt	
Within wiin	
Withinforth wiinfrth	
Withinside wiinsd	
Without wiout	
Withouten wioutn	
Withoutforth wioutfrth	
Withstand wistnd	
Withstood wistd	

NOTE.—The above method of expressing the words satisfy, satisfied, satisfaction and satisfactory may be written across *any* preceding word in a similar manner.

SUFFIXES.

REMARKS ON THE USE OF SUFFIX SIGNS.

In general a single suffix sign will serve to express an entire class of suffixes; as, the words sub-tract, sub-tracts, sub-tracted, sub-tracting, sub-traction, may all be represented by *sub*, with *tr* written near it, relying on the context to determine the part of speech, tense or participle. That this is not only possible but safe, is evident from the following illustrative sentence, in which the same form is used for the various forms of *subtract*, and the learner will readily supply the correct word: Can you sub-tr this? Have you sub-tr this? Are you sub-tr this? Can you perform this sub-tr?

Take the various forms of *indicate*: Can you ind-c (indicate) it? Will you ind-c (indicate) it? Have you ind-c (indicated) it? This clearly ind-c (indicates) that. What is the ind-c (indication)? What are the ind-c (indications)? There is no ind-c (indication) that it will. There are ind-c (indications) of it. The signs are all ind-c (indicative) of a storm. The signs ind-c (indicate) a storm. There is every ind-c (indication) of a storm.

Take *elect* in its various forms: We will el-e him. We have el-e our ticket. We can el-e our ticket. The el-e is in progress. We are el-e our ticket. The independent exercise of the el-e franchise. He was el-e to serve as one of the presidential el-e.

Take *adapt* with its various forms: It is not ad-a to him. It is very well ad-a. With ad-a facility. A perfect ad-a of the means to the end. We are ad-a it, or trying to ad-a it.

Hopeful ho*fl		**Carelessly** carls	
Hopefully ho*fl		**Carelessness** carls	
Hopefulness ho*fl		**Childish** ch*ldsh	
Hopeless ho*ls		**Childishly** ch*ldsh	
Hopelessly ho*ls		**Childishness** ch*ldsh	
Hopelessness ho*ls		**Foolish** foolsh	
Faithful fathfl		**Foolishly** foolsh	
Faithfully fathfly		**Foolishness** foolsh	
Faithfulness fathfl		**Slavish** slavsh	
Faithless fathls}		**Slavishly** slavsh	
Faithlessness fathls		**Slavishness** slavsh	
Healthful helthfl		**Clownish** clownsh	
Healthfully helthfly		**Clownishly** clownsh	
Healthfulness helthfl		**Clownishness** clownsh	
Artful artfl		**Methodic** methdc	
Artfully artfly		**Methodical** methdcl	
Artfulness artfl		**Methodically** methdcl	
Artless artls		**Poetic** petc	
Artlessly artls		**Poetical** potcl	
Artlessness artls		**Poetically** potcly	
Careful carfl		**Angelic** anjl-i	
Carefully carfly		**Angelical** anjl-i	
Carefulness carfl		**Angelically** anjl-i	
Careless carls		**Alphabetic** alfbt-i	

Alphabetical a/fbt-i	
Alphabetically a/fbt-i	
Changeable chanjbl	
Changeably chanjbl	
Changeableness chanjbl	
Changeability chanjbl	
Accept acspt	
Accepting acspt	
Acceptable acsptbl	
Acceptably acsptbl	
Acceptableness acsptbl	
Acceptability acsptbl	
Commutable comu-tbl	
Commutably comu-tbly	
Commutableness comu-tbl	
Commutability comu-tbl	
Blamable blambl	
Blamably blambl	
Blamableness blambl	
Blamability blambl	
Resistible resstbl	
Resistibly resstbl	
Resistibility resstbl	
Compressible compre-sbl	

Compressibleness pre-sbl	
Compressibility pre-sbl	
Defensible deinsbl	
Defensibleness deinsbl	
Defensibility deinsb	
Contractible tra-ctbl	
Contractibleness tra-ctbl	
Contractibility tra-tcbl	
Dangerous danjrs	
Dangerously danjrs	
Dangerousness danjrs	
Glorious glors	
Gloriously glors	
Gloriousness glors	
Slanderous slandrs	
Slanderously slandrs	
Slanderousness slandrs	
Ruinous runs	
Ruinously runs	
Ruinousness runsns	
Attractive a/rc-t	
Attractively a/rc-t	
Attractiveness a/rc-t	
Diffusive dif-s	

Diffusively
di̇f-s

Diffusiveness
di̇f-s

Oppressive
op̌r-s

Oppressively
op̌r-s

Oppressiveness
op̌r-s

Coercive
coer-s

Coercively
coer-s

Dependence
depndns

Dependent
depndnt

Dependently
depndnt

Indulgence
indljns

Indulgent
indljnt

Indulgently
indljnt

Confidence
fi-dns

Confident
fi-dnt

Confidently
fi-dntly

Difference
difr

Different
difrnt

Differently
difrnt

Muffle
mufl

Muffled
mufl

Muffler
muflr

Muffling
mufl

Ramble
rambl

Rambled
rambl

Rambler
rambl

Rambling
rambl

Swindle
swindl

Swindled
swindl

Swindler
swindlr

Swindling
swindl

Grumble
grumbl

Grumbled
grumbl

Grumbler
grumblr

Grumbling
grumbl

Aliment
almnt

Alimental
almnt

Alimentary
almnt

Elemental
elmnt

Elementary
elmnt

Supplement
suplmnt

Supplemental
suplmnt

Supplementary
suplmnt

Realize
relis

Realized
relisd

Realizes
relis

Realizing
relis

Realization
rel-z

Civilize si̇vlis		**Confusedly** confu-sdly
Civilized si̇vlis		**Conceit** consc-t
Civilizes si̇vlis		**Conceited** consc-t
Civilizing si̇vlis		**Conceitedly** consc-t
Civilization si̇vlis		**Content** conte-nt
Moralize morlis		**Contented** conte-nt
Moralized morlis		**Contentedly** conte-nt
Moralizes morlis		**Refine** refn
Moralizing morlis		**Refined** refnd
Moralization morlis		**Refinedly** refn
Obligate obl-g		**Clarify** clarf
Obligated obl-g		**Clarified** clarf
Obligating obl-g		**Clarifying** clarf
Obligation obl-g		**Clarification** clarf-c
Indicate ind-c		**Gratify** gratf
Indicated ind-c		**Gratified** gratf
Indicating ind-c		**Gratifying** gratf
Indication ind-c		**Gratification** grat-c
Accelerate ac-slrt		**Modify** mod-f
Accelerated ac-slrt		**Modified** mod-f
Accelerating ac-slrt		**Modifying** mod-f
Acceleration ac-slrt		**Modification** mod-c
Confuse confu-s		**Sanctify** sanctf
Confused confu-s		**Sanctified** sanctf

Sanctifying
sanctf

Sanctification
sanct-c

National
nashn

Nationality
nashn

Constitutional
con-st

Constitutionality
con-st

Formal
forml

Formality
formlt

Contradictory
contra-dctry

Contradictorily
contra-dctrly

Interrogate
introgt

Interrogatory
intr-g

Interrogatorily
intr-g

Derogatory
dcrgrty

Derogatorily
dcrgtrly

Troublesome
trublsm

Troublesomely
trublsmly

Troublesomeness
trublsmns

Delightsome
deltsm

Delightsomely
deltsmly

Delightsomeness
deltsmns

Methodist
methdst

Methodism
methdsm

Federalist
fdrlst

Federalism
fdrlism

Formalist
formlist

Sharpen
sharp

Sharpened
sharpnd

Sharpening
sharpn

Quicken
qicn

Quickened
qicn

Quickening
qicn

Hardening
hardn

Active
ac-t

Actively
ac-t

Activity
ac-t

Receptive
rescp-t

Receptivity
rescp-t

Receptively
rescp-t

Adaptive
adp-t

Adaptively
adp-t

Adaptivity
adp-t

Destructive
de-str

Destructively
de-str

Destructiveness
de-str

Enlarge
enlrj

Enlarged
enlrjd

Enlarging
enlrj-i

Invested invst	**Obeyed** obad
Investing invst	**Obeying** oba
Investment invst	**Delayed** delad
Allure a/r	**Delaying** dela
Allured a/rd	**Envious** envs
Alluring a/r-ing	**Enviously** envs
Allurement a/rmnt	**Melodious** meldus
Entombed entmd	**Melodiously** meldus
Entombing entm-ing	**Penurious** penurs
Entombment entmnt	**Penuriously** penurs
Helped help	**Piteous** pitus
Helper help	**Piteously** pitus
Helping help	**Beauteous** beuts
Helpful help	**Beauteously** beutsly
Helpless help	**Mortifying** mortf
Taxed taxt	**Mortifyingly** mortf
Taxer taxr	**Satisfying** st-f-ing
Taxing tax	**Satisfyingly** st-f
Wished wishd	**Healthy** helthy
Wisher wishr	**Healthily** helthly
Wishing wish	**Healthiness** helthns
Traded tradd	**Destroy** destr
Trader tradr	**Destroyed** destr
Trading trad	**Destroyer** destrr

Manly manly		**Immense** imns	
Manliness manlns		**Conveyance** con v	
Easy esy		**Annoyance** noyns, an-oy	
Easily esly		**Finance** finns	
Easiness esns		**Penance** penns	
Weary wery		**Permanency** permnns	
Wearily werly		**Fluency** flun-s	
Weariness werns		**Competency** comptnsy	
Noisy noi-s		**Potency** potnsy	
Noisily noi-s		**Impotency** imptnsy	
Noisiness noi-s		**Expectancy** xpectnsy	
Handy hand		**Pliancy** plinsy	
Handily handly		**Pretends** pretnds	
Handiness handns		**Offends** ofnds	
Cosey co-s		**Legends** lejnds	
Cosily co-s		**Frequents** fre-q	
Cosiness co-s		**Expends** xpends	
Commerce comrs		**Viands** vnds	
Intense intns		**Amends** amnds	
Suspense suspns		**Portends** portnds	
Suspends suspnds		**Extends** xtnds	
Decadence decdns		**Intends** intnds	
Confidence confdns		**Inference** infrns	
Pretence pretns		**Inferences** infrnss	

Faints	fants		**Differences**	dıfrnss
Saints	sants		**Incendiary**	insndry
Paints	pants		**Commentary**	comn-tr
Senses	snss		**Country**	coun-tr
Census	snss		**Momentary**	momn-tr
Dances	danss		**Sedentary**	sedn-tr
Evince	erns		**Promontory**	promn-tr
Events	ernts		**Elementary**	elmn-tr
Evinces	ernss		**Exclamatory**	xclam-tr
Agents	ajnts		**Inflammatory**	inflm-tr
Agencies	ajnss		**Parliamentary**	parlmn-tr
Exigencies	xijnss		**Voluntary**	voln-tr
Accents	acsnts		**Salutatory**	sal-tr
Accidents	acsdnts		**Salutary**	sal-tr
Pencil	pensl		**Adulatory**	adl-tr
Tensile	tensl		**Breviary**	brevry
Utensil	utnsl		**Plenary**	plenry
Utensils	utnsls		**Binary**	binry
Prehensile	prensl		**Canary**	canry
Immensely	imnsly		**Contrary**	cntrry
Immensity	imnst		**Freedom**	fredm
Immenseness	imsnns		**Kingdom**	cindm
Intenseness	intnsns		**Serfdom**	serfdm
Difference	difrns		**Wisdom**	wisdm

Random	randm		Variety	vart

Random
randm

Thralldom
thraldm

Plethoric
plethrc

Bishopric
bishprc

Choleric
colrc

Turmeric
turmrc

Morose
moros

Varicose
varcos

Jocose
jocos

Adipose
adpos

Boyhood
boyhd

Manhood
manhd

Girlhood
girld

Womanhood
womnhd

Penmanship
penmnshp

Horsemanship
hersmnshp

Friendship
frenshp

Pestiferous
pestfrs

Herbivorous
erbvrs

Carnivorous
carnvrs

Graminivorous
gramnvrs

Pity
pity

Piety
pie-t

Polity
polt

Variety
vart

Humanity
humn-t

Community
comnt

Committee
com-it

Insanity
insnt

Infancy
infns

Decency
desns

Pittance
pitns

Idealism
idlism

Truism
truism

Heroism
heroism

Favoritism
favrtism

Exorcism
xorssm

Realism
rclism

Solecism
solsism

Syllogism
syljsm

Puerile
pucrl

Projectile
pro-j

Dactyl
dactl

Ductile
ductl

Volatile
v-ltl

Versatile
verstl

Bombast
b-mbst

Iconoclast
icnclst

Ballast		**Jurist**
balst		jurst
Debased		**Endorsee**
debst		endrse
Canvassed		**Fiancee**
canvst		fnse
Fuller		**Nominee**
fulr		nome
Droller		**Payee**
drolr		pae
Greater		**Engineer** .
gratr		enjnr
Nearer		**Financier**
nerr		finnsr
Purer		**Gazetteer**
purr		gaztr
Redder		**Muleteer**
redr		multr
Sooner		**Privateer**
soonr		privtr
Truer		**Pioneer**
trur		pinr
Address		**Bipartite**
adrs		biprtt
Undress		**Expedite**
undrs		xpedt
Caress		**Hematite**
cars		hemtt
Digress		**Theodolite**
digrs		thedlit
Express		**Auditor**
xpres		audtr
Ingress		**Editor**
ingrs		edtr
Duress		**Exterior**
durs		xterr
Baptist		**Interior**
baptst		intrr
Casuist		**Inferior**
casust		infrr
Dramatist		**Superior**
dramtst		suprr
Duelist		**Imitator**
· dulst		imttr
Fatalist		**Artisan**
fatlst		artsn
Formalist		**Partisan**
formlst		partsn

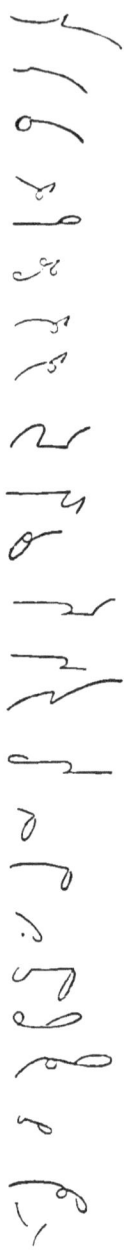

Citizen s/tzn		**Enacted** en-a
Denizen d·nzn		**Enactment** en-a
Horizon h·rzn		**Enacts** en-a
Barrister b·rstr		**Inapt** in-a
Minister m/nstr		**Inaptly** in-a
Registrar rejstrr		**Inaptness** in-a
Forester f·rstr		**Adapt** ad-a
Chorister c·rstr		**Adapting** ad-a
Potentate p·tntat		**Adapted** ad-a
Magistrate m·jstrt		**Adaptation** ad-a
Laureate l·urat		**Adaptive** ad-a
Magnate m·gnat		**Elect** el-e
Magnet m·gnt		**Elected** el-e
Catkin c·tcn		**Electing** el-e
Lambkin l·mcn		**Election** el-e
Bantling b·ntl-ing		**Elective** el-e
Fatling f·tl-ing		**Elects** el-e
Youngling ungl-ing		**Except** xcpt
Gauntlet g·untlt		**Excepting** xcpting
Wristlet r/slt		**Excepted** xcptd
Corselet c·rslt		**Excepts** xcpts
Globule gl·bl		**Exception** xcpshn
Ferrule f·rul		**Addict** ad-i
Enact en-a		**Addicted** ad-i

Evict		**Abate**
ev-i		a-b
Evicted		**Abated**
ev-i		a-b
Evicts		**Abating**
ev-i		a-b
Evicting		**Abatement**
ev-i		a-b
Eviction		**Ambition**
ev-i		am-b
Evictment		**Ambitious**
ev-i		am-b
Tuition		**Ambitiously**
tu-i		am-b
Intuition		**Retribution**
int-i		retri-b
Adopt		**Retributive**
ad-o		retri-b
Adopts		**Abrade**
ad-o		a-br
Adopted		**Abraded**
ad-o		a-br
Adopting		**Abrading**
ad-o		a-br
Adoption		**Abrasion**
ad-o		a-br
Induct		**Indicate**
ind-u		ind-c
Induction		**Indicates**
ind-u		ind-c
Inductive		**Indicating**
ind-u		ind-c
Product		**Indication**
prod-u		ind-c
Production		**Indicative**
prod-u		ind-c
Products		**Occasion**
prod-u		oc-c
Productive		**Occasions**
prod-u		oc-c
Interrupt		**Occasional**
intr-u		oc-c
Interrupts		**Occasionally**
intr-u		oc-c
Interrupted		**Execrate**
intr-u		xc-cr
Interruption		**Execrates**
intr-u		xc-cr

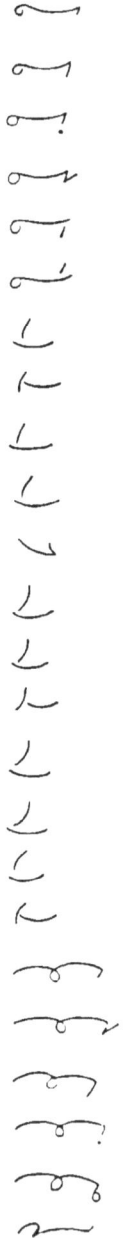

Execration xe-cr		**Recite** resit	
Execute xe-c		**Recited** resitd	
Executes xe-c		**Reciting** resiting	
Executed xe-c		**Recites** resits	
Executing xe-c		**Recitation** resi-t	
Execution xe-c		**Recitations** resi-t	
Executive xe-c		**Antedate** ant-d	
Exclude xclud		**Antedates** ant-d	
Excludes xclud		**Antedated** ant-d	
Exclusive xclu-s		**Antedating** ant-d	
Excluding xclud-ing		**Edition** edshn	
Exclusion xclushn		**Indite** in-d	
Incur incr		**Indited** in-d	
Incurred incr		**Indites** in-d	
Incurs incr		**Inditing** in-d	
Incurring in-cr		**Indictment** in-d	
Incursion in-cr		**Antidote** ant-d	
Incursive in-cr		**Antidotes** ant-d	
Succeed susd		**Forfeit** forft	
Succeeds susd		**Forfeits** forfts	
Succeeded susd		**Forfeited** forftd	
Succeeding susd		**Forfeiting** forfting	
Success sucss		**Forfeiture** forftr	
Succession su-s		**Profess** profs	

Profession pro-f	**Apprehend** apr-h
Professor pro-f	**Apprehended** apr-h
Professors pro-f	**Apprehensive** apr-h
Profuse pro-f	**Apprehension** apr-h
Profusion pro-f	**Prohibit** pro-h
Inflate in-fl	**Prohibited** pro-h
Inflates in-fl	**Prohibits** pro-h
Inflated in-fl	**Prohibiting** pro-h
Inflating in-fl	**Prohibition** pro-h
Inflation in-fl	**Inject** in-j
Aggregate agr-g	**Injected** in-j
Aggregates agr-g	**Injectment** in-j
Aggregated agr-g	**Injection** in-j
Aggregation agr-g	**Object** obj
Congregation congr-g	**Objected** ob-j
Congregational congr-g	**Objection** ob-j
Congregationalists congr-g	**Objectionable** ob-j
Integrated int-gr	**Objective** ob-j
Integrating int-gr	**Objects** objs
Integration int-gr	**Subject** sub
Annihilate an-hl	**Subjected** su-j
Annihilates an-hl	**Subjection** su-j
Annihilated an-hl	**Subjective** su-j
Annihilation an-hl	**Subjects** su-j

Collate		Ignites
co-l		ig n
Collated		Ignited
co-l		ig n
Collation		Ignition
co-l		ig-n
Collates		Ammunition
co-l		am-n
Collide		Diminution
co-l		dim-n
Collided		Comminute
co-l		com-n
Collision		Comminuted
co-l		com-n
Collude		Comminutes
co-l		com-n
Collusion		Comminuting
co-l		com-n
Evolute		Anticipate
ev-l		ants-p
Evolution		Anticipated
ev-l		ants-p
Intimate		Anticipation
int-m		ants-p
Intimated		Anticipates
int-m		ants-p
Intimates		Emanciate
int-m		emns-p
Intimation		Emancipates
int-m		emns-p
Commit		Emancipated
com-m		emns-p
Commission		Emancipation
com-m		emns-p
Commute		Compete
com-m		compt
Commuted		Competed
com-m		comptd
Terminate		Competing
term-n		compt-ing
Terminates		Competition
term-n		comp-t
Terminating		Dispute
term-n		disput
Termination		Disputed
term-n		disputd
Ignite		Disputing
ig-n		disput-ing

Disputation
dispu-t

Contemplate
contem-pl

Contemplating
contem-pl

Contemplated
contem-pl

Contemplates
contem-pl

Contemplation
contem-pl

Explode
xplod

Explodes
xplod

Exploded
xplodd

Explosion
xploshn

Explosive
xplosv

Complete
com-pl

Completed
com-pl

Completion
com-pl

Complexion
com-plx

Equate
e-q

Equated
e-q

Equates
e-q

Equating
e-q

Equation
e-q

Loquacious
lo-q

Antiquated
ant-q

Adequate
ad-q

Adequately
ad-q

Adequateness
ad-q

Obdurately
obd-r

Obdurateness
obd-r

Duration
du-r

Deride
de-r

Derided
de-r

Deriding
de-r

Derides
de-r

Derision
de-r

Derisive
de-r

Derisively
de-r

Corrode
cor-r

Corrodes
cor-r

Corroding
cor-r

Corrosive
co-r

Corrosion
cor-r

Compensate
compn-s

Compensated
compn-s

Compensating
compn-s

Compensation
compn-s

Compensates
compn-s

Decide
de-s

Decided
de-s

Decision
de-s

Decisive — dc–s	
Precision — prc–s	
Insulate — ins-l	
Insulated — ins-l	
Insulating — ins-l	
Insulation — ins-l	
Devastate — devs-t	
Devastated — devs-t	
Devastating — devs-t	
Devastation — devs-t	
Devastates — devs-t	
Dentition — den-t	
Restitution — rest-t	
Penetrate — pen-tr	
Penetrated — pen-tr	
Penetrates — pen-tr	
Penetration — pen-tr	
Penetrative — pen-tr	
Distort — distrt	
Distorted — distrtd	
Distortion — distrshn	
Intend — intnd	
Intended — intndd	
Intention — intnshn	
Persuade — per-sw	
Persuaded — per-sw	
Persuades — per-sw	
Persuasion — per-sw	
Persuasive — per-sw	
Persuasively — per-sw	
Persuasiveness — per-sw	
Perpetuate — perpt-w	
Perpetuated — perpt-w	
Perpetuation — perpt-w	
Evacuate — erc-w	
Evacuated — erc-w	
Evacuates — erc-w	
Evacuation — erc-w	
Situate — sit-w	
Situated — sit-w	
Situating — sit-w	
Situation — sit-w	
Extenuate — xten-w	
Extenuating — xten-w	
Extenuates — xten-w	
Extenuation — xten-w	
Octogenarian — octj-n	
Latitudinarian — lattd-n	

COMMERCIAL TERMS.

In the first three following vocabularies there are necessarily some repetitions, from the fact that certain terms are common to the three classes.

In words beginning with *com*, *con*, it may be optional with the student to choose either method of expression, but the outlines given authorize the use of *c lengthened*, while those who write a fine hand may prefer and use the prefix form.

Abatement
abtmnt

Acceptance
acsptns

Acceptor
acsptr

Account
acnt

Accountant
acntnt

Account current
acntcrnt

Accommodation
acm-d

Adjustment
justmnt

Administrate
ad-trt

Ad valorem
advlrm

Annually
anly

Appraisement
aprsmnt

Arbitration
arb-tr

Articles of agreement
artclsgrmnt

Articles of copartner-
artclscprtnrshp [ship]

Assessment
sesmnt

Assignment
sinmnt

Association
sa-s

Assurance
asrns

Average
avrj

Balance-sheet
balnsht

Bank-book
bankbk

Bank-draft
bankdrft

Bank-note
banknt

Bank discount
bankdscnt

Bill-book
bilbc

Bills of exchange
bilsxchnj

Bills of lading
bilsldng

Bills of parcels
bilsprsls

Bills payable
b p

Bills receivable
b r

Blotter
blotr

Board of brokers
bord brokrs

Borrow
boro

Breakage
brakj

Business paper
bisns papr

Cashier's statement
cashrs statmnt

Certified
srtfd

Certificate of deposit
srtfctdp

Certificate of member-
srtfctmmbrshp [ship]

Certificate of stock
srtfctstc

Charged
chargd

Check-book
chcbc

Circulars
sircirs

Circulation
src-l

Collaterals
cltrls

Collections
col-e

Collection register
colrjstr

Commercial
cmrshl

Commission
com-m

Company
co

Compensate
compnst

Compensation
compn-s

Compound interest
compnd intrst

Comptroller
contrlr

Computations
comp t

Concern
consrn

Contributory
contrb-tr

Consignee
consne

Consignment
consnmt

Consignor
consnr

Consideration
consd-r

Conveyance
convns

Corrected bill
cor-cbl

Correspondence
cor-sp

Coupons
coupns

Credit
credt

Currency
crn-s

Current
crnt

Customers
custmrs

Custom-house
custmhs

Damages
damjs

Day-book
dabk

Days of grace
dasgrs

Debited
debtd

Debits and credits
debtscrdts

Delivery
delvry

Demurrage
demrj

Depositors
depstrs

Directors
dirctrs

Disbursements
disbursmnts

Discrepancy
discrcpn-s

Dishonored
disonrd

Dividend
divdnd

Dollars
dolrs

Domestic
domestc

Drawee
drawee

Drawer
drawer

Due bill
dubl

Exchange
xchang

Exhibit
xibt

Export
xport

Expectation
xpctshn

Express order
xpresrdr

Equation
e q

Estimate
estmt

Fictitious
fic t

Financial
finnshl

Fixtures
fixtrs

Foreign bill
f rnbl

Foreign draft
f rndift

Foreign exchange
f rnxchng

Foreign money
f rnmny

Furniture
furntr

Guarantee
garnt

Hazardous
hazrds

Held for collection
heldfrci-e

Imaginary
imjnry

Import
imprt

Importation
impr-t

Incorporation
incrprshn

Indebtedness
indtdns

Indemnify
indmnf

Indemnity
indmnt

Indorsee
indrse

Indorser
indrsr

Industries
indstrs

Inland bill
inlndbl

Installment
instlmnt

Installment receipts
instlmntrsts

Instructions
in-str

Insurance
inshrns

Inventions
in-vn

Investment
invsmnt

Invoice
invs

Journal
jurnl

Judgment note
jumntnt

Leakage
lekj

Ledger
lejr

Legacy
leg-y

Liquidations
liq d

Offerings
ofr-ings

Officers
ofsrs

Orders
ordrs

Outstanding
oustnd-ing

Overplus
ovrpls

Package
pacj

Partial payment
parshl pamnt

Partnership
partnrshp

Payee
pae

Payer
par

Payment
pamnt

Pecuniary
pecnry

Per cent
prsnt

Power of attorney	**Resources**	**Surplus**
partrny	resrss	surpls
Premium	**Resources and liabili-**	**Trade-mark**
prenm	resorssndlblts [ties	tradmrc
President	**Railroad**	**Trade price**
prcs	ralrd	tradprs
Products	**Rates of interest**	**Trade sale**
prod-u	ratsntrst	tradsl
Profit and loss	**Real estate**	**Trades union**
proftndls	relstt	tradsunn
Promissory note	**Remainder**	**Trade wind**
premsrnt	remandr	tradwnd
Property	**Revenue**	**Traffic**
propr-t	revnu	trafc
Proprietary	**Schedule**	**Trafficless**
propr-tr	scedl	trafcls
Proprietor	**Secretary**	**Transact**
preprtr	scc	t-ct
Protect	**Security**	**Transaction**
protct	secr t	t-cshn
Protest	**Set of exchange**	**Transcribe**
protst	setxchng	t-scrb
Protest book	**Share-holder**	**Transfer**
protsbc	sharhldr	t-fr
Purchase	**Signature**	**Transfer-book**
purchs	signtr	t-frbc
Rebate	**Solvent**	**Transmission**
rebat	solvnt	t-mshn
Receipts	**Speculation**	**Transmit**
rescts	spec-l	t-mt
Receivable	**Statement**	**Transportation**
rescvbl	statmnt	t-portshn
Received	**Statutory**	**Warden**
rescvd	statu-tr	wardn
Receiving book	**Storage**	**Warehouse**
rescv-ingbʹʹ	storj	warous
Recourse	**Stocks**	**Warehouseman**
recors	stocs	warousmn
Redemption	**Stock-broker**	**Warehousing**
redcmshn	stocbrcr	warousing
Re-exchange	**Stock-exchange**	**Warrantee**
rexchang	stocexchng	warnte
Refunded	**Stockholder**	**Warrantor**
refundd	stockhldr	warntr
Reimburse	**Stock investment**	**Warranty**
reimbrs	stocvsmnt	warnty
Remittance	**Sundries**	**Weights**
remitns	sundrs	wats

RAILWAY TERMS.

Acting president act-ingprs	**Baggage** bagj	**Chain brakes** chanbrcs
Accommodation train a-dtrn	**Baggage car** bagjcr	**Charges** charjs
Advance charges vanchrjs	**Basing rates** bas-ingrts	**Check value** chcvlu
Air line arln	**Belt line** beltln	**Chief surgeon** chfsrjn
Ash pan ashpn	**Bill of lading** b l	**Claim agent** clam-a
Asst. gen. auditor ssntjnaudtr	**Board of transporta-** [tion berd t-prtshn	**Claim department** clamprtmnt
Assistant superin- [tendent ssntspt	**Box car** boxcr	**Second-class car** scndclscr
Assistant secretary ssntsc	**Boiler** boilr	**Close car** clscr
Auditor's office audrs ofs	**Brakes** bracs	**Coaches** cochs
Aud. of passenger [receipts audpsrsts	**Bridges** brijs	**Collision** colshn
Aud. of transportation [receipts audtr t-rsts	**Broad gauge** brodgj	**Collect on delivery** c o d
Auditor of disburse- [ments auddsbrsmnts	**Buffet smoking car** buftsmc-ingcr	**Commercial freight** [agent comrshlfrt a
Automatic brakes autmtcbrks	**Buffer spring** bufrspr-ing	**Commutation ticket** com-t tict
Axles acsls	**Bumpers** bumprs	**Conductor** cndctr
Axle box aslbx	**Car accountant** carcntnt	**Connecting rod** cn n crd
Axle guard acslgrd	**Car service agent** carsrvs-a	**Connections** cnncc
Back eccentric bac ecsntrc	**Cattle car** catlcr	**Cond. time table** cndnstmtbls
Bad order badrdr	**Car wheel** carwhl	**Construction train** cnstrtran
Ballasting balst-ing	**Chair car** charcr	**Consignment** cnsnmnt

Contractor's rail
con-tr ral

Corrected bill
cor-ebl

Contractor
con-tr

Coupling
cup-ling

Coupons
cupns

Culverts
culvrts

Cylinder
silndr

Day coach
dach

Depot check
dapchc

Depot connections
dapcn-c

Derailed
derld

Dispatches
spachs

Ditches
dichs

Demoralization of
demrl-zrts [rates

Distributing points
distrbtng points

Dining car
din-ingcr

Directors
dir-c

Director's car
dir-ecar

Direct route
dir-ert

Disaster
disastr

Dividends
divdnds

Division superin-
di vspt [tendent

Domestic rates
dem-erts

Down grade
dezngrd

Drag bolts
dragblts

Drag link
draglnk

Drag bar
dragbr

Draw head
drawhed

Draw link
drawlnk

Draw spring
drawsprng

Driving boxes
driv-ingbxs

Driving shaft
driv-ingshft

Drawing room cars
draw-ingrmcrs

Driving wheel
driv-ingwhl

Earnings
ern-ings

Eastern division
estrn-v

East bound freight
esbnfrt

West bound freight
wesbnfrt

Elevated road
el-vrd

Emigrant cars
emgrnt-crs

Emigrant agent
emgrnt-a

Empty cars
em-tcrs

Engine
enjn

Engineer
enjnr

Engine crank
enjncrnc

Equitable
ectbl

Equalizing beam
eclis-ingbm

Excavation
xca-v

Excess baggage
xcsbgj

Exchange coupon
xchang cupn

Executive depart-
xec-tprtmnt [ment

Excursion train
xcurtrn

Expedition
xpe-d

Export traffic
xpert trafc

Express train
xprestrn

Express messenger
xpresnjr

Express car
xprescr

Export rates
xportrts

Extra
xtra

Fast mail
fastml

Fast freight
fastfrt

Fed and watered
f w

Feed pipe
fedpp

First-class car
frsclscr

Flange
flanj

Flat car
flatcr

Fluctuating rates
fluct-wrts

Foreman
formn

Fore eccentric
for ecsntrc

Free on board
f o b

Freight
frat

Freight department
fratprtmnt

Freight bill
fr*a*tbl

Freight car
fr*a*tcr

Freight depot
fr*a*tdpo

Freight traffic man'gr
fr*a*t trafcmnjr

Freight conductor
fr*a*tdctr

Freight handlers
fr*a*thnlrs

Frog
fr*o*g

Gate keeper
g*a*tcpr

General attorney
j*e*ntrny

General auditor
j*e*naudtr

Gen. baggage agent
j*e*nbg-a

General claim agent
j*e*nclm-a

General freight agent
j*e*nfrt-a

Gen. passenger agent
j*e*nps-a

General counsel
j*e*ncnsl

Gen. superintendent
j*e*nspt

Gen. traveling agent
j*e*ntrvl-a

Gen. traffic manager
j*e*ntrfcmnjr

General ticket agent
j*e*ntct-a

Going east
g*o*-ingest

Going west
g*o*-ingwst

Grading
gr*a*d-ing

Grain car
gr*a*ncr

Gross earnings
gr*o*srn-ings

Gauger
g*a*jr

Half fare
h*a*fr

Hand brake
h*a*ndbrk

Hand car
h*a*ndcr

Head light
h*e*d l*i*t

Hot box
h*o*tbx

Hub
h*u*b

Inland rates
i*a*lnrts

Inter state rates
i*a*trsttrts

Investment
i*a*vsmnt

Junction
j*a*nshn

Land commissioner
l*a*ncm-m

Lanterns
l*a*ntrns

Lost car
l*o*stcr

Legal department
l*e*gldprtmnt

Lifting rod
l*i*ft-ingrd

Limited express
l*i*mtdxprs

Local business
l*o*clb

Local express traffic
l*o*clxprstrfc

Local traffic
l*o*cltrfc

Local rates
l*o*clrts

Locomotive
l*o*cm-t

Locomotive engineer
l*o*cm-tnjnr

Locomotive engine
l*o*cm-tnjn

Locomotive street rail
l*o*cm-tstrtrl

Long haul
l*o*ng h*a*ul

Lumber car
l*u*mbrcr

Mail car
m*a*lcr

Main line
m*a*nln

Master car builder
m*a*strcrbldr

Master mechanic
m*a*strmcnc

Maximum basis
m*a*xnmm b*a*ss

Message
m*e*s-a

Mileage
m*i*l-a

Minimum basis
m*i*nmm b*a*ss

Net weight
n*e*twt

New standard time
n*e*wstnrtm

Observation car
o*b*sr-vcr

Open car
o*p*ncr

Operating depart-
o*p*-rprtmnt   [**ment**

Operator
o*p*-r

Ore car
o*r*cr

Overcharge
o*r*rchrj

Passes
p*a*ss

Passenger
p*a*snjr

Passenger agent
p*a*s-a

Passenger conductor
p*a*sdctr

Passenger car
p*a*scr

Passenger depart-
pasprtmt	[ment

Parlor car
parlrcr

Paymaster
pamstr

Paymaster's car
pamstrscr

Percentage basis
persntbss

Perishable freight
pershblfrt

Personal baggage
persnlbgj

Piston rod
pstnrd

Platform
platfrm

President
pres

President's car
prescr

Profitable
prcftbl

Profits
prcfts

Pro rata
prorta

Pullman palace car
pulmnplscr

Purchasing agent
purchs a

Pullman sleeping car
pulmnslp-cr

Railroad commis-
ralrdcm-m	[sioner

Railway truck
ralwtruc

Rails
rals

Railway ties
ralwts

Rebate
rebat

Restoration of rates
rest-rrts

Reshipment
reshipmnt

Right of way
ritvw

Road master
rodmstr

Rolling stock
rol-stc

Round trip ticket
roundtrpct

Safety valve
saf-tvl

Safety switch
saf-tswch

Sand box
sandbx

Smoking cars
smok-crs

Scalpers
scalprs

Section boss
secshnbs

Section hands
secshn hands

Semaphore
semfor

Shipment
shipmnt

Short haul
shorthl

Short line
shortln

Signal
signl

Side track
sidtrc

Sleeper
slepr

Sleeping car
slep-cr

Slide valve gear
sldvlvgr

Smoke consumer
smoccnsmr

Smoke stack
smocstc

Spark arrester
sparcrstr

Special car
speshlcr

Special train
speshltrn

Spikes
spics

Stage connections
stajcn-e

Standard central time
standrdsntrltm

State rates
statrts

State tariff
stat tarf

Station
stashn

Steam chest
stemchst

Strap rail
straprl

Steel rail
stel ral

Stock car
stoccr

Stock-holders
stckhldrs

Stop over checks
stopvrchks

Stop over ticket
stopvrtct

Street rail
stret ral

Subscriptions
su-scr

Suburban time table
subrbntmtbl

Suburban trains
subrbntrns

Supt. of bridges and
suptbb	[buildings

Supt. of motive power
suptm-tpr

Supt. of telegraphing
supttlsg [and signals

Supt. of machinery
suptmshnry

Supt. of rolling stock
suptrlstc

Swing beam
swingbm

Switching
swich-ing

Switch lights
swich l/ts

Telegram
tel-g

Telegraph
tel-g

Tender
tendr

Through bill
thrnbl

Through freight
thrnfrt

Through car arrange-
thrncrnjmnt   [ment

Through car service
thrncrsrvs

Through train
thrntrn

Through traffic
thrntrfc

Traffic manager
trafcmnjr

Train dispatcher
tran-spchr

Traveling passenger
travlingps-a   [agent

Trip shaft
tripshft

Truck frame
trucfrm

Trainmen
tranmn

Trailing driver
tral-ingdrvr

Transshipment
t-shpmnt

Trans-continental
t-cntntl

Transportation
t-prtshn

Transportation facili-
t-fslts   [ties

Traveling auditor
travl-audtr

Trucks
trucs

Tunnel
tunl

Turn table
turntbl

Unloading station
unld-ingstshn

United States express
u s xprs

Up grade
u/grd

Valve gear
valvgr

Valve rod
valvrd

Vice-president
vispris

Ventilators
vent-l

Wagner dr'w'ng room
wagnrdr-ingrmcr   [car

Wagner sleeping car
wagnr-slepcr

Water tank
watrtnk

Way freight
wafrt

Way bill
wabl

Warehouse
warous

Warehouse receipts
warousrpts

Weighmaster
wamstr

Westward bound
westrdbnd

Western division
westrn-v

Wipers
wiprs

Whistle
whisl

PROMINENT RAILWAY LINES.*

Albert Lea Route
   a l r

Atchison, Topeka & Santa Fe
   a t s f r   [Railway

Baltimore & Ohio R. R.
   b & o r r

Burlington Route
   b r

Canadian Pacific Railway
   c p r

Chicago & Alton Railroad
   c & a r

Chicago, Rock Island & Pacific
   c r i & p r   [Ry.

Cincinnati, Indianapolis, St. Louis
   c i s t l & c r   [& Chicago Ry.

Grand Trunk Railway
   g t r r

Lake Shore & Michigan Southern
   l s & m s r   [Ry.

Michigan Central Railroad
   m c r

Milwaukee, Lake Shore & West-
   m l s & w r   [ern Ry.

Missouri & Pacific
   m & p

Monon Route
   m n n r

New York Central & Hudson
   n y c & h r r   [River Ry.

New York, Lake Erie & Western
   n y l e & w r   [R. R.

Nickel Plate Line
   n p l

Northern Pacific Railroad
   n p r

Ohio & Mississippi R. R.
   o & m r

Pacific & Great Eastern
   p & g e

Pennsylvania Railroad
   p r

Pittsburgh & Fort Wayne R.R.
   p & f w r

Pittsburgh, Cincinnati & St. Louis
   p c & s t l r   [R. R.

St. Louis, Vandalia, Terre Haute
   s t l v t h & i r   [& Ind.

Syracuse, Binghamton & New
   s b & n y r   [York Ry.

Texas & Pacific Railroad
   t & p r

Toledo, St. Louis & Kansas City
   t s t l & k c r   [Ry.

Union Pacific
   u p

Wabash, St. Louis & Pacific Ry.
   w s t l & p r

* Other lines may be indicated in a similar manner.

INSURANCE TERMS.

Abstract
ab-str

Accumulation
acm-l

Actual results
actlrslts

Actuary
actry

Additional insurance
ad-dshrns

Adjustment
jusmnt

Advisory board
advsrybrd

Agreements
grcmnts

Annual cost
anlcst

Annual dues
anldus

Annual premiums
anlprmms

Annuity
anu-t

Artificial premium
art-fprmm

Assessment insur- [ance
scsmntshrns

Assessment life
scsmntlf

Assessment note
scsmntnt

Assets
asts

Assignments
sinmnts

Assumed examples
sumdxmpls

Average yearly cost
avrjyrlcst

Benefits
bnfts

Beneficiaries
ben-f

Brokerage
brocrj

Calculated
calc-l

Cash dividends
cashdvdnds

Cash surrender value
cashsrndrvl

Certificate of member- [ship
srtfctmmbrsh

Cheap insurance
chepshrns

Commissioners
com-m

Compound interest
compnd intrst

Conditional
con-d

Contingent surplus [fund
conti-ngsrplsfn

Consideration
considrshn

Contribution
contri-bshn

Contribution divi- [dends
contri-bshndv

Co-operation
coprshn

Corporation
corprshn

Correct basis
cor-cbss

Current death fund
curntdthfnd

Death fund
dethfnd

Death losses
dethlss

Death rate
dethrt

Distribution
distr-b

Dividend
div-d

Dividends
div d

Duration of human [life
du-rhmnlf

Economy
conmy

Endowment insur- [ance
dowmntshrns

Endowment premium
dowmntprmm

Equalized
eclisd

Equitable
ectbl

Examiner
xamnr

Examination
xamnshn

Examining physician
xamngf s

Expectancy
xpectnsy

Expectation of life
xpctlf

Experience table
xpcrnstbl

305

Face value
fasvl

Fifteen payment life
fztnpmnlf

Fire insurance
firshrns

Five payment life
fivpmnlf

Fluctuations
fluc-t

Forfeited
forftd

Forfeiture
fort:r

Full value
fulvl

General solicitor
jenrlslstr

Graduated assess-   [ment
grad-wssmnt

Graduation
grad-w

Gross annual pre-   [mium
grosnlprmm

Guaranty fund
garn-tfnd

Healthy
helthy

Heirs
ars

Home office
homfs

Income
incm

Inspection
in-sp

Insures
inshrs

Insured
inshrd

Insurer
inshrr

Insurable
inshrbl

Insurance com-   [mission
inshrn-cm

Investment
invsmnt

Kind of insurance
cinshrns

Lapse
laps

Legal claim
legl clam

Legal reserve
leglrsrv

Lim't'd pay'nt endorse-   [ment
lmtdpmntdrsmnt

Level premium
levlprmm

Liabilities
li-b

Life companies
lifcmpns

Life insurance
lifshrns

Life policy
lifplsy

Loading
lod-ing

Long lived
longlvd

Lower average
lorvrj

Marine
marn

Matured endowments
maturd dozmnts

Medical examination
medclxmnshn

Misappropriated
misproprtd

Mixed companies
mixtcmpns

Mortuary payments
mor-trpmnts

Mortality tables
mortlt tabls

Mutual benefits
mutlbnfts

Mutual reserve fund
mutlrsrvfnd

Natural premium
natrlprmm

Net annual payment
net anlpmnt

Non-tontine
nontntn

Non-forfeiture
nonfrtr

Old line
oldln

Ordinary endowment
ordnry dozmnt

Option
ofshn

Ordinary life
ordnrlf

Participating
partsptng

Policy
pols

Policy-holders
polshldrs

Practical advantage
praclvntj

Probable cost
problcst

Probability of life
probl-t lif

Progressive premium
prcgr-s prcnm

Prohibitions
pro-hb

Proportional
pro-pr

Quarterly premiums
qarprmms

Receiver
rescvr

Reduction
re-dc

Re-examination
rexamnshn

Reinsured
reinshrd

Renewable
renæbl

Renewable term life
renæbl termlf

Representations
rcpsn-t

Reserve
rcstv

Reserves
resrvs

Reversionary divi- [**dends**
revrshn divdnds

Risks
risks

Safety fund
saf-tfnd

Semi-annual premi- [**ums**
sem anlprmms

Semi-tontine insur- [**ance**
sem-tntnshrns

Short lived
short livd

Single payment life
singl pmnlf

Sources of dividends
sorssdvdnds

Special reserve
speshl resrv

Splendid investment
splenddvsmnt

Stock companies
stocmpns

Suicide
susid

Surrender value
surndrvl

Surplus
surpls

Tabulated
tab-l

Ten payment life
tenpmnlf

Term life
termlf

Term insurance
termshrns

Term policy
termpls

Tontine insurance
tontnshrns

Tontine plan
tontnpln

Total premiums
totlprmms

Twenty payment life
twentpmnlf

Warrantees
warn ts

Working expenses
work-i xpss

Yearly renewable [**policy**
yerlnbl pols

LAW TERMS.

A.

Abandonment
abnnmnt

Abduction
ab-dc

Abeyance
abans

Abiding by
abd-ingb

Abnormal
abnrml

Absolute
abslt

Absolute conveyance
absltcn-v

Absolute estate
absltstt

Abuttals
abutls

Accordant
acrdnt

Acceptance supra pro-
acsptns suprprtst [test

Acceptor
acsptr

Accessory
acssry

Accomplice
a-pls

Account
acnt

Account current
acntcrnt

Account stated
acntsttd

Accretion
ac-cr

Accroach
acrch

Acknowledgment
acnlmntmny [money

Acquest
ac-q

Acquittance
ac-qt

Action
acshn

Actor
actr

Addition
ad-d

Adeem
adm

Ademption
admshn

Adherence
adhrns

Adjective law
aj-claw

Adjudication
ajd-c

Adjustment
jusmnt

Admeasurement of
admshrmntdowr [dower

Admeasurement of
admsrmntpstr [pasture

Adminicle
admncl

Administration
a-trshn

Administration suit
a-trshnsut

Administrator
a-trtr

Admiralty
admrl-t

Admittance
admtns

Adult
adlt

Advancement
vansmnt

Adventure
advntr

Advisement
advsmnt

Advocate
advct

Advocation
adv-c

Advowee
advowe

Advowson
advowsn

Advowtry
advow-tr

Affiant
afnt

Affiliation
aflashn

Affirmant
afrmnt

Affirmation
afr-m

Affray
afra

Aftermath
aftrmth

Age
aj

Agent and patient
ajntpshnt

309

Aggravation	**Ancestor**	**Arrest of judgment**
agr-v	ansstr	arstjmnt
Agrarian	**Ancestral action**	**Arrestment**
agrrn	ansstrl-a	arstmnt
Aid	**Anchorage**	**Arson**
ad	ancr-a	arsn
Aids	**Ancient domain**	**Article**
ads	anshntdmn	artcl
Aider by verdict	**Ancillary**	**Assault**
adrbvrdct	anslry	aslt
Alibi	**Annuity**	**Assayer**
alib	anu-t	asar
Alien	**Answer**	**Assembly unlawful**
alyn	ansr	asmbly unlfl
Aliment	**Apostles**	**Assets**
alimnt	apsls	asts
Alimony	**Apparent heir**	**Assignee**
almny	afrnt ar	asne
Allegation	**Appeal**	**Assign**
al-g	afl	asn
Alleging diminution	**Appearance**	**Assignment**
alj-ingdm-n	afrns	asnmt
Allision	**Appellate**	**Assistance**
alsyn	aflat	sistns
Allocation	**Appendant**	**Association**
alo-c	afndnt	so-s
Allodial	**Appointment**	**Assumpsit**
alodl	afntmnt	asmpst
Allotment note	**Apprentice**	**Assurance**
letmntnt	afrnts	asrns
Alnage	**Appropriation**	**Astitution**
alnj	afr-pr	ast-t
Altarage	**Approver**	**At arm's length**
altr-a	afrvr	armslnth
Alternative	**Appurtenant**	**At bar**
altrn-t	afrtnnt	atbr
Amalphitan code	**Appurtenances**	**At large**
amlftncd	afrtnnss	atlrj
Ambiguity	**Arbitrament and**	**Attach**
amb-g	arbtrmntndwrd [award	atch
Amenable	**Archdeacon**	**Attachment**
amnbl	archdcn	atchmnt
Amercement	**Argumentative**	**Attainder**
amrsmnt	argmntv	atndr
Amicable action	**Arraign**	**Attaint**
amcbl-a	aran	atant
Amotion	**Array**	**Attendant terms**
a-m	ara	atndnt terms

Attestation
a/s-t

Attorney
a/rny

Attorney general
a/rnyjnrl

Audience court
audnscrt

Auditor
audtr

Augmentation
augmn-t

Adventure
advntr

Aver
avr

Average
avr-a

Aver-corn
avrcrn

Aver-land
avrlnd

Aver-peny
avrpny

Averment
avrmnt

Avoidance
avdns

Avow
avow

Avulsion
avlshn

Award
award

B.

Back bond
bacbnd

Backing
bac-ing

Bail
bal

Bailee
bale

Bail below
balblo

Bail bond
balbnd

Bailiff
balf

Bailment
balmnt

Bailor
balr

Bail piece
balps

Bankrupt courts
bancrptcrts

Bar
bar

Bargain and sale
bargnsl

Barratry
bara-tr

Barrister
barstr

Base fee
basfe

Bastard
bastrd

Battery
ba-tr

Bedel
bedel

Bench
bench

Benchers
benchrs

Benefice
benfs

Beneficiary
ben-f

Benefit of clergy
benft clrj

Benevolence
benvlns

Bequeath
beqth

Betterment
betrmnt

Bigamy
bigmy

Bill for cancellation
biltcnslshn

Bill in chancery
bilnchnsry

Bill in equity
belnqt

Bill of conformity
bilcnfrm t

Bill of costs
bilcsts

Bill of discovery
bildiscovry

Bill of exceptions
bilxpshns

Bill of indictment
bilndtmnt

Bill of interpleader
bil intrpldr

Bill for a new trial
bilfrntrl

Bill of particulars
bilprtclrs

Bill of peace
bilps

Bill of privilege
bilprvlj

Bill of review
bilrvcu

Bill of revivor
bilrvr

Bill of attainder
bil tandr

Bill of indemnity
bildmn t

Bill of mortality
bilmrtl t

Bill of rights
bilrts

Bill of adventure
biladvntr

Bill of credit
bilcrdt

Bill of debt
bildt

Bill of exchange
bilxchng

Bill of lading
bild ing

Bill of sale
bilsl

Bill single
bilsngl

Bill penal
brlpnl

Blackmail
blacml

Blank bar
blancbr

Bond
bond

Booty
boo-t

Breach of close
brech cls

Breach of peace
brechps

Breach of privilege
brechprvlj

Brief
bref

Brokerage
brokrj

Burglar
burglr

Burking
burc-ing

Butts and bounds
butsndbnds

Buying of titles
bi ing ttls

By-laws
blas

C.

Cambist
cambst

Canon
cann

Capias
caps

Capita
capta

Capital
captl

Caput
capt

Carrier
carr

Cartel
cartl

Carvage
carv-a

Castigatory
castg-tr

Castle guard
caslgrd

Casual ejector
casuljctr

Catchpole
cachpl

Causa
causa

Caveat
cavat

Cert money
certmny

Certificate into chan-
sertfct intchnsry [cery

Certified check
sertfchc

Challenge
chalnj

Chamber
chambr

Champarty
champr-t

Chancellor
chanslr

Chancellor of a dio-
chanslrdss   [cese

Chancellor of the ex-
chanslrxcher [chequer

Chancery
chansry

Chantry
chan-tr

Charge and discharge
charjnddschr

Charta
carta

Charter land
chertrlnd

Charter party
chartrpr-t

Chattel
chatl

Chaud-medley
chaudmdly

Chief justice
chefjsts

Chief rents
chefrnts

Chief pledge
chefplj

Chirograph
cir-gr

Circuit
sirct

Civil action
sivl-a

Civil corporation
sivlcrprshn

Civil death
sivldth

Civil injury
sivlinjry

Civil law
sivl law

Civil liberty
sivl librty

Civil list
sivl list

Clause
claus

Clearance
clrns

Close writs
closrts

Close rolls
clesrls

Close copies
closcps

Cocket
cocet

Code civil
codsvl

Codex
codx

Codicil
codsl

Cognizance
censns

Coif
ccif

Collateral
c-ltrl

Color	**Common jury**	**Consanguinity**
colr	*comnjry*	*consngn-t*
Combat	**Common law**	**Conscience**
combt	*comnlaw*	*consins*
Commissary	**Common nuisance**	**Consensual**
comsry	*comn nusns*	*consushl*
Commission	**Common pleas**	**Consent rule**
com-m	*comnpls*	*consntrul*
Commission of assize	**Commonable**	**Consideration**
com-tnoss	*comnbl*	*consdrshn*
Com. to examine wit-	**Commonality**	**Consistory**
com-mxmnnss [**nesses**	*comnalt*	*conss-tr*
Commitment	**Commons**	**Consolidation rule**
comtmnt	*comns*	*consl-drul*
Committee	**Compensation**	**Consols**
com-i	*compn-s*	*consls*
Common appendant	**Composition**	**Conspiracy**
comupndnt	*comp-s*	*conspr-s*
Common appurtenant	**Compound larceny**	**Constructive**
comnprtnnt	*compndlrsny*	*con strc*
Common in gross	**Conclude**	**Contentious**
comngros	*concld*	*contnshs*
Common of estovers	**Condition compul-**	**Contingency with a**
comnstvrs	*con-d complsry* [**sory**	[**double aspect**
Common of piscary	**Condition expressed**	*contn-sdblaspct*
comnp-cry	*con-dxprst*	**Contingent**
Common of turbary	**Condition inherent**	*contnjnt*
comntrbry	*con-dhrnt*	**Continual claim**
Common in the soil	**Condition insensible**	*contnl clam*
comnsoil	*con-dsnsbl*	**Continuance**
Common assurances	**Condition precedent**	*contnns*
comnshrnss	*con-dprsdnt*	**Contra**
Common bail	**Condition subsequent**	*contra*
comnbl	*con-dsbsqnt*	**Contract**
Common bar	**Conditional fee**	*contrct*
comnbr	*con-dfe*	**Aleatory contract**
Common carrier	**Conditional limita-**	*al-trcntrct*
comncrr	*con-dlm-t* [**tion**	**Bilateral contract**
Common courts	**Conduct money**	*biltrlcntrct*
comncrts	*condctmny*	**Unilateral contract**
Common day	**Cone and key**	*unltrlcntrct*
comnda	*con and ce*	**Consensual contract**
Common fine	**Confession and avoid-**	*consnslcntrct*
comnfn	*con-fndvoidns* [**ance**	**Executed contract**
Common form	**Confirmation**	*xcutdcntrct*
comnfrm	*cnfr-m*	**Executory contract**
Common intendment	**Conformity**	*xcutrvcntrct*
comntndmnt	*confrm-t*	**Oral contract**
		orlcntrct

Parol contract
parlcntrct

Simple contract
simplcntrct

Special contract
speshlcntrct

Contract of benefi-
c-n-trbnlsns   [cence

Contracts of record
con-trrcrd

Contribution
ccntr-b

Contributory
contrb-tr

Contumacy
ccntm-s

Conversion
can-vr

Convey
cenva

Conveyance
cenvans

Conveyance by record
cenvansrcrd

Coparcenary
ceprsnry

Copyhold
copyhld

Co-respondent
cerspndnt

Corody
c rody

Coroner
cernr

Corporal oath
cerprl oth

Corporation
cerprshn

Corruption of blood
cer-ubld

Corsepresent
cersprsnt

Cotland
cotlnd

Count
caunt

Counterplea
cauntrple

Counter-roll
countr rol

County corporate
coun-tcrprt

Court of appeals
cortapls

Court of chancery
cortchnsry

County courts
coun-tcrts

County sessions
coun-t-s

Coroner's court
coronrscrt

Court of sessions
cort-s

Courts-martial
certsmrshl

American courts
amrcnerts

Courts of the United
certs u s   [States

Circuit court
srctcrt

District court
distrct

Court of claims
cort clams

Supreme court
suprmcrt

Supreme court of ap-
suprmcrtapls   [peals

Supreme judicial
saprmj-dcrt   [court

Court of errors
certerrs

Court of common
certcmnpls   [pleas

County court
ceun-tcrt

Court of probate
certprbt

Surrogate's court
surgtscrt

Court of oyer and
certoyrtrmnr [terminer

City court
si-tcrt

Municipal court
munsplcrt

Court lands
certlnds

Covenant
cuvnnt

Covert
cuvrt

Coverture
cuvrtr

Covin
cuvn

Creditor's bill
crcdtrsbl

Crim con
crim cen

Criminal information
crimnlinfr-m

Croft
croft

Cross-bill
crcsbl

Crown land
crewnlnd

Cumulative
cuml-t

Cure of souls
cursls

Custom of merchants
custm merchnts

Customary estate
custmry estt

D.

Damages
damjs

Dative
da-t

Dead freight
dedfrat

Death's part
dethsprt

Dead pledge
dedplj

Dean and chapter
denndchptr

Debt
det

Debentures
dcbntrs

Debtor
dctr

Debt of record
detrcrd

Debt by specialty
det speshl-t

Decedent
desdnt

Deceit
dest

Declaration of inten-
dccl-rintnshn [tion

Declaration of trust
dccl-rtrst

Declare
declr

Declinatory plea
dcclntryple

Decree
dccre

Decretal order
dccrtl o/r

Deed
ded

Defeasance
defsns

Defend
defnd

Defensive allegation
defn-s a/-g

Degree of relation-
degr re-l [ship

Deliverance
delvrns

Demandant
demndnt

Demise
demes

Demonstrative
demnstr-t legs [legacy

Demurrage
demr-a

Demurrer
demrr

Denizen
densn

Deodand
deodnd

Departure
deprtr

Depone
depn

Deposit
depst

Deposition
dep-s

Deputy
dep-t

Determine
detrmn

Dereliet
derlct

Dernier ressort
dernr resort

Descent
desnt

Detainer
detnr

Determine
detrmn

Devise
deviz

Dictum
dictm

Dignity
dign-t

Dilapidation
dilp-d

Dilatory plea
dil-tr ple

Diligence
diljns

Diminution of the
dim-nrcrd [record

Diocese
diss

Diriment impedi-
dirmntimpdmnts [ments

Disability
disbl-t

Disbar
disbar

Discharge
discharj

Disclaimer
disclmr

Discontinuance
d-tnuns

Discontinuous servi-
d-tnussrv-t [tude

Discovery
discovry

Disentailing deed
disentil-ingdd

Disgavel
disgavl

Dishonor
disonr

Disjunction
disjunshn

Disparagement
disparjmnt

Disseisin
disseczn

Distrain
distrn

Distress
distrs

Distribution
distr-b

Disturbance
distrbns

Diversity
divrs-t

Divest
divst

Divorce
divrs

Divorce courts
divrscrts

Docket
dect

Doctor's commons
dectrscmns

Doom
dem

Domicil of origin
dmslorjn

Dominant tenement
d-mnnttnmnt

Dormant partners
d-rmntprtnrs

Double bond
dubl bnd

Double cost
dublcst

Double damages
dubldmjs

Double fine
dublfn

Double plea
dubl ple

Double voucher
dublvchr

Double waste
dublwst

Dower
dower

Dower by the com-mon law
dowercmnlaw

Dower by custom
dowercstm

Dowry
dowry

Dry exchange
dryxchng

Dry rent
dryrnt

Due bill
dubl

Duplicity
dupls-t

Dying without issue
dr-ingwoutisu

E.

Easement
esmnt

Ecclesiastical cor-porations
clesclcrp-r

Ecclesiastical courts
clesclcrts

Ecclesiastical law
clescl law

Ejectment
ej e

Eleemosynary
elemsnry

Elisors
elisrz

Embezzlement of goods
embslmntgdz

Emblements
emblmnts

Embracery
embrsry

Encroach
encrch

Endorsement
endrsmnt

Endowment
dowment

Enfeoff
enft

Enfranchisement
enfrnchsmnt

Engross
engrs

Enlarge
enlrj

Enroll
enrl

Entail
entl

Entry
en-tr

Right of entry
rito en-tr

Equitable assets
ectbl asts

Equitable estate
ectbl estt

Equitable mortgage
ectbl morgg

Equitable plea
ectbl ple

Equitable defence
ectbldfns

Equity
ec-t

Equity of a statute
ec-tsttu

Equity of redemption
ec-trdmshn

Error
err

Escape warrant
escpwrnt

Escheat
escht

Escheator
eschtr

Escrow
escro

Estate for life
esttfrlf

Estate in possession
esttinp-s

Estate in remainder
esttinrmndr

Estate for years
esttfryrs

Estate at will
esttatwl

Estate at sufferance
esttatsfrns

Estate from year to year
esttfrmyryr

Estoppel by deed
estplbdd

Estoppel by record
estplbrcrd

Estray
estra

Estreat
estrt

Eviction
ev-i

Exaction
xacshn

Exceptions
xcpshns

Exchange
xchanj

Exchequer
xchecr

Exensable homicide
xcusbl homsd

Executed estate
xcutdstt

Executed trust
xcutdtrst

Executed use
xcutdus

Executory use
xcutryus

Executory devise
xectrydvs

Execution
xcushn

Executory
xectr

Exemplary
xemplry

Exemplification
xempl-c

Expire
xpir

Extend
xtend

Extent
xtent

Extortion
xtorshn

F.

Factor
factr

Factorizing process
factrisingpross

Failing of record
fal-ingorcrd

Faint action
fant-a

Faint pleading
fantpld-ing

False imprisonment
falsprsnmt

False judgment
falsjjmnt

Fealty
fel-t

Fee simple
fesmpl

Feigned issue
fend isu

Felony
felny

Feoffment
fefmnt

Feudal system
fudlsstm

Fiat in bankruptcy
fiatbkrpt-s

Fides
fides

Filiation
filashn

Fiduciary
fi-d

Fine for alienation
finfral-n

Fine of lands
finolnds

First fruits
firstfrts

Fixture
fixtr

Flotsam
flotsm

Folio
folo

Forcible entry
forsbln-tr

Foreclosure
forclsr

Foreign attachment
fogntchmnt

Foreign bill
fornbl

Forejudge
forjj

Forestall
forstl

Forgavel
forgvl

Forgery
forjry

Forisfamiliated
forsfmlatd

Formed action
formd-a

Formedon
formdn

Forprise
forpris

Forthcoming bond
forthcm-ingbnd

Forum
form

Franchise
franchs

Francus homo
francs homo

Frank bank
francbnc

Frank fee
francfe

Frank law
franclaw

Frank tenant
franctnnt

Free alms
frcams

Free bench
frebnch

Freehold
frehld

Free services
fresrvss

Free ships
freshps

Free tenure
fretnyr

Fresh disseisin
freshdsszn

Fresh fine
freshfin

Fresh force
freshfrs

Fresh suit
freshsut

Full age
ful-a

Full blood
fulbld

Half blood
hafbld

Full court
fulcrt

Full life
ful lif

Full right
fulrt

Fungible
funjbl

Further assurance
furthrshrns

G.

Gabel
gabl

Gage
gaj

Gaol delivery
jaldlvry

Gard
gard

Garner
garnr

Garnishee
garnshe

Garth
garth

Gavelkind
gavlcnd

Gavelet
gavlt

General agent
jenrl-a

Good abearing
gud abring

Grand assize
grandass

Grand bill of sale
grandblsl

Grand distress
granddstrs

Grange
granj

Grassum
grasm

Great seal
gratsl

Great council
gratcnsl

Gross average
gros arrj

Ground rent
groundrnt

Guaranty
garn-t

Guardian
gardyn

H.

Habeas corpus
habscrps

Half blood
hafbld

Hanaper office
hanapr ofs

Handborow
handbro

Handsale
handsl

Hanse towns
hanstowns

Hearth-money
harthmny

Heir apparent
ar afrnt

Heir presumptive
arprsm-t

Heir by custom
arbcstm

Heir by devise
ar by devs

Heirloom
arlm

Hereditament
herdtmnt

High treason
hitrsn

High court
hicrt

Holograph
holo-g

Homage
omj

Homestead
homstd

Homologation
homol g

Hotchpot
hochpt

House of Lords
houslrds

Hue and cry
handcry

Hustings
hust-ings

I.

Illusory appointment
ilsry pointment

Immemorial
immmorl

Impanel
impnl

Imparlance
imprlns

Impeachment
pechmnt

Imprisonment
prisnmnt

Impropriation
impr-pr

Imputation of pay-
imp-tpmnts   [ments

In action
in-a

In bank
inbnk

In blank
inblnc

In mercy
inmr-s

Inchoate
incoat

Inclosure
inclsr

Incumbent
incmbnt

Indefeasible
indfsbl

Indemnity
indmn-t

Indenture
indntr

Independent
indpndnt

Indorsement
indrsmnt

Inducement
indsmnt

Induction
in-dc

Infant
infnt

Infirmative
infrm-t

Information
infr-m

Inheritance
inhrtns

Inhibition
inh-b

Initiate
in-sh

Injunction
injnshn

Inland bill of ex-
inlndblxchng [change

Innovation
ino-v

Innuendo
inndo

Inquest
inqst

Insurance
inshrns

Intendment of law
intndmntlaw

Intercommoning
intrcmn-ing

Interdict
intr-d

Interlocutor
intrlctr

International law
intr-nlaw

Interpleader
intrpldr

Interrogatories
intr-og

Intromission
intro-m

Intrusion
in-tr

Investiture
invstur

Issuable
isubl

Issue
isu

J.

Jail
jal

Jettison
jetsn

Joinder
joindr

Joint bonds
jointbnds

Joint stock company
jointstcmpny

Joint tenants
jointtennts

Jointure
jointur

Judgment debt
jumntdt

Judgment note
jumntnt

Judgment paper
jumntppr

Judicial admission
ju-d ad-m

Judicial committee
ju-d cm-i

Judicial sale
ju-dsl

Judicial separation
ju-dsprshn

Judicial writ
ju-drit

Juridical
jurdcl

Jury
jur

Grand jury
grandjr

Common jury
cmnjr

Special jury
speshljr

Coroner's jury
crnrsjr

Justice
justs

Justice of the peace
justsps

Juxta
jux-t

K.

King's bench
cingsbnch

King's court
cingscrt

King's council
cingscnsl

L.

Label
labl

Laches
lachs

Land-gable
landgbl

Lapse
laps

Larceny
larsny

Simple larceny
simplrsny

Petit larceny
pettlrsny

Law day
lawda

Law merchant
lawmrchnt

Law of the land
law land

Law of nations
law nashns

Lawful
lawfl

Lawless court
lawlscrt

Law days
lawds

Leading question
led ingq

Lease
les

Legacy
legsy

General legacy
jenrl leg-s

Specific legacy
spɛsi-i lɛgɛy

Demonstrative legacy
dɛmnstr-t lɛg-s

Cumulative legacy
cɛm-l lɛg-s

Lapsed legacy
lɛpsd lɛg-s

Residuary legacy
rɛsdry lɛg-s

Letters of credit
lɛtrsɛrdt

Letters of request
lɛtɛrsrqst

Letters testamentary
lɛtrststmnɛtr

Levitical degrees
lɛvtɛl dɛgrs

Levy
lɛvy

Libel
lɛl

Liberate
lɛbrɛt

Liberty
lɛbr-t

Liege
lɛj

Lien
lɛn

Special lien
spɛshl lɛn

General lien
jɛnrl lɛn

Vendor's lien
vɛndrs lɛn

Mechanic's lien
mɛcn-i lɛn

Maritime lien
mɛrtm lɛn

Limited company
lɛmtdcmpny

Lineal
lɛnl

Liquidated
lɛq-l

Litigious right
lɛtjsrt

Littleton
lɛtltn

Livery in law
lɛvry lɛw

Location
lɔ-c

M.

Magistrate
mɛjstrt

Mainsworn
mɛnswrn

Maintenance
mɛntnns

Maintenant
mɛntnnt

Malice
mɛlis

Malicious prosecution
mɛ-l pr s-c

Mandamus
mɛndms

Mandant
mɛndnt

Mandatory
mɛnd-tr

Mandate
mɛndt

Manifest
mɛnfst

Manor
mɛnr

Manorial court
mɛnrlcrt

Manslaughter
mɛnsltr

Market overt
mɛrct ovrt

Marksman
mɛrksmn

Marque and reprisal
mɛrcrprsl

Marriage
mɛr-a

Marriage articles
mɛr-artcls

Marriage brokerage
mɛr-abrcr-a

Marriage license
mɛr-alsns

Marriage settlement
mɛr-astlmnt

Martial law
mɛrshl lɛw

Master in chancery
mɛstrchnsry

Matter in deed
mɛtrindd

Mayor
mɛr

Lord mayor
lɔrdmr

Medical jurispru-
mɛdcljrsprd   (dence

Merger
mɛrjr

Messuage
mɛsw-a

Metropolitan
mɛtrpltn

Military court
mɛltrycrt

Military law
mɛl-tr lɛw

Misadventure
mɛsdvntr

Miscontinuance
m-t s

Misdemeanor
mɛsdmnr

Misfeasance
mɛsfsns

Misjoinder
mɛsjndr

Misnomer
mɛsnmr

Mispleading
mɛspld-ing

Misprision
mɛsprsn

Mixed action
mɛxt-a

Money counts
mɛnycnts

Moot
mɔt

Mortgage
mrgj

Mortmain
mrtmn

Mortuary
mr-tr

Motion
mshn

Multifarious
multfrs

Municipal corpora-
mnsplcrprshn   **tion**

Municipal law
mnspl law

Municipal court
mnsplcrt

N.

Naturalization
natrl-z

Navigable
nav-g

Navigation act
nav-g act

Negative pregnant
neg-tprgnnt

Negotiable
ne-g

Negotiate
ne-g

New assignment
newsnmnt

Next of kin
nexten

Nominal partner
n mnlprtnr

Nomination
n m-n

Nonage
n n-a

Non-claim
n nclm

Non-feasance
n nfsns

Non-joinder
n njndr

Non-juror
n njrr

Non-suit
n nst

Non-tenure
n ntnr

Non-term
n ntrm

Normal law
n rml law

Not found
n tfnd

Notary
no-tr

Nuisance
nsns

Nuncupative will
nncptvwl

O.

Oblations
ob-l

Obligations
obl-g

Obligor
oblgr

Occupant
ocpnt

Office
ofs

Office found
ofsfnd

Office copy
ofscpy

Olograph
ol-gr

Onerous
onrus

Onomastic
onmstc

Open law
ofn law

Open policy
ofnpl-s

Option
ofshn

Orator
ortr

Ordeal
ordl

Order
ordr

Ordinary
ordnry

Original bill
orjnlbl

Original writ
orgnlrt

Orphans' court
orfnscrt

Outlaw
oulaw

Outlawry
oulawry

Outstanding term
outstn-ingtrm

Overt
ort

Oyer
oir

Oyer et terminer
oirtrmnr

P.

Parliamentary cases
p c

Palace court
palscrt

Palatine
pdln

Panel
panl

Paper book
paprbk

Parage
par a

Paramount
parmnt

Paraphernalia
partrnly

Particular average
partclr avrj

Partition
par t

Partnership
partnrsh

Party wall
partywl

Party jury	**Plaint**	**Post-note**
partjr	plant	pstnt
Party witness	**Plaintiff**	**Poundage**
partywtns	plaf	poundj
Patent	**Plaintiff in error**	**Pound breach**
patnt	plaferr	poundbrch
Patron	**Calling the plaintiff**	**Power**
patrn	calng plaf	pour
Payments appropria-	**Plea**	**Power of appoint-**
pamnts afr-pr [tion	ple	pourpntmnt [ment
Penal	**Pleader**	**Power of attorney**
penl	pledr	pourtrny
Peremptory	**Pleading**	**Prebendary**
permtry	pled-ing	prebndry
Perfecting bail	**Pledge**	**Precedent**
per fcbl	plej	presdnt
Perjury	**Plenary**	**Precept**
perjry	plenry	prespt
Perpetuating testi-	**Plenarty**	**Premises**
perpt-wtstmny [mony	plenr-t	premss
Perpetuity	**Poinding**	**Premium**
perp-t	pound-ing	premm
Personable	**Police court**	**Prerogative**
persnbl	polscrt	prerg-t
Personal	**Policy**	**Prescribe**
persnl	pol-s	prescrb
Personality	**Poll**	**Prescription**
persnl-t	pol	pre-scr
Petit jury	**Pollicitation**	**Present**
pettjry	polis-t	presnt
Petit larceny	**Pontage**	**Presentation**
pettlrsny	pontj	presn-t
Petit treason	**Popular action**	**Presentative**
pett tresn	poplr-a	presnt-t
Petition	**Popular court**	**Presentment**
pet	poplrcrt	presntmnt
Petitory suit	**Portgreve**	**Presumptive heir**
pettry sut	portgrv	presmp-t ar
Piccage	**Positive law**	**Primage**
picj	pos-t law	primj
Pickery	**Possessory**	**Primer fine**
picry	pssry	primrfn
Pin-money	**Possibility**	**Principal**
pinmny	posbl-t	prinspl
Piscary	**Possibility on a possi-**	**Private act statute**
piscry	posbl-t posbl-t [bility	privt act statut
Pixing the coin	**Possibility of re-**	**Private corporation**
pxing coin	posbl-trvrtr [verter	privtcrprshn

Private law
privt law

Private nuisance
privt nusns

Privilege
privlj

Privileged communi- [cation
privljdcmn-c

Privileged debts
privljddts

Privity
priv-t

Privity of estate
priv-tstt

Privy council
privycnsl

Probate
probt

Procedure
prosdur

Process
.pross

Proclamation
procl-m

Proctor
proctr

Procurations
proc-r

Prohibition
pro-hb

Promissory note
promsrynt

Promoters
pro-m

Proponent
proponnt

Propound
propnd

Prosecutor
prosctr

Protection
pro-tc

Protestation
prots-t

Prothonotary
prothntry

Public act
publc act

Public corporation
publc corprshn

Public law
publcla

Public nuisance
publcnsns

Publication
publ

Purchase
purchs

Purgation
pur-g

Purlieu
purlu

Pursue
pursu

The queen's bench
quensbnch

Q.

Qualified fee
qualfd fe

Quarantine
qaarntn

Quarter session
quartr-s

Quit-claim
quit clam

R.

Rack rent
racrnt

Real action
rel-a

Real chattels
relchtls

Real contract
relcntrct

Reasonable part
resnbl part

Reassurance
resurns

Rebellion
rebelyn

Rebutter
rebutr

Recaption
recapshn

Receipt
reset

Receiptor
resetr

Receiver
resevr

Recognition
r-nshn

Recognizance
r-nsns

Recognize
r-ns

Record
recerd

Recoupment
recupmnt

Recourse
recors

Recovery
recuvry

Redemption
re-dm

Reduction into pos- [session
re-dc po-s

Regrating
regrating

Rejoinder
joindr

Relator
reltr

Release
reles

Remainder
remandr

Remitter
remitr

Remoteness
remotns

Renounce probate
renouns probt

Rent services
rentsrvs

Repleader
repledr

Replevin
replevn

Replication
repli-c

Requests
quests

Resceit
resct

Residuary
residry

Resolutive
resl-t

Respondent
respndnt

Respoudentia
respndnsh

Restitution
rest-t

Resulting trust
result-ingtrst

Return
return

Reversion
revershn

Review
revew

Rhodian law
rodnla

Riot act
riot act

Roman law
romnla

Royal court
roylcrt

Running with the
run-ingwlnd [land

S.

Sacrilege
sacrlj

Safeguard
safgrd

Salvage
salvj

Sanctuary
sanctry

Scienter
scintr

Scot
scot

Scroll
scrcl

Sea letter
se letr

Section
secshn

Seigniory
senyry

Seized
sezd

Senate
senat

Sequestration
seqs-tr

Serjeant
srjnt

Service
servs

Settlement
setlmnt

Several
sevrl

Severance
sevrns

Shifting use
shift-ingus

Ship's husband
shpshsbn

Shire-mote
sher mot

Sign manual
srnmnl

Simony
srmny

Simple
srmpl

Single bill
singlbl

Slander
slandr

Sold note
soldnt

Sovereign
sevrn

Special agent
speshl ajnt

Special issue
speshl isu

Special pleading
speshl pledng

Special property
speshl preprty

Special traverse
speshl-travrs

Specialty
speshl-t

Specific legacy
spesfc legsy

Specific performance
spesfc perfrmns

Spiritualities
spiritalts

Stallage
stalj

Standing mute
standing mut

Star chamber
starchmbr

State's evidence
stats evdns

Statute merchant
statumrchnt

Statutory release
statu-tr rels

Stipulation
stip-l

Stoppage in transitu
stopj transtu

Strict settlement
strict setlmnt

Striking a jury
stric-ingjr

Subletting
sublt-ing

Subornation
subr-n

Subrogation
subr-g

Subsequent
subs-q

Substantive law
substn-t law

Subtraction
sub-trc

Sufferance
sufrns

Suffragan
sufrgn

Suggestion
su-js

Suit
sut

Suitor's fund
sutrsínd

Summary
sumry

Superior
supr

Superstitious uses
supr-st uss

Supplemental bill
suplmntbl

Suppletory oath
supl-tr oth

Supremacy act
suprm-s act

Supreme
suprm

Surcharge
surchrj

Surety
shur-t

Surrebutter
surbtr

Surrejoinder
surjndr

Surrender
surndr

Surrogate
surogt

Suspensive
suspnsv

Swearing the peace
swar-ingps

Synod
sind

Syngraph
sin-gr

T.

Tacking
tac-ing

Tail general
taljnl

Tail male
talml

Tail female
talfml

Tanistry
tans-tr

Temple
templ

Temporalities
temprlts

Tenant
tennt

Tenant-right
tenntrt

Tender
tendr

Tenement
tenmnt

Tenths
tenths

Tenure
tenyr

Term
term

Timber
timpr

Time immemorial
timimmrl

Tipstaff
tipstf

Tithes
tiths

Tithing
tith-ing

Traverse
travrs

Treason
tresn

Treble costs
trebl costs

Trespass
tresps

Trial
tril

Triers
trirs

Triplication
tripl-c

Tronage
tronge

Trover
trovr

True bill
trubl

Trust deed
trustdd

Trustee process
trusteprss

U.

Underlease
undrles

Unilateral
unlatrl

Unity of interest
un-t intrst

Unity of title
un-t titl

Unlawful assembly
unlflsmly

Usage
us-a

Usance
usns

User
usr

Usufruct
usfrct

Usury
usry

Uterine
utrn

V.

Vacant succession
vacntsc-s

Valuable considera- [tion
valb consdrshn

Valued policy
valudpl-y

Variance
varns

Vassal
vasl

Vendee
vende

Vendor
vendr

Vendue vendu	**Void** void	**Waive** wav
Vendor's lien vendrsln	**Voidable** voidbl	**Ward-holding** wardhldng
Vendee's lien vendsln	**Voidance** voidns	**Ward-mote** wardmt
Verdict verdct	**Voluntary** veln-tr	**Warden** wardn
Verification verf-c	**Volunteer** volntr	**Warrant** warnt
Vested use vestd us	**Vouch** vouch	**Warranty deed** warn-tdd
Vested legacy vestdlgsy	**Voucher** vouchr	**Warren** warrn
Vested remainder vestdrmndr	**W.**	**Whole blood** hulbld
Vesting order vest-ingordr	**Wage** waj	**Widow's chamber** widoschmbr
Vicar vicr	**Wage law** wajla	**Withdrawing a juror** widr-ingjrr
Vice-chancellor vischnslr	**Wager of law** wajrdaw	**Without day** wioutd
View vew	**Wager-policy** wajr pel-s	**Without recourse** wioutrcrs
Villanous judgment vilnsjmnt	**Waif** waf	**Witness** witns
Violent presumption vilntprsmsln	**Wainable** wanbl	**Writ of inquiry** rituqry
Violent profits vilntprfts	**Wainage** wan-a	

TERMINATIONS OF MEDICAL TERMS.

THE regular formation of this class of words makes it possible to greatly abbreviate their shorthand representation by adopting signs for the more common terminations. The signs consist of one or more of the initial letters of the terminations and are hence very suggestive and easily memorized.

On the following five pages is a list of terminations with their signs, given in both Roman and shorthand characters, alphabetically arranged for ready reference.

In practice the sign is drawn across the last character of the initial part of the word, except in words having terminations common to other words, as *sation, tation, fusion*, etc., which signs are to be written under or over the previous characters, as in other words.

327

æmatoma cmt		**cephalocele** sflsl	
æmia cm		**chroses** crss	
æresis cr		**chysis** css	
æcons ass		**cinia** sn	
agogue ag		**citis** c	
agra agr		**clitis** clt	
algia al		**cognosis** cg	
alysis al		**cology** · cl	
anæsthesia ans		**comphalus** cm	
aphysis af		**comus** co	
asmas as		**copæia** ce	
athesis ath		**copathy** cp	
atrophy atr		**eoses** cs	
blepharon blf		**cotomy** ct	
bleparos bl		**cranium** crn	
blepsis blp		**crisis** cr	
biosis bos		**crotomy** crt	
brachial br		**dectomy** dc	
canthropy cn		**demic** dc	
cardium cr		**dermotomy** drot	
cele sl		**disia** d	
cephaloma stlo		**disiac** dis	
cephalus sf		**drimia** drm	
cephalites sfli		**dritis** drt	

droses dros		**graphy** gr
dynamics dnam		**hœmia** h
dynia dn		**hexia** x
ectasia ec		**iferous** ifrs
ectasy ects		**inia** in
ectasis ectss		**iparous** ip
ectopia ecto		**itis** i
emea em		**isis** i
enery e		**lactia** lc
facient f		**lepsy** lp
fugue fg		**lescence** ls
ganie gn		**lites, litis** li
gastrea gs		**lises** li
gastrocele gsl		**lithiases** lths
genesis jss		**lithic** lth
genetic jn		**logy** lj
genous j		**lophagous** lf
gensia jns		**losis** los
gesea js		**losity** lo
gismus gs		**lysis** lis
gitis ji		**malacia** mlc
globous glb		**mania** m
glottis glo		**mopathy** mp
gotamy got		**morphosis** mr

morphopsis
  mrp

moses
  mos

myelites
  ml

namia
  n

nanthropy
  nn

nemues
  nnes

nervia
  nr

nesia
  ns

neumonia
  ncu

neurosis
  nrss

nitis
  nt

nocular
  nclr

nology
  nl

noma
  nma

nosis
  ns

nucleated
  ncl

octomy
  oc

odyne
  odn

odynia
  odn

ography
  og

ogenes
  oj

ometer
  or

omphalocele
  omsl

omphalos
  om

onomy
  on

ontriptic
  ontr

opathy
  op

opathic
  opc

opexia
  ox

ophobia
  ofo

ophyma
  of

opolypus
  opls

opsy
  os

opthalmia
  opth

ophyta
  ott

orexia
  orx

ormia
  orm

orrhæa
  orh

ositis
  osi

osmose
  osms

ossious
  oss

osteatoma
  ostt

ostosis
  ost

otica
  otc

otomy
  ot

otraphy
  otrf

otrophy
  otrf

pathia
  pth

pectorial
pc

pepsia
pps

phogia
fj

phasia
fas

phatic
fat

phobia
fb

phoca
fc

phonia
fn

phosis
fss

phralgia
frl

phritic
frt

phritis
fri

physasis
fs

physis
fi

physemia
fsm

plasmatica
plsm

plastic
plst

plegia
plj

pitis
pi

prosis
prss

ptysis
tss

pyrotic
prtc

raphi, raphy
rf

raphe
rf

rasthema
rasth

resis
rss

rexia
rx

rhœa
re

riferous
rfrs

ritis
ri

roma
rm

ropathy
rop

rosthemia
rosth

rotica
rc

ruginous
rj

sarca
sr

sarcoma
src

scope
sc

scopo
sco

scopy
scy

section
sc

septic
sp

splanchnia
splnc

spasmus
sps

spastic
spst

stases
stss

stoma
stm

tality
tl

tastasis tas	**tomia** tm
tatrophy ttr	**tomosis** tmss
tergent trj	**tomy** tmy
tescence ts	**tonea** tn
thæmia them	**tonos** tns
thalmia thl	**topia** tp
thalmity thlmt	**tozoa** tz
thema thm	**tripsy** trps
thermal thr	**tritis** tri
thesia thes	**tropia** trp
thesis this	**trophic** trfc
thiasis thas	**trophes** trfs
thopia thp	**trophy** trf
thoses thos	**uria** ur
thotonos thtns	**varem** vrm
thritis thri	**vesica** vs
throsis thros	**vitis** v
throlis thro	
ticulus tc	
tidium td	
tisis tss	
titis ti	
tology to	
tolysis tlss	

MEDICAL TERMS.

A.

Abdomen
abdmn

Abduction
ab-dc

Abductor
abdctr

Aberration
abr-r

Abiosis
aboss

Ablation
ab-l

Ablution
ab-l

Abnormal
ab-nr

Abnormity
ab-nr

Abortion
abrtion

Aborticidium
abrtsdm

Abortives
abr-t

Abrasion
ab-r

Abrosia
abrosha

Abruptio
abrpto

Abscess
abss

Abscission
ab-s

Absorption
ab-srp

Abstemious
abstmys

Abstinence
abstnns

Abstergent
abstrjnt

Abulia
abula

Abvacuatio
ab-vc

Acamsia
acmsia

Acantha
acntha

Acardia
acrda

Acardiohæmia
acrd-h

Acardionervia
acrd-nr

Acarus
acars

Acatalepsy
act-lp

Acclimation
acl-m

Accucuchement
acchmnt

Acephalous
asfls

Acephalocyst
asflsst

Acephalopedia
asflpda

Acephalorrhachia
asflrca

Acescency
asssn-s

Acetated
asttd

Acheilia
acela

Acheiria
aceria

Acholia
acola

Achor
acr

Achoristus
acrsts

Achroma
acrma

Achromatopsia
acrmtpsa

Acinesia
acnesa

Acinus
acins

Acne mentagra
acn mentgra

Acnemia
ac-ne

Acology
ac-o

Acopria
acopra

Acraipala
acrapla

Acralea
acrala

Acrasia
acrasia

Acratia
acrata

Acraturesis
acrtrss

335

Acrid acrd	**Adynatus** adnats	**Albuminosis** a/bmnoss
Acrinia acrnia	**Ædœa** edea	**Alcoholism** a/chlsm
Acrisia acrisia	**Edœitis** ede-i	**Aleus** ales
Acritical acrtcl	**Esthetica** esthtca	**Algid** a/jd
Acromion acromn	**Etiology** eti o	**Alkalinuria** a/kln ur
Acrothecium acrthsm	**Afiluxus** afixs	**Allantois** a/ntois
Acupressure acuprsr	**Agalactia** aga-lc	**Allopathy** a/-op
Acupuncture acupnctr	**Agenesis** a/ness	**Allotriuria** a/ot-ur
Acyesis asiess	**Agenosomus** a/nosoms	**Alogotrophia** a/go-trf
Adacrya adacria	**Ageusia** a/usia	**Alopecia** a/opsia
Aden adn	**Aglutition** aglu-t	**Alterative** a/tr-t
Adenalgya adn-al	**Agnesia** ag-ns	**Alveus** a/vus
Adenectopia adn-ecto	**Agomphosis** agm-fss	**Alveoli** a/voli
Adenitis adn-i	**Ahypnia** a/pnia	**Alvine** a/vn
Adenocele adn-sl	**Ague** agu	**Amaurosis** amross
Adenoma ad-nma	**Air cells** arsls	**Ambustial** ambstl
Adenotomy adn-ot	**Akinesia** ak-ns	**Ametropia** ame-trp
Adenoid adenoid	**Albinism** a/bnsm	**Amorphous** amrfs
Adipose adpos	**Albuginea** a/bjnea	**Amphiarthrosis** amfr-thros
Adipsia adpsia	**Albumen** a/bmn	**Amputation** amp-t
Adolescence ado-ls	**Albumeniparous** a/bmn-ip	**Amygdalitis** amgd-li
Adros adros	**Albuminoid** a/bmnoid	**Amyotrophic** amy-trfc
Adustion adustion	**Albuminose** a/bmnos	**Anabasis** anabss
Adynamie ad-n	**Albuminuria** a/bmn-ur	**Anacathartic** ancthrtc

Anæmia
an-em

Anæmotrophy
anm-otrf

Anæsthesia
ans-thes

Analepsy
an-lp

Analgesia
anl-js

Anaphrodisia
anfr-d

Anapieratic
anapcrtc

Anaplasmatic
ana-pls

Anasarca
ansrca

Anastomosis
anas-tm

Anatomy
anatmy

Anconeus
ancons

Anconal
anconl

Anencephalous
ann-sf

Aneurism
anrsm

Aneurismal varix
anrsmlvrx

Anfractuous
anfrctus

Angeiectasia
anj-ec

Angeileucitis
anjl-c

Angeiography
anj-og

Angeitis
anj-i

Angina
anjna

Angiocarditis
anjcrdts

Angionoma
anj-nma

Angioscope
anj-sc

Anhelation
anh-l

Anhydrimia
anh-drm

Anhydrosis
anhdross

Anhydrous
anhdrs

Anima
anima

Aniridia
anrdia

Ankyloblepharon
ancl-blf

Ankylosis
anc-los

Anodyne
anodn

Anophthalmia
ant-thl

Anopsia
an-op

Anorganic
anr-gn

Anorthopia
anr-th

Anosmia
anosma

Anotos
anots

Antacid
antasd

Antaphrodisiac
antfr-dis

Anthelmintic
anthlmntc

Anthracosis
anthr-cs

Anthrax
anthrx

Antidote
antdt

Antigalactic
antg-lc

Antilithic
ant-lth

Antiphlogistic
antlljstc

Antiplastic
ant-plst

Antipyic
antpic

Antipyrotic
ant prt

Antiseptic
ant-sp

Antrum
antrm

Anuria
an-ur

Aperient
afrint

Aphagia
afaj

Aphasia
afasa

Aphthæ
afthe

Apnœa
afnea

Apoplexy
afplxy

Apostasis
afstss

Apostax
afstx

Apsethyria
afsthria

Apyretic
afrtc

Apyrexia
af rx

Aqua capsulitis
acweps li

Aqueous humor
acwshmr

Arachnoid
arcnoid

Arbores
arbres

Areotic
ar-tc

Arsenicism
arsnssm

Arteriae
artiac

Arteriotomy
artr ot

Arteritis
ar-ri

Arthritis
ar thri

Arthrodynia
arthr dn

Arthropathy
arth-rop

Articulation
artc l

Ascaris
ascrs

Ascites
ascits

Asphyxia
asfxa

Assimilation
asm-l

Asthenia
asthna

Asthenology
asthn-o

Asthenopia
asthnopa

Asthma
asma

Astigmatism
astgmtism

Astriction
astrcshn

Astringent
astrinjnt

Atavism
atvism

Atheroma
ath-rm

Athetosis
athtoss

Atrabiliary
atrblry

Atrichia
atrca

Atrophy
atrfy

Atropia
atropa

Attenuation
atn-w

Audition
aud d

Aura
aura

Auriscalp
auscIp

Auscultation
ascl-t

Autophony
aut-f

Axilla
acsila

Azote
azot

Azygos
azgos

B.

Bacillus
baslus

Bacteria
bactra

Balneotherapia
balnthrapa

Bantingism
bantngism

Baryphonia
bar-f

Bdellometer
del-or

Bechies
bechcs

Binocular
bi-nc

Bittos
bitos

Biventral
bi-v

Blennogenous
blen oj

Blennophthalmia
blen-op

Blennorrhœa
blen-orr

Blennoes
blenoes

Blepharitis
blef-ri

Blepharadenitis
blefrdn-i

Blepharoncosis
blefrn-cs

Blepharopyorrhœa
blefrf-orr

Blepharospasm
blefrspsm

Bothriocephalus
bothro-sf

Boulimia
beul-im

Bromism
br mism

Bronchia
branca

Bronchiectasis
brenc-cc

Bronchitis
bron-c

Bronchocele
bronc-sl

Bronchophony
bren-cf

Bronchoplasty
branc-pls

Bronchorrhœa
bren-crr

Bronchotomy
bron-ct

Brygma
brigma

Bubo
bubo

Bubonalgia
bubn-al

Bunion
bunyn

Bursa
bursa

Bursa mucosa
bursmcosa

Butyraceous
but-r

C.

Cacæmia
cac-em

Cacation
ca-c

Cachexia
cachxa

Cacogalactia
cac-lc

Cacohymia
cachma

Cacophony
cac-f

Cacorrhachitis
cacrc-i

Cacosplanchnia
cac-spln

Cacothanasia
cac-thn

Caffein
cafn

Calcification
calsf-c

Calcigerous
calsjrs

Calculusvesicæ
calcls-vs

Calenture
calntur

Caligation
cali-g

Calisthenics
calsthn-i

Calippers
calprs

Callus
calus

Calmative
calm-t

Calorimeter
calrmtr

Campsis
campss

Canalicnlus
canliclus

Cancelli
cansli

Cancer
cansr

Cancroid
cancroid

Canthus
canths

Capillaceous
capi-l

Capillary
caplry

Capitulum
capitlm

Capsule
capsl

Carbonaceous
carb-n

Carbonated
carb-n

Carbuncle
carbncl

Carcinomatous
carcnomts

Cardiac
card-a

Cardiagra
cardagra

Cardiocele
card-sl

Cardio stenosis
cardstnoss

Cardiodyne
cardodn

Carditis
car-di

Cariated
caratd

Caries
caries

Carious
carius

Carminative
carmntv

Carnosity
carns-t

Carphology
carf-o

Carotids
carotids

Carpotica
carpotc

Cartilage
cartlj

Carunculate
carnclat

Casein
casn

Castratus
castrats

Catagma
catgma

Catagmatic
catgmtc

Catalepsy
cat-lp

Catalysis
cat-li

Cataphora
cat-fr

Cataplasm
catpls

Cataract
catrct

Catarrh
catr

Cathartic
cathrtc

Cathartin
cathrtn

Catheter
cathtr

Catopsis
catpss

Cauterant
cautrnt

Cellulitis
sclul-i

Cenosis
scnoss

Cenotica
scn-otc

Cephalæmatoma
scfl-emt

Cephalæmia
scfl-em

Cephalalgia
scfl-al

Cephalagra
sefl-agr

Cephalodynia
seflo-dn

Cephalotripsy
sefl-trps

Ceratitis
ser-ti

Cerebelum
sereblm

Cerebration
sere-br

Cerebritis
ser-bri

Cervical
servcl

Cervicobrachial
serve-brc

Chalazonephritis
calzn-fri

Chancre
chancr

Cheilitis
che-li

Cheiloplasty
chel-pl

Cheloid
cheloid

Chin-cough
chincf

Chiragra
_hir-agr

Chirarthritis
chirar-thr

Chiropodist
chiropdst

Chirurgery
chirurjry

Chloasma
cloasma

Chloroma
clo-rm

Chlorosis

cleross

Chrondritis
cron-dr

Chondrogensia
condr-jns

Chondroid
condroid

Chondrosis
cen-dros

Chorditis
cor-di

Chorea
corea

Chromatics
cromtcs

Chromatodysopia
cromtdsopa

Chromatophobia
cromt-fb

Chronothermal
crono-thr

Chylaceous
ci-l

Chyle
cil

Chyliferous
cilfrus

Chyme
cim

Chymosin
cimosn

Cicatricula
sictrcla

Cicatrization
sictr-z

Cilia
silia

Ciliary
siliry

Cinchonism
sincnism

Cionitis
sion-i

Cirrhonosus
sironoss

Cirrhosis
cir-rss

Circocele
sirc-sl

Cirsomphalus
sirs-om

Cirsotomy
sirs-ot

Claviele
clavcl

Climacterie
climctre

Coccyodynia
cocs-dn

Coction
cocshn

Cœliaca
coelica

Cœlialgia
coel-al

Colitis
col-i

Collapse
cclaps

Colliquative
coliq-t

Collyrium
colirm

Coloboma
colbma

Colostrum
colostrn

Colostration
colos-tr

Colotomy
col-ot

Coma
coma

Comatose
comtos

Condyloma
condloma

Congenital
conjntl

Conjunctivitis
conjnct-vi

Constipation
const-p

Consumption
consmshn

Contagion
con-t

Contusion
con-t

Convalescence
conv-ls

Convulsion
con-vl

Cophos
cofos

Cophosis
co-fs

Coreclisis
corc-lis

Corectomia
corec-tm

Corectopia
corc-tp

Corectosis
corc-tss

Coredialysis
cored-al

Corelysis
core-lis

Coremorphosis
core-mr

Coreplasty
cor-pls

Coretomia
cor-tm

Coriaceous
cor-a

Corium
corium

Cornea
cornea

Corona
corona

Corpuscle
corpscl

Corrigent
corijnt

Corroborant
corobrnt

Corrosive
corosv

Coryza
corza

Costal
costl

Coxalgia
cox-al

Coxitis
cox-i

Cranial
cranal

Craniaclasm
cranclsm

Craniometer
cran-or

Craniotomy
cran-ot

Crassamentum
crasmntm

Crepitation
crepi-t

Crisis
criss

Crypta
cripta

Cyanhydrosis
sinh-drss

Cyanosis
sianoss

Cyclitis
si-clt

Cylindroma
silndrma

Cylitis
si-li

Cynanche
sinnke

Cynanthropy
si-nn

Cyotrophy
si-otr

Cystic
sist

Cystic sarcoma
sistcsrcma

Cystirrhagia
sist-rj

Cystitis
sys-ti

Cystocele
sist-sl

Cystodynia
sist-dn

Cysto-lithiasis
sisto-lths

Cystoma
sistma

Cystoplegic
sistpljc

Cystosarcoma
sistsrcma

Cystotomy
sist-ot

Cystovarem
sist-vrm

Cytoblast
sitoblst

Cytogenetic
sit-jn

D.

Dacryadenalgia
dacradn-al

Dacryadenitis
dacrad-nt

Dacryallososis
dacr-lss

Dacryoblennorrhœa
dacrbln-orr

Dacryocystalgia
dacrosst-al

Dacryocystitis
dacrss-ti

Dacryolite
dacryolt

Dacryolithiasis
dacrol-lths

Dacrops
dacrps

Dacryopyorrhœa
dacrp-orr

Dacryosoleneotis
dacrslnts

Dactylitis
dact-li

Daltonian
daltonin

Dartoid
dartoid

Dartos
dartos

Debilitants
debltnts

Decalcified
dclsfd

Decapitation
decp-t

Decollation
decl-l

Dedentition
dedn-t

Defecation
def-c

Defluxation
de-flx

Deglutition
degl-t

Dehiscence
dehsns

Dejection
de-j

Deligation
deli-g

Delirium
delrm

Delitescence
deli-ts

Dementia
demnsha

Demephitization
demit-z

Demomania
dem-m

Demulcents
demlsnts

Dengue
dengwe

Dentition
den-t

Deobstruent
deobstrnt

Deodorizer
deodrzr

Depilation
dep-l

Depletion
de-pl

Deradenitis
derad-nt

Dermal
derml

Dermatology
derm-to

Dermatoses
derm-tss

Dermatozoa
derm-tz

Dermophyte
derm-it

Dermotomy
derm-ot

Desmitis
des-mt

Desmodynia
desm-dn

Desmopathy
des-mp

Desudation
desu-d

Detergent
de-trj

Detruncation
detrn-c

Deuteropathy
deutr-op

Diabetes
dibts

Diacrises
dia-cr

Diagnosis
diagnss

Diapedesis
dipdess

Diaphoresis
dif-rss

Diaphragm
difram

Diaphragmalgia
difrgmlj

Diaphragmitis
difrg-mi

Diaphysis
dia-fs

Diarrhaemia
dir-h

Diarrhœa
direa

Diarthrosis
dir-thros

Diastaltic
diastltc

Diastasæmia
diasts-cm

Diastematencephalia
diasmtn-sfl

Diastematia
distmta

Diastematocaulia
distmt-cl

Diastematocheilia
distmt-chl

Diastematocrania
distmt-crn

Diastematocystia
distmt-sst

Diastematogastria
distmt-gs

Diastematoglossia
distmt-gls

Diastematognathia
distmtg-n

Diastematometria
distmtmtra

Diastematopyeleia
distmtpela

Diastole
diastl

Diathesis
di-ath

Digestion
di-js

Diluents
dilunts

Dimyary
dimary

Diphtheria
difthra

Diplomyelia
diplmla

Dipsomania
dips-mn

Dipsopathy
dips-op

Disarticulation
dirtc-l

Discission
dis-s

Discutient
disctnt

Disinfectant
d*i*sn-tc

Dislocation
d*i*sl c

Dispensary
d*i*spnsry

Dispensatory
d*i*spns-tr

Distocia
d*i*stosia

Distoma
d*i*stma

Diuresis
d*i*u-rss

Dolorifle
d*o*lr-i

Dorsal
d*o*rsl

Dorsum
d*o*rsm

Duodenum
d*u*dnm

Duramater
d*u*rmtr

Dysæmia
d*i*s-em

Dyschrœa
d*i*scrœa

Dyscrasy
d*i*scr-s

Dysentery
d*i*sen-tr

Dysmenorrhœa
d*i*smcn-or

Dysopsy
d*i*s-os

Dyspepsia
d*y*s-pps

Dysphagia
d*i*s-fj

Dysphonia
d*i*s-fn

Dysthetic
d*i*stht-i

Dystocia
d*i*s-to

Dysuria
d*i*s-ur

E.

Ecblepharos
e*c*-blf

Ecbolic
e*c*bl-i

Ecchinococcus
e*c*chnccs

Ecchondroma
e*c*cndrma

Ecchymosis
e*c*chmss

Eccoprotic
e*c*cprt-i

Eccrisionosis
e*c*cris-ns

Ecdemimonomania
e*c*dmno-m

Echoscope
e*c*oscp

Eclampsia
e*c*lmpsa

Ecphylsis
e*c*flss

Ecstaltic
e*c*stltc

Ecthyma
e*c*thma

Ectoparasites
e*c*tprsits

Ectophyte
e*c*tfit

Ectopia
e*c*tpa

Ectozoa
e*c*-tz

Ectropion
e*c*-trp

Ectrotic
e*c*trtc

Eczema
e*c*zma

Eczematoses
e*c*zm-tss

Edentate
e*d*ntat

Effluvium
e*f*lvm

Egesta
e*j*sta

Egophony
e*g*-tn

Eisanthema
e*s*an thm

Elaboration
el*a*b-r

Eleosis
el-cs

Electrolysis
el*c*tro lss

Electropuncture
el*c*trpnctr

Elodes
el*o*ds

Elytritis
el-tri

Elytropasty
el-trp

Elytrorrhaphy
el*t*rrfy

Emasculation
em*a*sc l

Emboly
em*b*ly

Embolus
em*b*ls

Embrocation
em*b*r c

Embryalcia
em*b*ral-s

Embryo
em*b*ro

Embryoctomy
em*b*r-oc

Embryography
em*b*r og

Embryotomy
em*b*r ot

Embryotrophy
em*b*r-otr

Embryulcia
em*b*r ul

Emesis
em*e*ss

Emetic
em*c*tc

Emetise	**Eucolpitis**	**Enterocolitis**
emetis	encl-pi	entrc-lt
Emetology	**Encysted**	**Enterocystocele**
eme-tol	ensstd	entross-sl
Emiction	**Endangium**	**Enteroepiplocele**
emcshn	endnjm	entrosppl-sl
Emenologia	**Endermatic**	**Enterography**
emn-o	endrmtc	entero-g
Emollients	**Endermic**	**Entero hydrocele**
emlnts	endrmc	entrohd-sl
Empasm	**Endermism**	**Enterolith**
empsm	endrmsm	entrolth
Emphylsis	**Endoarteritis**	**Enterology**
emf-li	endort-ri	entr-o
Emphratic	**Endocardium**	**Enteromphalocele**
emirtc	end-crd	entr-omsl
Emphraxis	**Endodontitis**	**Enteroplasty**
emfrxs	endon-ti	entro-pls
Emphyma	**Endoenteritis**	**Enteroses**
em-fm	endont-ri	entross
Emphysema	**Endogastritis**	**Enterostenosis**
em-fsm	endogs-tri	entrostnss
Empiricism	**Endolymph**	**Enterotomy**
empirssm	endo-lm	entr-ot
Empyema	**Endometritis**	**Enterozoa**
emp-em	endom-tri	entr-oz
Empyesis	**Endosteitis**	**Entophyte**
em ess	endos-ti	entfit
Emulgent	**Enema**	**Entoptics**
emljnt	enema	entoptcs
Enantiopathic	**Enepidermie**	**Entorrhagia**
enant-op	enep-dr	entr-rj
Enarthrosis	**Enervation**	**Entozoa**
enr-thrs	enr-v	en-tz
Encanthis	**Enostosis**	**Entropion**
encnths	ens-tss	entropn
Encephalitis	**Entasia**	**Enucleation**
ens-li	entasa	enu-cl
Encephalocele	**Enteralgia**	**Enuresis**
ensfl-lsl	entr-al	emu-rss
Encephaloid	**Enterica**	**Ephidrosis**
ensfloid	entrca	ef-drss
Encephaloma	**Enteritis**	**Epicanthis**
en-sflo	entr-i	efcnthis
Enchondroma	**Enterobrosia**	**Epicystitis**
encndrma	entrbrosa	efss-ti
Encœlitis	**Enterocele**	**Epichrosis**
ensœ-li	entro-sl	efcross

Epidemic
ef-dc

Epidermata
efdrmata

Epididymitis
efdd-mt

Epigastralgia
efgs-tral

Epigastrium
efgstrm

Epigastrocele
efgstr-sl

Epiglottis
ef-glo

Epilation
ef-l

Epiglottitis
efglt-ti

Epilepsy
ef-lp

Epiphora
ef-fr

Epiphysis
ef-fi

Epiphyte
effit

Epiplocele
efpl-sl

Epiploic
efplo-i

Epiploischiocele
efploischo-sl

Epiploitis
efpl-i

Epiplomerocele
efplomr-sl

Epiploon
efpln

Epiploschiocele
efplos-sl

Episiohæmatoma
efisohm-t

Episioitis
efso-i

Episiorraphy
efsr-ra

Epispadias
efspds

Episplenitis
efsp-nt

Epistaxis
efstxs

Epithelioma
efthlma

Epithelium
efithlm

Epizoa
efpza

Epulis
efuls

Epulotic
eful-o

Equina
ecwna

Ergotism
ergtism

Eructation
eruc-t

Erysipelas
erspls

Erythema
erthma

Eschar
escr

Escharotic
escr-o

Etherization
ethr-z

Eupeptic
ufptc

Eventration
ern-tr

Exacerbation
xacr-b

Exangia
xanja

Exanimation
xany-m

Exarticulation
xartc-l

Excarnation
xcar-n

Excoriation
xco-r

Excreation
xcrc-a

Excrement
xcremnt

Excrescence
xcresns

Exenterismus
xentrsms

Exfætation
xfe-t

Exfoliation
xfo-l

Exhalation
xa-l

Exinanition
xina-n

Exitial
xitial

Exocardial
xocrdl

Exodic
xod-i

Exolution
xo-l

Exomphalos
ecs-om

Exophthalmia
ecs-of

Exormia
ecs-or

Exosmose
ecs-os

Exosseous
ecs-oss

Exostosis
ecs-ost

Exotic
ecs-o

Expectorant
ecs-pc

Explorator
xplrtr

Exsanguine
xangwn

Exstrophy
ecs-trf

Extravasation
xtrav-s

Extroversion
xtro-vr

Extuberance
xtubrns

Exudation
xu-d

Exulceration
xul-sr

F.

Fallopian
falopn

Fascicle
fascl

Fauces
fauss

Febricity
febrs-t

Febricula
febrcla

Febriculosity
febrc-los

Febrifacient
febri-f

Febriferous
febrfrs

Febrifugal
febrfgl

Febrile
febrl

Fellifluous
felflus

Femur
femr

Ferine
ferin

Ferrein
ferrin

Ferruginous
fer-rj

Fester
festr

Fibril
fibrl

Fibrin
fibrn

Fibrination
fibr-n

Fibro-cartilage
fibrcrtlj

Fibroma
fib-rm

Fibronucleated
fibr-ncl

Fibro-plastic
fibr-pls

Fibrous
fibrus

Fibula
fibla

Filaria
filara

Fistula
fistla

Flatulence
flatlns

Floccilation
flocs-l

Fluxion
fluxn

Fœtation
fœ-t

Fœticide
fœtsid

Fœtus
fœtus

Fomentation
fomn-t

Fontanel
fontanl

Fonticulus
fon-tc

Formication
frm-c

Foyer
foyer

Fracture
fractr

Frontal
frntl

Fundament
fundmnt

Fungoid
fungoid

Fungosity
fungs-t

Fungus
fungs

Furunculoid
furncloid

G.

Gala
gala

Galactæmia
galct-cm

Galactia
ga-lc

Galactirrhœa
galctrea

Galactocele
galct-sl

Galactophoritis
galctf-ri

Galactosis
galc-tss

Ganglionitis
ganglo-nt

Gangrene
gangrn

Gargarism
gargrsm

Gastralgia
gast-rl

Gastric
gastrc

Gastritis
gas-tri

Gastrobrosis
gastrbrss

Gastrocele
gastr-sl

Gastrocnemius
gastrc-nms

Gastrodynia
gastr-dn

Gastrolith
gastrlth

Gastromalaxia
gastrmlxy

Gastromenia
gastr-mn

Gastropathy
gastr-pth

Gastroperiodynia
gastrpro-dn

Gastroraphy
gastr-rf

Gastroses
gastrss

Gastrostomy
gastrstmy

Gastrotome
gastr-tm

Gastrotomy
gas-trt

Generation
jen-r

Genesial
jenesl

Genesiology
jenes-o

Genetica
jenetca

Geniculated
jenc-l

Genioplasty
jeno-pls

Genital
jentl

Genyantritis
jenan-tri

Genyoplastic
jeno-pls

Genyoplasty
jenio-pls

Gestation
jes-t

Gingivitis
ginj-vi

Glandule
glandul

Glandulosity
gland-los

Glancina
glansina

Glaucoma
glaucma

Glioma
glioma

Globulin
globln

Glossalgia
glcs-al

Glossitis
gles-i

Glossocele
gles-sl

Glottis
glots

Glucohæmia
gluc-h

Glucosuria
glucs-ur

Glutitis
glu-ti

Glycogenesis
glico-jn

Glycorrhœa
glic-rc

Glycosuria
glics-ur

Gnathalgia
nath-al

Gnathitis
nath-i

Gnathoplasty
nath-pls

Goitre
goitr

Gomphiasis
gomf-fi

Gomphosis
gom-fo

Gonarthritis
gonr-thr

Granulation
granu-l

Granule
granul

Graphospasmus
graf-sps

Gravel
gravl

Gravidin
gravdn

Gravidus
gravds

Gummata
gumata

Gustation
gus-t

Gustatory
gusta try

Gynaecology
gine-col

Gyrus
girus

II.

Hæma
hema

Hæmachroses
hem-crss

Hæmadynamics
hem-dym

Hæmagogue
hemgj

Hæmal
heml

Hæmantlion
hemntln

Hæmaphæin
hemafn

Hæmarthron
hemrthrn

Hæmastaties
hem-stt

Hæmatelæum
hemtlm

Hæmatemesis
hemtmss

Hæmatica
hemate

Hæmatine
hematn

Hæmatobium
hemtobm

Hæmatocele
hemto-sl

Hæmatochizia
hemtchza

Hæmatography
hem-tog

Hæmatolyses
hemtlss

Hæmatophthores
hemtfthrs

Hæmatophyta
hemtftə

Hæmatosis
hem-tss

Hæmatothorax
hemtthrx

Hæmatozoa
hem-tz

Hæmitis
hem i

Hæmoglobin
hemglbn

Hæmoptysis
hemop-tss

Hæmorrhage
hem-rj

Hæmorrhœa
hem-re

Hæmospastic
hemspstc

Hæmostatic
hemsttc

Hapontismus
hapntsms

Haphonosi
hafonos

Haptogen
haptjn

Hectisis
hec-tss

Heleology
hel-cl

Heleoplasty
hele-pls

Heliencephalitis
heln-sfli

Heliosis
helioss

Helminthagogue
helmth-gj

Helminthiasis
helmn-thi

Helosis
heloss

Hemianæsthesia
hemi-ans

Hemianalgesia
hemi-anal

Hemicrania
hemi-crn

Hemiopia
hemopa

Hemiphalacrosis
hemtl cr

Hemiplegia
hem-plj

Hemorrhage
hem-rj

Hepatalgia
hep-tal

Hepatic
hepatc

Hepatica
hepatc

Hepatorrhœa
hept-orr

Hepatitis
hepa-ti

Hepatization
hept z

Hepatocele
hept-sl

Hepatolith
hepatlth

Hepatolithiasis
hept-lths

Hepatomphalus
hep-tom

Hepatophyma
hep-tof

Hernia
herna

Heterochymeusis
hetrchmeuss

Hiccough
hicp

Hidrosis
hi drss

Hippocampus
hipcmps

Histogeny
his-toj

Histology
his-tol

Histolysis
histlss

Histrionic
his-trn

Humerus
hmmrus

Humor
hmmr

Hyalitis
hi-li

Hydatid
hidatid

Hydradinitis
hidr-ni

Hydragogue
hidrgj

Hydrargism
hidrrjsm

Hydrarthrosis
hydr-thrs

Hydrencephalocele
hydrn-sdsl

Hydrenterocele
hydrntr-sl

Hydroa
hydroa

Hydroæmia
hidr-em

Hydrocephalus
hydr-sf

Hydrochyes
hydroces

Hydrohymenitis
hidrmen-i

Hydromeningitis
hidrmn-ji

Hydronephrosis
hidrn-frss

Hydropericardium
hidrprcrdm

Hydrophobia
hidr fb

Hydropic
hidrpc

Hydropneumothorax
hidrnmthrx

Hydropyretic
hidrprtc

Hydrothorax
hidrthrx

Hydrotis
hidrots

I.

Hygrology
h*i*gr-o

Hygroma
h*i*grma

Hymenitis
h*i*mn-i

Hyperinosis
h*i*pr-nos

Hypermetropia
h*i*prm-trp

Hyperoitis
h*i*pro-i

Hyperostosis
h*i*pros-tss

Hypertrophy
h*i*prtr*i*y

Hyphæmia
h*i*f-em

Hypinosis
h*i*p-nos

Hypnagogie
h*i*pn-gj

Hypnic
h*i*pnc

Hypnotism
h*i*pntism

Hypochondriac
h*i*p-cn

Hypochondrium
h*i*pcndrm

Hypodermatomy
h*i*p-drot

Hypodinia
h*i*p-dn

Hypogastrium
h*i*p-gs

Hypogastrocele
h*i*p-gsl

Hypohæmia
h*i*p-h

Hypostasis
h*i*p-ost

Hysteria
h*i*stera

Hysterocele
h*i*ster-sl

Hysterotrismus
h*i*stro-trs

Iatraleptic
a*t*rlptc

Ichor
i*c*r

Ichthyoisis
i*c*thoiss

Ichthyosis
i*c*thoss

Ileitis
i*l*-i

Ileus
i*l*es

Immedicable
i*mm*dcbl

Imposthumation
i*m*posth-m

Impotence
i*m*ptns

Imputrescible
i*m*p-trs

Inanitiation
i*n*ani-sh

Incarnation
i*n*cr-n

Inconcoction
i*n*cn-cc

Indigestion
i*n*d-js

Infection
i*n*-fc

Inflammation
i*n*flm-m

Influenza
i*n*flnza

Infusoria
i*n*fsra

Ingesta
i*n*jsta

Ingravidation
i*n*grv-d

Inhalation
i*n*h-l

Inhumation
i*n*hu-m

Initis
i*n*-i

Injection
i*n*-j

Innervation
i*n*r-v

Innominata
i*n*nm-n

Inoculable
i*n*-ocbl

Inoculation
i*n*-ocl

Inohymenitis
i*n*hmn-i

Inoma
i*n*oma

Inopexia
i*n*-px

Inopolypus
i*n*-plps

Inosite
i*n*osit

Inosteatoma
i*n*-ostm

Insalivation
i*n*sl-v

Insalubrious
i*n*salbrs

Insaniferous
i*n*sn-itrs

Insanitary
i*n*sn-tr

Insomnia
i*n*snma

Inspiration
i*n*sp-r

Inspissant
i*n*spst

Insufflation
i*n*sf-fl

Intention
i*n*-tn

Intertrigo
i*n*trtrgo

Intestine
i*n*tstn

Introcession
i*n*tro-s

Intumescence
i*n*tumsns

Intussusception
intsss-sp

Inunction
in-unc

Invermination
invrm-n

Invertebral
invrtbrl

Involuntary
invln-tr

Iodined
iodnd

Iodism
iodsm

Iodomethe
iodmth

Iridectomedialysis
irdctmd al

Iridectomy
ird-ec

Iridocele
ird-sl

Irido-cyclitis
irds-cli

Iridoplagia
ird-plj

Iritis
ir-i

Ischæmia
isch-em

Ischiagra
isch-agr

Ischialgia
isch-al

Ischiocele
ischo-sl

Ischuretic
ischr-e

Ischuria
isch-ur

Isomorphous
ismrfs

Isophathy
is op

Isthmitis
isth-mi

Itis
itis

J.

Jaundice
jaunds

Jecoral
jecrl

Jugular
jugulr

Jumentous
jumntus

K.

Kelis
celis

Keloid
celoid

Keratitis
cera-ti

Keratocele
cerat-sl

Keratoconus
cerat-co

Keratoglobus
certo-glo

Keratoplasty
certo-pls

Kerion
cerin

Kiesteine
ciestin

Kinesipathy
cinsipthy

Kyllosis
ciloss

Kymographion
cimo-gr

L.

Lactifuge
lactfj

Laparo-enterotomy
laproentr-ot

Laparotomy
lapr-ot

Laryngismus
larin-js

Laryngitis
larn-ji

Laryngophony
larng-f

Laryngoscopy
larng-gos

Laryngotomy
larng-got

Larynx
larnx

Latibulum
latblm

Latica
latca

Laxative
lax-t

Leiphæmia
lef-em

Leipothymie
lepthm-i

Lenitive
len-t

Lentigo
lentgo

Leontiasis
len-ta

Leposteophyton
lepost-of

Lepra
lepra

Leptomitus
lept-mi

Leptothrix
leptthrx

Lesion
leshn

Lethargy
lethrj

Lethiferous
leth-frs

Leucæmia
leuc-em

Leucine
leusn

Leucitis
leu-c

Leucocytes
leuccts

Leucocytosis
leucos-tss

Leucoma
leucoma

Leucopathy
leu cp

Leucophlegmatic
leuc-flg

Leucorrhœa
leuc-re

Leucoses
leu cs

Lichen
lien

Lienculus
linculs

Lienitis
lin-i

Lientery
lintry

Ligament
ligmnt

Ligation
li-g

Ligature
ligtr

Limitrophes
lim-trf

Limnemic
limnm-i

Limisis
lim-i

Linctus
lincts

Lingua
linga

Linitis
lin-i

Lipæmia
lip-em

Liparocele
lipro sl

Lipoma
lipoma

Liquamumia
liqamuma

Liquefacient
liqfshnt

Listerism
listrism

Lithagogue
lithgj

Litheeboly
lithebly

Litheetasy
lith-ees

Lithia
lithia

Lithiatry
lithatry

Lithica
lithca

Litholapaxy
lithlpxy

Litholysy
lithlosy

Lithometra
lith or

Lithontriptic
lithn-t:p

Lithospasty
liths-ps

Lithotomy
lith-ot

Lithotripsy
lith-trps

Litre
litr

Liverfluke
livrflc

Lochia
locia

Loimology
l im-o

Lordosis
lordoss

Lotion
lshn

Lumbago
lumbgo

Lumbar
lumbr

Lunacy
lun-s

Lupus
lupus

Lurid
lurid

Luscitas
lus ci

Lycanthropy
li-cnthr

Lymph
limf

Lymphadenitis
limfd-nt

Lymphatic
lim fa

Lypemania
lip-m

Lyterian
litern

XI.

Macrobiotic
macrb-o

Macrocephalous
macr-sf

Maculæ
macle

Magrums
magrms

Malacia
malash

Malaria
malara

Malassimilation
malasm-l

Maliasma
mal-as

Malignant
malgnnt

Malis
malis

Mammitis
mam-i

Marasmus
marasms

Maschaladenitis
masclad-ni

Massage
mas a

Mastitis
mas-ti

Mastodynia
m rst-dn

Matrix	**Melosis**	**Methæmata**
matrx	meloss	me-thm
Maxilla	**Melyalgia**	**Metralgia**
maxla	mely-al	met-ral
Mazodynia	**Membrane**	**Metritis**
maz-dn	membrn	me-tri
Measles	**Meniddrosis**	**Metrophlebitis**
mesls	meni-drss	me-tr-flb
Meconismus	**Meningeal**	**Microcosmography**
mecnisms	mennjel	micrcsm-gr
Medicable	**Meningina**	**Microdosie**
medcbl	menjna	micrdos-i
Medicament	**Meninginitis**	**Micturition**
medcmnt	mennj-ni	mict-r
Medication	**Meningitis**	**Milaria**
med-c	menn-ji	milara
Medullitis	**Meningocele**	**Molluscum**
medul-li	menn-gsl	mdscm
Megrim	**Meninguria**	**Monoblepsis**
megrm	menn-gur	mono-blp
Melanæmia	**Meniscus**	**Monomania**
meln-cm	menscs	mon-m
Melanagogue	**Menopause**	**Monopathy**
melangj	menopaus	mon-op
Melancholy	**Menophania**	**Morbid**
melncly	meno-fan	morbd
Melanismus	**Mentagra**	**Morbific**
melnisms	mentgra	morpf-i
Melanosis	**Mephitic**	**Morbility**
melnoss	meftc	morbl-t
Melanurin	**Mephitism**	**Morbose**
melnurn	meftism	morbos
Melasma	**Mercurial**	**Morbulent**
mel-as	mercurl	morblnt
Meliceris	**Mesenteritis**	**Morbus**
melcris	mesn-tri	morbs
Melitæmia	**Mesentery**	**Monoplastic**
melt-em	mesntry	mon-pls
Melitis	**Mesodmitis**	**Morphœa**
mel-i	mesd-mi	mor-fe
Melituria	**Mesotica**	**Mortiferous**
melt-ur	mesotca	mort-ifrs
Meloæmia	**Metamorphopsia**	**Mortification**
mel-em	meta-mrf	mort-c
Meloplastic	**Metastasis**	**Mucitis**
melo-pls	me-tas	muc-c
Melosalgia	**Metatrophy**	**Mucocele**
mels-al	me-ttr	muc-sl

Mumps
mumps
Mundificant
mundfcnt
Myalgia
mi-al
Mydriasis
midrass
Myelitis
mie-li
Myeloma
mi-lo
Myodynia
mi-dn
Myolemma
mio-le
Myoma
mioma
Myopathic
mipthc
Myopia
miopa
Myosalgia
mios al
Myosarcoma
mio-src
Myosis
mioss
Myositis
mios-i
Myotility
mitl-t
Myringitis
mirn-ji
Myringoplasty
mirng-pls
Myxoma
mixma
Myxosarcoma
mx-src

N.

Naera
nacra
Narcotic
narctc
Narcotism
narctism

Nasitis
nas-i
Nausea
nausa
Nausiosis
nausoss
Nebulosity
nebls-t
Necraemia
necr-em
Necropsy
necrpsy
Necrosis
ne-cr
Necrotic
necrtc
Necrotomy
ne-crt
Neeusia
necusa
Nekrobiosis
necr-bo
Neogala
neogla
Nephralgia
nef-rl
Nephralmintic
nefrlmntc
Nephria
nefria
Nephritic
nefrtc
Nephritis
ne-fri
Nephrolithiasis
nefr-lths
Nephrolithic
nefr-lth
Nephrology
nef-rl
Nephropyic
nefropic
Nephrospastic
nefro-spst
Nephrotomy
ne-frot
Nervine
nervn

Nervousness
nervsns
Neuraemia
neu-rem
Neural
nural
Neuralgia
neu ral
Neurasthenia
neu rasth
Neuricity
neurs ty
Neurilemmitis
neurlm-i
Neurine
neurn
Neurodynia
neuro-dn
Neuritis
neu-ri
Neuroglia
neut-og
Neuroma
neu-rm
Neuropathy
neu-rop
Neuroses
neuross
Neurosthenia
neu-rosth
Neurotica
neu-rtc
Neurotrasis
neu-rtrss
Neurotomy
neu-rot
Nodosity
nedos t
Non compos mentis
n psmnts
Nosogeny
nesogny
Nosography
neso gr
Nosology
nes o
Nosonomy
nes-on

Nosophyta
nos-oft

Nosopoetic
nospo-e

Nosotaxy
nostxy

Nostalgia
nes-tal

Nostrum
nostrm

Notalgia
no-tal

Nutation
nu-t

Nutrition
nu-tr

O.

Obesity
obes-t

Obstetric
obsttrc

Obstipation
obst-p

Obtundents
obtndnts

Odontagra
odn-tag

Odontalgia
odn-tal

Odontisis
odn-ti

Odontobothritis
odntb-thri

Odontogeny
odntgny

Odontography
odn-tog

Odontolithos
odn-tlths

Odontology
odn-tol

Odontechny
odntcny

Œdema
edema

Œsophagismus
esofjisms

Œsophagitis
esfjits

Œsophagocele
esfg-sl

Œsophagotomy
esf-got

Œsophagus
esfgus

Oinomania
oinomna

Olecranarthrotis
olcrnr-thro

Olfaction
ol-fc

Olophonia
ol-fn

Omentum
omntm

Omohyoid
omhoid

Omphalic
omflc

Omphalocele
omfal-sl

Omphalotomy
omfl-ot

Oncoses
on-cs

Oncotomy
on-ct

Onychia
onichia

Onychographosis
onicgrfss

Onychomycosis
onicm-cs

Ophthalmia
of-thl

Ophthalmic
ofthlmc

Ophthalmitis
ofthl-mt

Ophthalmoptosis
ofthlmptss

Ophthalmostasis
ofthlmstss

Opisthotonos
ofsthtons

Oppilatives
ofltvs

Orchiocele
orch-sl

Orchitis
or-chi

Organism
orgnsm

Orgasm
orgsm

Orgastica
orgstca

Orthopnœa
orthpnea

Oscheocele
osch-sl

Oscheoplasty
osch-pls

Oschitis
os-chi

Osmidrosis
osm-dr

Osseoid
ossoid

Osseous
ossus

Ossicle
osscl

Ossiferous
os-frs

Ossification
osf-c

Osteitis
os-ti

Osteoblast
osteblst

Osteocele
oste-sl

Osteocope
ostcp

Osteocystoid
ostsstoid

Osteogeny
ostogny

Osteoma
ostoma

Osteomalacia
ost-mla

Osteomyelitis
osto-ml

Osteopaedion
oętpdn

Osteoporosis
ostprosis

Osteo-sarcoma
ost-sarc

Osteo-struma
oststrma

Osteotrite
ostotrit

Osthexy
osthxy

Otalgia
ot-al

Othaematoma
othemtma

Otopathy
ot-op

Otoplasty
ot-pls

Otorrhagia
otr-rj

Otorrhœa
ot-rc

Otophone
ot-fn

Ourolgy
our-o

Ouroscopy
ourscpy

Ovariotomy
ozr-ot

Ovaritis
ozr-i

Oviduct
ozdct

Oxaluira
oxl-ur

Ozæna
ozna

P

Pachæmia
pac-em

Pachylosis
pacloss

Paedotrophy
pęd-trf

Palpation
pal-p

Palpitation
palp-t

Panhioma
panboma

Pancreas
pancrcs

Pandemic
pandm-i

Panidrosis
pan-drss

Panophthalmitis
panf-thlmi

Pantagogue
pantagj

Papilloma
paploma

Papula
papula

Paracentesis
parasn-tss

Parachrœa
parcrea

Paracineses
parc-nes

Paracrises
para-cri

Paracusis
parcuss

Paracycleses
pars-cles

Paraglossa
parglosa

Paralysis
parlss

Paralyzed
parlisd

Parametritis
parm-tri

Paranephritis
parn-fri

Paraphonia
par-fn

Paraphrenitis
parfr-ni

Paraplastic
par-pls

Paraplegia
par plj

Parapoplexy
parap-plx

Parapsis
parapss

Paratopiæ
partopie

Paratrophy
par-atrf

Parectama
parectma

Parencephalocele
parn-sflsl

Parenchyma
parncma

Paresis
par-es

Parietal
paritl

Parodontides
pardntds

Paromphalocele
par-omsl

Paronychia
parnica

Parosmis
parosms

Parostia
parosta

Parotid
parotd

Parotitis
par-ti

Paroxysm
parxsm

Parturition
part-r

Parulis
paruls

Paruria
par-ur

Patella
patla

Pathogeny
path-oj

Pathology
path-o

Pathophobia
path-ofo

Pathopœtic
path-pe

Peccant
pccnt

Pectoral
pcctrl

Pelagia
pelaj

Pelodera
pclodra

Pemphigus
pcmfgs

Pepastic
pcpastc

Peptic
pcptc

Periarticular
pcrrtclr

Pericarditis
pcrcr-di

Pericardium
pcr-cr

Perichondritis
pcrcn-dri

Pericolonitis
pcrcl-ni

Pericolpitis
pcrcol-pi

Pericranium
pcr-crn

Pericystitis
pcrss-ti

Periexcephalitis
pcrx-sfli

Periglottis
pcr-glo

Perihepatitis
pcrh-pti

Perilymph
pcrilmf

Perimysium
pcrmism

Perinæum
pcrincm

Periosteophyte
pcrostft

Periosteum
pcrostm

Periostitis
pcros-ti

Periostosis
pcros-to

Periostosteitis
pcrosts-te

Periproctitis
pcrprc-ti

Peristole
pcrstol

Peristroma
pcrstrma

Perisystole
pcrsstl

Peritonæum
pcrtnem

Peritonitis
pcrt-ni

Perityphlitis
pcrt-fli

Perizoma
pcrzoma

Peroneal
pcrnel

Perspiration
pcrsp-r

Pertussis
pcrtuss

Pestiferous
pcstírs

Pestilence
pcstlns

Petechiæ
pctcie

Phagedæna
fagdcna

Phakitis
fak-i

Phalanges
falnjs

Pharmaceutics
farm-seu

Pharmacodynamics
farmc-dnm

Pharmacognosis
farm-cg

Pharmacology
farm-cl

Pharmacopœia
farm-cp

Pharmacy
farm-s

Pharyngitis
farn-ji

Pharyngocele
farn-gsl

Pharyngotoma
farn got

Pharynx
farnx

Phlebectasia
flcbc-tas

Phlebismus
flcbsms

Phlebitis
flc-bi

Phlebobyst
flc bob

Phlebolite
flc-bol

Phlebology
flc-bo

Phlebotomist
flc-bot

Phlebotomy
flcb-ot

Phlegmon
flcjmn

Phlogistic
flojistc

Phlyctenulæ
flictnle

Phlyctidium
flic-td

Phonica
fonca

Phosphuria
fos-fur

Phrenic
frcnc

Phrenica
frcnca

Phrenics
fren-i

Phthises
thises

Phthisis
thiss

Phymatoid
fimtoid

Phymatoses
fim-tss

Physconia
fiscnia

Physic
fisc

Phytosis
fi-tss

Pia-mater
piamatr

Piarhæmia
piar-h

Pigment
pigmnt

Piles
pils

Pimeloma
pimlma

Pimelosis
pimlss

Pittota
pitota

Pituitary
pitu-tr

Pityriasis
pitrass

Placebo
plasebo

Plasma
plasma

Placenta
plasnta

Plethora
plethra

Pleura
plura

Pleuralgia
plu-ral

Pleurisy
pleur-s

Pleurocele
pleur-sl

Pleurodynia
pleur-dn

Pleuroperipneumony
pleupr-nmo

Pleurothotonos
pleuro-thtns

Plexus
plexs

Pneumathæmia
neum-them

Pneumarthrosis
neumr-thro

Pneumatocele
neumat-sl

Pneumogastric
neum-gs

Pneumohæmorrhagia
neumhem-r

Pneumonia
neumna

Pneumonitis
neumon-i

Pneumonomycosis
neumnm-cs

Podagric
podagrc

Polyæmia
pal-em

Polyclinic
polclnc

Polyphasia
pol-fa

Polypus
polps

Polysarcia
polsrsia

Polyuria
pol-ur

Porrigo
perigo

Posthitis
pos-thi

Præcordial
precrdl

Prepuce
prepus

Presbyopia
presbopa

Presystolic
presstlc

Proctica
proctc

Proctitis
proc-ti

Proctocele
proct-sl

Prodroma
prodroma

Prognosis
prog-ns

Prosopalgia
pros-pal

Prostatitis
prosta-ti

Prurigo
prurgo

Pruritus
prurts

Psammone
samone

Psoriasis
sori-a

Psychiatry
siciatry

Psychical
sicicl

Psychology
si-cl

Psychoses
sy-cs

Ptarmics
tarmcs

Pterygium
terijm

Ptosis
tss

Purgative
purgtv

Putrefaction
putr fc

Pyæmia
pi-em

Pyarthrosis
pyr thro

Pyelitis
pie-li

Pyine
piine

Pylorus
pilorus

Pyogenia
pio-j

Pyonephrosis
pion-fro

Pyorrhœa
pio-re

Pyostatic
piosttc

Pyrectica
pirctc

Pyrexia
pi-rx

Pyrosis
pi-ro

Pyuria
pi-ur

Q.

Quarantine
qarntn

Quartan
qartn

Quinsy
qinsy

Quintan
qintn

R.

Rabid
rabd

Rachalgia
rach-al

Rachidian
rachdn

Rachitis
rac-i

Radius
radus

Ranine
rañin

Ranula
ranla

Raucity
raus-t

Reclination
recl-n

Recrement
recrmnt

Recrudescence
recrdsns

Rectitis
rec-ti

Rectocele
rect-sl

Rectum
rectm

Recuperative
recpr-t

Redintegration
rednt-gr

Reduction
re-dc

Reflection
re-flc

Regimen
rejmn

Regurgitation
regrj-t

Rejuvenescence
rejvnsns

Relapse
relps

Relaxation
re-lx

Remission
re-m

Reproduction
repr-dc

Resection
re-sc

Resolution
res-l

Resorption
resrpshn

Respirable
resprbl

Respiration
resp-r

Resuscitation
ress-t

Retinitis
ret-ni

Revivifaction
revv-fc

Rheum
reum

Rheumatism
reumtsm

Rhinalgia
rin-al

Rhinitis
ri-ni

Rhinoliths
rinlths

Rhinoplasty
rino-pls

Rhinosis
ri-no

Rhonchus
roncus

Rickets
ricts

Rigor
rigr

Roborant
robrnt

Roseola
rosola

Roseolæ
rosole

Rotula
rctula

Rubefacient
rubfshnt

Rubeola
rubola

Rupia
rupa

S.

Saburral
sabrl

Saburation
sab-r

Sacharorrhœa
sacr-orr

Sacrum
sacrm

Salivation
sali-v

Salpingitis
salpn-ji

Saltation
sal-t

Sanable
sanabl

Sanatory
san-tr

Sanative
san-t

Sanguiferous
sangfrs

Sanies
sanes

Sanitarium
santrm

Sarcocele
sarcsl

Sarcoma
sarcma

Scabies
scabes

Sciatica
siatc

Scirrhus
scirus

Scirrhoid
sciroid

Sclerencephalia
sclernsfla

Scleroderma
sclerdrma

Sclerosarcoma
scler-src

Sclerotitis
scler-ti

Scoliosis
scaloss

Scorbutus
scarbuts

Scotomy
scotmy

Scrofula
scrofla

Scrotocele
scratsl

Semeiography
semi-og

Seminiferous
smnfrs

Septaemia
sept-em

Sequestrum
seqstrm

Serocolitis
serc-li

Serolin
scroln

Serum
serm

Silacea
si-la

Sibbens
sibns

Singultus
singlts

Skoliosis
scoloss

Smegma
smegma

Spanaemia
span-em

Sparallium
sparalm

Specific
spesic

Spermatocele
spermatsl

Spermatozoa
sperm-tz

Sphacelism
sfaclsm

Sphygmic
sfigmc

Spicillium
spirilm

Splanchnica
splanchnca

Splenempraxis
splennprxs

Splenitis
sple-ni

Splenization
splen-z

Splenohaemia
splen h

Spondylitis
spond li

Spondylolisthesis
spondlolsthss

Sputum
sputm

Squinancy
sqinn s

Staphyloplasty
stafl pls

Staphylorraphy
staflr-ra

Steatocele
steat-sl

Steatoma
stea to

Steatosis
stea tss

Stegnotic
stegnotc

Stereotica
ster-otc

Sterility
steril-t

Sternutative
sternt t

Stertor
stertr

Stomatitis
stam-ti

Stomatomykoses
stamtmcss

Stomatoplasty
stamt-pls

Strabotomy
strabtmy

Strangury
strangry

Strophulus
strofls

Styptic
striptc

Subsultus
sabslts

Sudoriparous
sudripars

Suggilation
sugj-l

Superfetation
suprf-t

Supinator
supnatr

Suppository
supstry

Suppression
sup-pr

Suppuration
supu-r

Sural
surl

Surdity
surd-t

Surdomutity
surdmu t

Suture
sutr

Swelling
swel-ing

Sycoma
sicma

Sycosis
sicss

Symphyotomy
simf-ot

Symptom
simptm

Synchysis
sincss

Syncope
sincp

Syndectomy
sin-dc

Syndesmitis
sinds-mi

Syndesmosis
sinds-ms

Syndesmotomy
sinds-mot

Synizesis
sinzss

Synneurosis
sinross

Synocha
sinca

Synosteosis
sinstss

Synovia
sinova

Synovitis
sin-vi

Syntosis
sin-tss

Syphilides
sifiids

Syphilis
sifis

Syphilization
sifil-z

Syphiloderma
sifil-dr

Syphilogeny
sifil-oj

Syphiloid
sifiloid

Syringitis
sirn-ji

Syspasia
sispasa

Sysarcosis
sisrcss

Systaltic
sistaltc

Systole
sistl

T.

Tabefaction
tab-fc

Tabes-dorsalis
tabsdrsls

Tabes-mesenterica
tabsmsntrc

Tænicide
tensid

Tænifuge
tenfj

Tarsorrhaphy
tarsr-rf

Tarsotomy
tarstmy

Taurine
taurn

Taxis
taxis

Tegument
tegmnt

Tenesmus
tenesms

Tenosynitis
tens-ni

Tensor
tensr

Tentorium
tentorm

Tergal
tergl

Tertian
tertn

Tetanus
tetans

Tetter
tetr

Thanatology
than-tol

Thecitis
thes-i

Thelitis
the-li

Therapeutics
therptcs

Thoracentesis
thorsentss

Thoracic
thorsc

Thrombosis
thrombss

Thrombus
thrombs

Thymiatechny
thimateny

Thymitis
thy-mi

Tic-douloureux
ticdlreu

Tinea
tinea

Tisane
tisan

Titubation
titu-b

Tocology
to-cl

Tonicity
tonis-t

Tophus
tofs

Tormina
tormna

Torpent
torpnt

Torpor
torpr

Torporific
torprfc

Torticollis
tortcls

Toxæmia
tox-em

Toxicohæmia
toxc-h

Toxicoses
toxcss

Trachea
tracea

Trachelismus
traclisms

Tracheotomy
trac-ot

Trachitis
tra-ci

Trachoma
tracma

Transfusion
trans-f

Transpiration
transp-r

Trauma
trauma

Traumatism
traumtsm

Trichinosis
tric-no

Trichogenous
tric-oj

Trismus
trisms

Trophoneuroses
trofnrss

Tubercle
tubrcl

Tuberculitis
tubrc-li

Tuberculosis
tubrc-lo

Tumefaction
tum-fc

Turgidness
turjdns

Tussicular
tusiclr

Tussive
tus-s

Tyloma
tiloma

Tympanic
timpnc

Tympanites
timpn-i

Typhinia
trina

Typhoid
tifoid

Typhomia
tito-m

Typhous
tifs

Tyroma
tiroma

Tyrosin
tirosn

U.

Ulatropia
u/a-trp

Ulcer
u/sr

Ulceration
u/s-r

Ulcuscule
u/cscl

Ulitis
u/its

Umbilical
umblcl

Unction
uncshn

Ungual
ungul

Upodermic
u/-dr

Uræmia
u-cm

Uraniscoplasty
unsc-pls

Ureteritis
utr-i

Urethritis
ur-thri

Urethroplasty
urethr-pls

Urethrotomy
ur-thrt

Uretica
uretca

Urination
ur-n

Uriniferous
urnfrs

Urodialysis
urod-al

Uroneus
uroncs

Urophanic
urofanc

Urorhodine
urorhdn

Uroscopy
uroscpy

Uroses
uross

Urticaria
urtcra

Ustion
ustn

Uterus
u/rs

Utricle
u/rcl

Uvea
ura

Uvula
urla

Uvulitis
ur-li**

V.

Vaccinal
vacsnl

Vaccination
vacs-n

Vaccinia
vacsna

Varicella
varsla

Varicoblepharon
varc-bl

Varicocele
varcel

Varicomphalus
var-cmf

Varicose
varcos

Variola
varola

Varioloid
varloid

Varix
varx

Vascular
vasclr

Venefice
venfs

Venenation
ven-n

Venenose
venos

Venereal
venerl

Venesection
ven sc

Venomous
venms

Vermicide
vermsd

Vermiculation
vermc l

Vermination
verm-n

Vertebrated
vertbrtd

Vertigo
vertgo

Vesical
vescl

Vesicant
vescnt

Vesiculae
vesicle

Viable
vibl

Virilescence
virlsns

Virulent
virlnt

Virus
virs

Visceral
visrl

Viscera
visra

Visual
visl

Vital
vitl

Vitals
vitls

Vitality
vitlt

Vivification
viv-c

Vivisection
viv-sc

Volition
vo-l

Vomica
vemca

Vomito
vemto

Vulnus
vulns

Vulvitis
vul-vi

W.

Welk
welc

Wen
wen

Whitlow
whitlo

Whooping-cough
hup-cf

Wirsung
wirsng

Wolffian bodies
wulfnbds

Wormian bones
wurmnbns

Wound
wound

Wrisberg
risbrg

X.

Xanthelasma
zanthlsma

Xanthopsia
zanthpsa

Xanthema
zanthma

Xanthosis
zanthss

Xanthuria
zanth-ur

Xerasia
zerasa

Xeroderma
zer-dr

Xerophthalmia
zerf-thl

Xiphopages
zif-op

Xylophagous
zi-lf

Z.

Zoobiology
zeb-o

Zoogeny
ze-og

Zoography
ze-gr

Zeotomy
ze-ot

Zumology
zum-o

Zymotic
zym-o